BEACON
BIBLE
EXPOSITIONS

BEACON BIBLE EXPOSITIONS

Editors' Preface

No Christian preacher or teacher has been more aware of the creating and sustaining power of the Word of God than the Apostle Paul. As a stratagem in his missionary endeavors, he sought out synagogues in the major cities where he knew Jews would gather to hear the Old Testament. No doubt he calculated that he would be invited to expound the Scriptures, and so he would have a golden opportunity to preach Christ. That peripatetic preacher was confident that valid Christian experience and living could not be enjoyed apart from the Word of God, whether preached or written. To the Thessalonians he wrote: "And we also thank God constantly for this, that when you received the word of God which you heard from us, you accepted it not as the word of men but as what it really is, the word of God, which is at work in you believers" (1 Thess. 2:13, RSV). Strong Christians—and more broadly, strong churches—are born of, and nurtured on, authentic and winsome exposition of the Bible.

Beacon Bible Expositions provide a systematic, devotional Bible study program for laymen and a fresh, homiletical resource for preachers. All the benefits of the best biblical scholarship are found in them, but nontechnical language is used in the composition. A determined effort is made to relate the clarified truth to life today. The writers, Wesleyan in theological perspective, seek to interpret the gospel, pointing to the Living Word, Christ, who is the primary Subject of all scripture, the Mediator of redemption, and the Norm of Christian living.

The publication of this series is a prayerful invitation to both laymen and ministers to set out on a lifelong, systematic study of the Bible. Hopefully these studies will supply the initial impetus.

—WILLIAM M. GREATHOUSE AND
WILLARD H. TAYLOR, *Editors*

Introduction to Mark's Gospel

Several generally accepted conclusions concerning the Gospel of Mark will be assumed in this commentary:

1. That the author was John Mark of Jerusalem, concerning whom the New Testament has a good deal to say.

2. That he completed his work between the years A.D. 65-70, after the death of Peter and before the fall of Jerusalem.

3. That Rome was the place of origin and that Mark wrote to inform and strengthen Gentile Christianity in a period of persecution and suffering.

4. That Mark was a close associate of Peter and of Paul, whose influence may be detected in this Gospel.

5. That Mark was a significant Christian historian and theologian in his own right and that he did his work with articulate purpose and consummate skill.

6. That Mark wrote what has been called a "witness-document," with profound spiritual understanding and pastoral solicitude, in order to evoke faith in "Jesus Christ, the Son of God" (1:1).

In the words of William L. Lane, "Mark's task was to project Christian faith in a climate of uncertainty where martyrdom had been a reality."*

---

*The author of the present volume acknowledges with appreciation the contribution of each writer cited in the bibliography. Special mention should be made of the work by William L. Lane, whose commentary represents a high-water mark in evangelical scholarship. The reader may also refer to the author's more comprehensive bibliography in the *Beacon Bible Commentary*, Vol. 6, pp. 415-16.

BEACON BIBLE EXPOSITIONS

VOLUME 2

MARK

by
A. ELWOOD SANNER

Editors
WILLIAM M. GREATHOUSE
WILLARD H. TAYLOR

BEACON HILL PRESS OF KANSAS CITY
Kansas City, Missouri

Permission to quote from the following copyrighted versions of the Bible
is acknowledged with appreciation:

New International Version of the New Testament (NIV), © 1973 by the
New York Bible Society International.

Good News Bible, Today's English Version (TEV). New Testament ©
American Bible Society, 1966, 1971, 1976.

The Living Bible (TLB), © 1971 by Tyndale House Publishers, Wheaton,
Ill.

New English Bible (NEB), © The Delegates of the Oxford University
Press and the Syndics of the Cambridge University Press, 1961, 1970.

New American Standard Bible (NASB), © The Lockman Foundation,
1960, 1962, 1968, 1971, 1972, 1973, 1975.

New Testament in Modern English (Phillips), Revised Edition © J. B.
Phillips, 1958, 1960, 1972. By permission of the Macmillan Publishing Co., Inc.

The *Revised Standard Version of the Bible* (RSV), copyrighted 1946,
1952, © 1971, 1973.

Contents

John Mark of Jerusalem

A. *What the New Testament Tells Us About Him*

Although Mark was not one of the Twelve, he does appear in the pages of the New Testament as a significant, influential person.

1. It is clear that Mark had a close association with the infant Christian Church and with several of its prominent leaders. We may cite the following factors:

a. His mother's home was "headquarters" in Jerusalem for the first believers. We read in Acts 12:12 that when Peter was miraculously released from Herod's prison, "he went to the house of Mary the mother of John, also called Mark, where many people had gathered and were praying" (Acts 12:12, NIV). A servant girl named Rhoda went to the door and recognized Peter's voice, although in the excitement she neglected to let him in.

From this scene a variety of inferences have been drawn. Mark's mother was obviously a leader in the young Church, with some degree of affluence. Was the "upper room" (Acts 1:13) in her home? Was this also the place where Jesus and the Twelve gathered for the Last Supper? (Mark 14:12-16). In any case, John Mark was thrust into the heart of the earliest Christian fellowship.

b. It is possible that the mysterious youth described in Mark 14:51-52 was John Mark. *The Oxford Annotated Bible* includes this intriguing note:

> *The young man's identity is not disclosed. Perhaps he was sleeping in the house where Jesus ate the Last Supper and rose hastily from bed to follow Jesus to Gethsemane. If the house was that of Mary, the mother of John Mark (where the disciples met at a later date; Acts 12:12) it is possible that the young man was the Evangelist himself.*

c. The Book of Acts and some of the Epistles describe Mark as a companion and helper of Barnabas, Paul, and Peter (see Acts 12:25; 1 Tim. 4:11; 1 Pet. 5:13).

2. It is also certain that as a young adult, Mark had a

traumatic experience of failure. He had come to Antioch of Syria with Barnabas and Saul and, consequently, was in that city when the church sent out its first missionaries (Acts 13:2-3). Mark accompanied Barnabas and Saul for only a part of the journey. When they came to Perga in Pamphylia, "John left them and returned to Jerusalem" (Acts 13:13).

Luke does not give us the reason for Mark's action, but it alienated Paul and became the occasion of a sharp dispute between the missionary friends (Acts 15:36-39). We can well imagine that, as a result, Mark had to cope with considerable stress.

3. Happily, perhaps through the compassionate care of his cousin Barnabas ("son of consolation," Acts 4:36), Mark found restoration and became a trustworthy and productive comrade of both Paul and Peter and, in time, a significant leader in the early Christian Church.

Years later Paul wrote to Timothy, "Get Mark and bring him with you; for he is very useful in serving me" (2 Tim. 4:11, RSV). Peter spoke affectionately of Mark as "my son" (1 Pet. 5:13).

B. *What Tradition Tells Us About Him*

By tradition is meant responsible historic records accepted as reflecting with accuracy the convictions of the early Christian Church.

A good example is the statement of Papias (ca. A.D. 140), Bishop of Hierapolis, preserved by Eusebius, the noted church historian (A.D. 260-340):

> The Elder said this also: "Mark, having become the interpreter of Peter, wrote down accurately whatever he remembered of the things said and done by the Lord, but not however in order." For neither did he hear the Lord, nor did he follow him, but afterwards, as I said, Peter, who adapted his teachings to the needs of his hearers, but not as though he were drawing up a connected account of the Lord's oracles. So then Mark made no mistake in thus recording some things just as

he remembered them. For he took forethought for one thing, not to omit any of the things that he had heard nor to state any of them falsely.

In addition to Papias, the tradition concerning Mark has come down to us from other sources in Asia Minor, Rome, Lyon, North Africa, and Alexandria (see bibliography for details).

This combined early Christian witness tells us the following:

1. That Mark was a close associate and interpreter of Peter, who was an eyewitness to the Gospel story. This assertion is supported by Peter's reference to "my son Mark" (1 Pet. 5:13) and by considerable internal evidence in the Gospel itself.

2. That Mark was not merely a mouthpiece, an echo of Peter, but also a creative "servant of the word" (Luke 1:2), adapting Peter's "teachings to the needs of his hearers."

Christian tradition is important and helpful but, of course, does not give us the whole story. Much of it is unclear and uncertain. As we shall see, the careful, insightful study of the Gospel itself reveals a great deal about the character and spirit of the author and of those "who from the first were eyewitnesses and servants of the word" (Luke 1:2, NIV).

John Mark: "Servant of the Word"

For most of Christian history, the Gospel of Mark waited in the background, overshadowed by Matthew and Luke. Many believed, Augustine among them, that Mark was a rather roughhewn abridgement of Matthew.

It was not until mid-19th century that devout scholarship established beyond reasonable doubt that Mark was the first Gospel to be written and that it became the primary source for Matthew and Luke. Since that time interest in Mark's Gospel has flourished. Scholars are saying that Mark was a talented historian, theologian, and pastoral evangelist.

A. *He Was a Historian*

Too long the Christian world has been bedeviled by critical studies of the Scriptures which have rent asunder history and faith. Our biblical faith has historical roots, and when those roots are severed, faith withers and dies.

In the hands of devout scholars, such studies have become an asset. These studies have shown that the Gospel story early circulated in both written and oral form and met the needs of the growing and expanding Christian community. The Gospel story, by the power of the Holy Spirit, created and nourished the Christian community, not the reverse.

With compassionate care, Mark gathered this account together and summarized the preaching and teaching which he had received from those who were participants and eyewitnesses.

For example, a remarkable parallel exists between the preaching of Peter, as summarized in Acts 10:36-40, and the outline of Mark's Gospel:

> *This is the message God sent to the people of Israel, telling the good news of peace through Jesus Christ, who is Lord of all. You know what has happened throughout Judea, beginning in Galilee after the baptism that John preached—how God anointed Jesus of Nazareth with the Holy Spirit and power, and how he went around doing good and healing all who were under the power of the devil, because God was with him.*
>
> *We are witnesses of everything he did in the country of the Jews and in Jerusalem. They killed him by hanging him on a tree, but God raised him from the dead on the third day and caused him to be seen* (Acts 10:36-40, NIV).

(A comparison of the foregoing scripture with the outline of Mark given at the close of this introduction, will illustrate their parallel structure.)

It is certain that one of the "servants of the word" which Luke consulted was the Gospel of Mark and that he did so in order to demonstrate "the certainty of the things you have been taught" (Luke 1:2, 4, NIV).

B. *He Was a Theologian*

The New Testament writers held Christian doctrine in high regard. The first fruitful "fallout" of our inspired Bible is *doctrine* (2 Tim. 3:16). The apostles warned against *false doctrine* and encouraged the teaching of *good doctrine* (1 Tim. 4:1-6).

Somewhat more implicitly, perhaps, Mark taught sound doctrine in his Gospel—that Jesus was the Messiah, the Son of God (1:1), but also that He was the Son of Man (2:28). He could forgive sin (2:7) and cast out Satan, but He could also grow weary and fall asleep (4:38).

He knew that the sins of man spring from a sinful heart (7:20-23), but He came to ransom men from that corruption (10:45). If the atonement was costly for Jesus, discipleship was costly also. He taught that this present age would always be fraught with stress, but He also knew of a time when He would come "with great power and glory" to deliver His own (13:24-27).

Like anyone Jesus drew back from the threat of death (14:34), but He made good on His promise that He would rise again from the dead (10:34). Mark taught all these things with an evangelistic purpose.

C. *He Was a Pastoral Evangelist*

As we have seen, the Gospel of Mark is a "witness-document," a new form of literature with a missionary purpose.

Throughout his work Mark has one overriding purpose: to evoke and strengthen faith in Jesus as the Messiah of Israel, the Son of God who is adequate for all human need.

Mark wrote in a time of uncertainty, suffering, and

martyrdom. External and internal evidence point to the Neronian persecution as the occasion for Mark's Gospel. The Roman historian, Tacitus, has recorded the circumstances. In a brutal effort at "urban renewal," Nero set flame to the city of Rome and destroyed 10 of 14 wards. Because suspicion persisted that he was the culprit, Nero sought and found a scapegoat in the Christians. The persecution which followed was vicious—wild beasts and burning crosses were often the instrument of death.

Christians went underground. Treachery and defection were common. Families turned on each other. It was obvious to those who knew the gospel story that Christians were facing a period of suffering much like that Jesus experienced.

In a vivid, colorfully detailed, and rapidly moving style, Mark put together the gospel narrative, known throughout the Early Church, that Jesus came to preach and teach the Good News, to destroy the kingdom of Satan, to heal the sick and raise the dead, to engage hollow religiosity in mortal struggle, to call all men to follow Him to the Cross, to die and rise again as Victor over all foes. Christians in Rome must have gathered strength for their ordeal from Mark's Gospel.

Mark accomplished his work with consummate skill. By midpoint in his Gospel (8:29), Peter and the rest of the Twelve had seen that Jesus was the Christ. By the end of the Gospel (15:39), the Roman centurion had seen that Jesus was the Son of God. Israel and the Gentile world all bore witness to the truth that Jesus is the Christ, the Son of God (1:1).

But through his Gospel, Mark calls to us as well. What will our response be to this call for discipleship of this sort?

In the oft-quoted words of Laurence Housman, Mark was

> *The saint who first found grace to pen*
> *The life which was the Life of men.*

A man who had worked through an experience of humiliation and disgrace to become a comrade of the great apostles Peter and Paul, and who became the instrument of God to preserve for all time the inspired account of Jesus of Nazareth, a prophet mighty in word and deed, the Messiah, the Son of God, towers namelessly behind his Gospel and invites us to believe, to obey, to follow the Savior, whatever the cost.

Topical Outline of Mark

The Ministry in Galilee and Environs

The Ministry in Galilee and Environs

Mark 1:1—9:50

The Gospel Begins

Mark 1:1-8

> 1 The beginning of the gospel of Jesus Christ, the Son of God;
> 2 As it is written in the prophets, Behold, I send my messenger before thy face, which shall prepare thy way before thee.
> 3 The voice of one crying in the wilderness, Prepare ye the way of the Lord, make his paths straight.
> 4 John did baptize in the wilderness, and preach the baptism of repentance for the remission of sins.
> 5 And there went out unto him all the land of Judaea, and they of Jerusalem, and were all baptized of him in the river of Jordan, confessing their sins.
> 6 And John was clothed with camel's hair, and with a girdle of a skin about his loins; and he did eat locusts and wild honey;
> 7 And preached, saying, There cometh one mightier than I after me, the latchet of whose shoes I am not worthy to stoop down and unloose.
> 8 I indeed have baptized you with water: but he shall baptize you with the Holy Ghost.

In simplest terms, *the gospel* (1) means "joyful tidings" or "good news." In a world where newspapers and newscasts proclaim very little but bad news, the gospel should be heartening.

Christians did not coin the term "gospel," for it was then in circulation and was a part of their cultural and religious heritage. Glad reports of Roman festivals, such as those associated with the emperor, were "joyful tidings," "evangels." In predicting the release of Judah from exile, Isaiah brought "good tidings of good" (Isa. 52:7).

For the *beginning* of the gospel there was a preparation, a proclaimer, whose proclamation was full of *promise.*

1. *There was a preparation for the gospel* (2-3). To what point in time does Mark refer when he writes, *The beginning of the gospel of Jesus Christ* (1)? In what sense does the gospel begin with John the Baptist, in what sense before him?

Mark intends to say that the gospel begins with the ministry of John the Baptist. The preaching of the early Christian Church linked John and Jesus: *The word which God sent . . . and began from Galilee, after the baptism which John preached* (Acts 10:37). It has been suggested that no man had a greater influence over Jesus than did John the Baptist.

However, Mark sees the coming of John as the fulfillment of prophecy: *Behold, I send my messenger before thy face, which shall prepare thy way* (2). In vv. 2 and 3, Mark blends together quotations from the Law and the Prophets (Exod. 23:20; Isa. 40:3; Mal. 3:1). This blending of Old Testament references is highly significant and makes clear the unity of the Hebrew and Christian Scriptures. John, the greatest of all the prophets, and Jesus are one in the unfolding of God's purpose.

In a very real sense, the gospel of Jesus Christ began with the preaching of John the Baptist, but if John came as the fulfillment of Old Testament prophecies, and the prophets spoke *as they were moved by the Holy Ghost* (2 Pet. 1:21), we may say that the gospel was in the mind of God from eternity.

2. *There was a proclaimer of the gospel* (4-6).

a. Mark writes that the gospel is *about* Jesus Christ, the Son of God, but that in the ministry of John the Baptist, the gospel truly entered history and had its *beginning* (1). This was the persuasion of the first Christians. As the disciples were waiting in the Upper Room, before Pentecost, they spoke of the ministry of Jesus as "beginning from the baptism of John" (Acts 1:22).

b. History so soon buries the dead and obliterates the memory even of the great. This is almost the case with John the Baptist. His influence was enormous. In his *Antiquities,* the Jewish historian Josephus records that Herod became alarmed when he learned of John's popularity. He feared that such eloquence "might lead to some form of sedition." Sometime after his death, John's stature was still so great, the leaders of Judaism feared him and his message (11:27-33).

c. The emphasis of John's powerful preaching was upon righteousness—repentance, confession of sins, rectitude: *make his paths straight* (3). "Confessing their sins, they were baptized by him in the Jordan River" (5, NIV). This is remarkable, for the Jew believed it was the Gentile who needed the washing of baptism, not the sons of Abraham, but John required a *cleansed* life.

d. The locale of John's preaching was also significant. Israel began her life, as the people of God, in the wilderness. It was there Israel received the Law, followed the pillar of cloud and of fire, and experienced the bounty of God's generosity. Dressed like the rugged prophet Elijah, and subsisting on the food a bleak desert could afford, John called Israel to a new Exodus and a new deliverance.

If we were to liken John the Baptist to the great evangelists of modern times—such as George Whitefield, Dwight L. Moody, Billy Graham, as influential as they have been, the Baptist would tower above them.

3. *There was a promise in the gospel* (7-8).

a. However great John the Baptist was, his life and ministry were incomplete and preparatory: *There cometh one mightier than I after me* (7). John was an example of humility and unselfish dedication with few parallels.

Jesus must have had great affection and admiration for John. "I tell you the truth," Jesus said of John, "Among those born of women there has not risen anyone greater than John the Baptist" (Matt. 11:11, NIV; cf. Luke 7:24 ff.). Nevertheless, Jesus recognized that John's work was to prepare the way for the gospel (Matt. 11:10).

b. The proclamation of John included the most significant promise of this age: *I have baptized you with water; but he will baptize you with the Holy Spirit* (8, RSV). To use William Barclay's expression, John's baptism *drenched* men in water, but Jesus would *drench* men in the Holy Spirit.

According to H. Orton Wiley, P. F. Bresee used to say that this promise is the primary truth of our dispensation: *Jesus baptizes men and women with the Holy Spirit and fire.*

c. Mark is at this point laying the groundwork for what is to follow in the life and ministry of Jesus. Three times in the Prologue (1:8, 10, 12), Mark alludes to the Holy Spirit in the experience of Jesus. Conceived by the Holy Spirit (Luke 1:35), anointed by the Spirit (1:10), led by the Spirit (1:12), Jesus ultimately returned to the Father in order to send the Holy Spirit to His disciples (John 15:26). The promise of the gospel is that the power, wisdom, purity, and holiness of Pentecost are available to all repentant believers!

The Baptism and Temptation of Jesus

Mark 1:9-13

> 9 And it came to pass in those days, that Jesus came from Nazareth of Galilee, and was baptized of John in Jordan.
> 10 And straightway coming up out of the water, he saw the heavens opened, and the Spirit like a dove descending upon him:
> 11 And there came a voice from heaven, saying, Thou art my beloved Son, in whom I am well pleased.
> 12 And immediately the spirit driveth him into the wilderness.
> 13 And he was there in the wilderness forty days, tempted of Satan; and was with the wild beasts; and the angels ministered unto him.

Why did Jesus insist upon His own baptism? Matthew tells us that when Jesus came to John for His baptism, the Baptist "forbad him, saying, I have need to be baptized of thee" (Matt. 3:14). But Jesus prevailed. He who had no sin submitted to the baptism of repentance.

What are we to learn from the temptation of Jesus? Was His temptation real? We are assured that Jesus "was in all points tempted like as we are, yet without sin" (Heb. 4:15).

We shall look for answers to these questions.

1. *The baptism: friendly skies.* The hour had struck. For three decades Jesus had lived and worked, thought and prayed in the obscure village of Nazareth (cf. Luke 2:51-52). No one really knew who He was. But now the years of waiting and preparation were at an end. When news of John the Baptist's ministry reached Galilee, the Spirit must have impelled Jesus to lay aside His carpenter's tools and join the crowds following the Baptist.

a. But the question lingers: why did Jesus insist upon receiving John's baptism, when all other candidates came *confessing their sins* (5)? It is thought-provoking to learn that the New Testament contains no systematic discussion of the baptism of Jesus. However, some answers to the questions suggest themselves.

For one thing, Jesus wanted to identify himself with John the Baptist. Jesus knew that John was His own forerunner. "This is the one about whom it is written," Jesus said: "I will send my messenger ahead of you, who will prepare your way before you" (Matt. 11:10, NIV). Jesus recognized that He and John were one in the unfolding plan of God. John may have been the greatest among the prophets and the least in the kingdom of heaven (Matt. 11:11), but the Old Covenant and the New Covenant were both under the control of the one God. Jesus of Nazareth wanted to identify with and support "the Elijah who was to come" (Matt. 11:14, NIV).

Also, and more importantly, Jesus went into the wilderness as God's true Son to bear, in John's baptism, the judgment and sin of Israel and of the world. As Glenn W. Barker has written, in *The New Testament Speaks,* "Jesus in the waters of Jordan . . . takes upon himself God's judgment against Israel so that Israel might go forth to a new Exodus from the slavery of sin and death." Jesus was indeed, as Isaiah prophesied, "numbered with the transgressors; and . . . bare the sins of many" (Isa. 53:12).

b. The baptism of Jesus was a high point—perhaps the highest—in His earthly life. It was a time of conscious, deliberate dedication to His mission in the Father's will. Jesus *chose* to accomplish that mission: "I have a baptism to be baptized with, and how I am constrained until it is accomplished!" (Luke 12:50, RSV).

His baptism was also a special time of enduement and approbation. The people of God had long prayed that He would "rend the heavens and come down" (Isa. 64:1, RSV). They had read in the prophets that a special anointing would be on the Messiah to empower Him for His ministry (Isa. 61:1-3). Now this was all fulfilled; the heaven was torn open, the Spirit descended, and the Father spoke: "Thou art my beloved Son."

In his commentary on Mark, William L. Lane explains the significance of these words. They "express an eternal and essential relationship . . . Jesus did not *become* the Son of God, at baptism or at the transfiguration, he *is* the Son of God, the one qualified to bestow the Holy Spirit."

What power, strength, steadfastness, and zeal this experience must have afforded Jesus for the tasks yet before Him!

2. *The temptation: the hostile desert.* The Spirit, who led Jesus to the high point of heavenly approval, now drives Him to the place of severe testing. G. Campbell Morgan summarizes: "The Spirit after His anointing, drove Him to face the forces that ruin and blast and spoil humanity."

The proximity of two such contrasting events—the baptism and the temptation—is a parable, a commentary on life. The baptism was for Jesus a "mountain peak" of assurance and power. The temptation was for Him one of the darkest valleys. The believer should remember that the servant is not above his Master.

> *In the hour of trial, Jesus, plead for me,*
> *Lest by base denial I depart from Thee.*

We are thus to visualize Jesus as striding into the wilderness with a sense of urgency, perhaps determination. He who came "that he might destroy the works of the devil" (1 John 3:8), must seek out and encounter the enemy at the start. Mark's bare and stark account of the temptation is given in 30 words, but it is pungent and vigorous. Matthew (4:1-11) and Luke (4:1-13) give the details we are familiar with.

When one has a fiery trial or crushing burden to cope with, he wants to be alone and, with God, to wrestle with the problems, to sort out possible decisions, to think through and disentangle issues, to discover his "marching orders."

So it was with Jesus. Satan thrust before Him alternatives to the role of the Suffering Servant (cf. Isaiah 53) and offered an easier and *deadlier* route to world conquest. But Jesus reaffirmed the way of vulnerable love. He chose the road to Golgotha and the Cross, not only there in the wilderness but repeatedly during His ministry (cf. John 6:15).

The place of desolation (perhaps a harsh locale such as the Qumran community had earlier claimed) was one of loneliness but also of fellowship and comfort.

Mark alone records that Jesus *was with the wild beasts* (13). This may carry a hint of the hostility which Christians faced in Rome during the decade in which Mark wrote. According to the Roman historian, Tacitus, in his *Annals,* Christians "dressed in wild animal skins . . . were torn to pieces by dogs, or crucified, or made into torches." Roman Christians would have taken heart from Mark's account.

However, Mark also records that the *angels ministered unto him* (13). In describing the praying of Jesus in Gethsemane, on the eve of the Crucifixion, Luke reports, "there appeared an angel unto him from heaven, strengthening him" (Luke 22:43). The Father does not always remove the cup of trial and suffering, but He does provide comfort and strength that we may drink it. St. Paul found that "as the sufferings of Christ abound in us, so our consolation also aboundeth by Christ" (2 Cor. 1:5).

The Merging of the Old and the New

Mark 1:14-20

> 14 Now after that John was put in prison, Jesus came into Galilee, preaching the gospel of the kingdom of God,
> 15 And saying, The time is fulfilled, and the kingdom of God is at hand: repent ye, and believe the gospel.
> 16 Now as he walked by the sea of Galilee, he saw Simon and Andrew his brother casting a net into the sea: for they were fishers.
> 17 And Jesus said unto them, Come ye after me, and I will make you to become fishers of men.
> 18 And straightway they forsook their nets, and followed him.
> 19 And when he had gone a little farther thence, he saw James the son of Zebedee, and John his brother, who also were in the ship mending their nets.
> 20 And straightway he called them: and they left their father Zebedee in the ship with the hired servants, and went after him.

Change and transition are inevitable. "God buries His workmen but carries on His work." Herod Antipas, in rancor, may have muzzled John the Baptist, but God, in holy love, released His Son to preach the gospel.

Change and transition are painful, but in God's plan and order they bring improvement. Under the Law and the Prophets none was greater than John, but even the "least in the kingdom of heaven is greater than he" (Matt. 11:11, NIV). The new covenant was a marked improvement over the old (Jer. 31:31-34). Even Jesus said, "It is expedient for you that I go away" (John 16:7). How painful that change was for the disciples! The result, however, was the coming of the Holy Spirit. "In ev'ry change He faithful will remain."

1. *The muzzling of John* (14). The details of John's imprisonment and martyrdom are given later (6:14-29) in a "flashback," but two observations may be made here:

a. *The offence of righteousness.* In preparing the way for the Lord (3), John the Baptist stressed personal and social righteousness, rectitude, holiness (cf. Luke 3:7-20).

This put him on a collision course with Herod Antipas, the ruler of Galilee and Perea." John rebuked Herod the tetrarch because of Herodias, his brother's wife, and all the other evil things he had done" (Luke 3:19, NIV). This offended Herod and prompted him to lock up John in prison. That offence has not ceased (John 3:19).

b. The divine signal. When Herod silenced John, Jesus began His public ministry (14). It was as if an angry listener had turned off his radio or television set with no effect upon thousands of others still playing. The light shines on in the darkness, for the darkness has no power to extinguish the light (John 1:5).

2. *The ministry of Jesus.* As we have seen, the new does not destroy the old but fulfills it (Matt. 5:17). John the Baptist later had his problems with doubt about the true identity of Jesus (Matt. 11:2), perhaps understandably so. Jesus reassured and comforted him (Matt. 11:4-15). At this point, the ministry of Jesus involved two activities:

a. Preaching the kingdom. Jesus was both a teacher ("Rabbi," John 1:38) and a preacher. The New Testament words for "teaching" and "preaching" are not the same. *Preaching* involved the proclamation of the gospel and was addressed to the world, whereas *teaching* involved instruction in doctrine and ethics and was addressed to the church. *Jesus came . . . preaching the gospel of the kingdom of God* (14).

The *kingdom* had come near in the person of Jesus. The rule of God, so long anticipated by the prophets (1 Pet. 1:10-11), was now impinging upon men. The Kingdom as a *realm* is yet to come. The Kingdom as a fact of God's *reign* or sovereignty is a present reality (cf. BBC, VI, 277). The "last days" (Acts 2:17) have begun. The message is urgent.

The appropriate response to the approach of the Kingdom is to *repent . . . and believe the gospel* (15). This means a break with, a renunciation of, the past and an acceptance of the gospel with mind and heart. What we believe, or give assent to, is crucial. The mission and message of Jesus carried a sense of urgency: *The kingdom of God is at hand* (15).

b. Preparing the followers. This preparation began with an unqualified call and an unquestioned response. Jesus was ready now to recruit His disciples and begin their preparation. He issued an unqualified call: "Come, follow me" (17, NIV), but with a promise of adequacy. *I will make you to become fishers of men* (17).

It is seldom noted that more than a play on words is involved in the call to become fishers of men. Much is said in the Old Testament about God as a fisher of men and in the atmosphere of judgment (Jer. 16:16; Ezek. 32:3). William L. Lane explains this content: "The summons to be fishers of men is a call to the eschatological task of gathering men in view of the forthcoming judgment of God."

When Christ calls, and thy nets would have thee stay,
To cast them well's to cast them quite away.

The unqualified call met with an unquestioned response. It is probable that these first disciples—Simon and Andrew, James and John—had previous knowledge of Jesus through the ministry of John the Baptist. It is clear that Simon and Andrew, at least, had been introduced to Jesus by the Baptist (John 1:40-41). In any case, their response to the call of Jesus was immediate and without compromise. In Mark's view, this is the ideal reaction to the invitation of Jesus. "When the voice of Jesus calls, we should drop everything and respond." It is startling to visualize the Son of Man confronting Everyman with the direct, friendly, firm call, *Come, follow me* (17).

Mighty in Word and Deed

Mark 1:21-28

21 And they went into Capernaum; and straightway on the sabbath day he entered into the synagogue, and taught.
22 And they were astonished at his doctrine: for he taught them as one that had authority, and not as the scribes.

23 And there was in their synagogue a man with an unclean spirit; and he cried out,

24 Saying, Let us alone; what have we to do with thee, thou Jesus of Nazareth? art thou come to destroy us? I know thee who thou art, the Holy One of God.

25 And Jesus rebuked him, saying, Hold thy peace, and come out of him.

26 And when the unclean spirit had torn him, and cried with a loud voice, he came out of him.

27 And they were all amazed, insomuch that they questioned among themselves, saying, What thing is this? what new doctrine is this? for with authority commandeth he even the unclean spirits, and they do obey him.

28 And immediately his fame spread abroad throughout all the region round about Galilee.

Mark tells his story in a matter-of-fact way, using few adjectives and adverbs, but the thoughtful reader will soon discover that the Evangelist has a deliberate purpose—to describe Jesus in such a way as to elicit faith and obedience. The Prophet of Nazareth already begins to loom as the Son of God, whose authority and power are awesome.

1. *The authority of Jesus.* Those who listened to Jesus as He taught and who looked on as He cared for human needs were consistently *astonished* (22).

a. They were astonished at what He taught, i.e., *his doctrine* (22). Mark records more of the works of Jesus than of His teachings, but he makes it clear, as do the other Evangelists, that "never man spake like this man" (John 7:46). To this day, the parables and stories of Jesus permeate and color our culture and civilization. How many hospitals, e.g., bear the name "Good Samaritan"?

b. However, the people were especially astonished at the way He taught, *for he taught them as one that had authority* (22). His authority was intrinsic to His own person and not, as with the scribes, derived and secondary. The scribes quoted earlier sources and debated endlessly the complexities of their burdensome tradition.

Jesus came, as did the prophets, with *thus saith the Lord* upon His lips. But He was more than a prophet, for as the unique Son of God, He was also the "Word [who] was made flesh" (John 1:14).

We have some understanding of such authority from our experience of the self-authenticating power of truth and character. The scientist who discovers and publishes truth speaks with authority. The musician who composes from what he has discovered of reality, speaks, in his idiom, with authority. The writer—poet, playwright, philosopher—who has seen through the veil of the flesh to the world of the spirit, speaks with authority. And so the works of Einstein, Beethoven, Milton, Shakespeare, and Plato have a self-authenticating quality about them.

Likewise also the preacher, who has labored to divide rightly "the word of truth" (2 Tim. 2:15) and who proclaims "the gospel . . . with the Holy Ghost sent down from heaven" (1 Pet. 1:12), speaks with *authority, and not as the scribes* (22).

2. *The power of Jesus.* The authority of Jesus appeared not only in His teachings but also in His works. The authority of His words was confirmed by the power of His deeds.

a. On this Sabbath in Capernaum, Jesus appeared as a provocative Presence. A man "who was possessed by an evil spirit" (23, NIV) cried out in recognition of Jesus. Ordinary sick folk usually called upon Jesus with such terms as, "Master" (9:17) or "Son of David" (10:47), whereas the demoniacs addressed Him as *the Holy One of God* (24) or "the Son of the most high God" (5:7). They had a superior knowledge of His person and understood they were in conflict with Him.

Hitherto the *man with an unclean spirit* (23) had been neither disturbed nor helped *in their synagogue* (23), but now he will be both disturbed and helped.

It is ironic that, in our day, Satan worship, interest in the occult, and talk of the demonic flourish along with the sophisticated rejection of belief in demon possession. But what evil, unclean spirits impair the mind and defile the soul of mankind! The universal presence of greed and malice and impurity testify to the reality of Satan and his kingdom. The *Holy One of God* (24) still engages the enemy to disturb and to destroy him.

The answer to the question, *Art thou come to destroy us?* is yes! Mark wants us to understand that "the Son of God came to earth with the express purpose of liquidating the devil's activities" (1 John 3:8, Phillips).

b. The righteous Exorcist encountered the foe as no other exorcist then or now. Using no devices, spells, or incantations, Jesus rebuked the evil spirit and commanded him to leave the man. "'Be quiet!' said Jesus sternly. 'Come out of him!'" (25, NIV).

The action of Jesus in exorcising the unclean spirit aroused a mixed reaction. The realm of the demons responded with consternation, anger, and conflict. The evil spirits may have sought to counter the power of Jesus by calling His name and thus, as some supposed, gain the upper hand. The command of Jesus, *Hold thy peace* (25), was a rebuke to an opponent. Furthermore, it was not yet time to reveal His messiahship. When that revelation was made it would not come from an unworthy witness.

The response of the people was always one of amazement, perhaps with a touch of alarm. "What is this? A new teaching with authority!" (27, NASB). They had no means by which to classify Him. He was *sui generis,* unique. Their categories did not fit Him.

We may well remember that Mark was writing a missionary document. The young church was perhaps 30 to 40 years old and struggling to grow in spite of bitter persecution, ostracism, and discouragement. Defections did occur. Mark wanted these young Christians to join the crowds who followed Jesus in Galilee, to sense their awe as He taught, and to hear them gasp as they saw His mighty works. Perhaps believers today should become a part of those crowds and recover again their astonishment and amazement at the words and works of Jesus.

A Healing Ministry in Capernaum

Mark 1:29-34

> 29 And forthwith, when they were come out of the synagogue, they entered into the house of Simon and Andrew, with James and John.
> 30 But Simon's wife's mother lay sick of a fever, and anon they tell him of her.
> 31 And he came and took her by the hand, and lifted her up; and immediately the fever left her, and she ministered unto them.
> 32 And at even, when the sun did set, they brought unto him all that were diseased, and them that were possessed with devils.
> 33 And all the city was gathered together at the door.
> 34 And he healed many that were sick of divers diseases, and cast out many devils; and suffered not the devils to speak, because they knew him.

Mark wastes no time in showing that Jesus almost literally burst in upon the Galilean scene with astonishing words and deeds. It is not surprising that *immediately his fame spread abroad* (28) and that everyone came looking for Him.

These verses describe a Sabbath day in Capernaum, the hometown of Simon and Andrew and, increasingly, something of a home base for Jesus. The Great Physician devoted much of that Sabbath to a healing ministry. The publicity which naturally followed created problems.

1. *The Great Physician.* If Paul called Luke "the beloved physician" (Col. 4:14), what should we call Jesus? Perhaps the following lines are appropriate:

> *The Great Physician now is near,*
> *The sympathizing Jesus.*

As we see Jesus touching the many who came to Him and healing them of "various diseases" (34, RSV), we may call to mind a considerate, unselfish family doctor who gives himself to his patients almost to the breaking point.

a. The healing ministry of Jesus in Capernaum began in a home and spread to the town. The little party of Jesus and the four (presumably) disciples evidently went directly to the home of Simon and Andrew from the synagogue service, *where they found Simon's wife's mother . . . sick of a fever* (30). We are not told in the Gospels about Peter's wife, although Paul makes reference to her in his correspondence with the Corinthian church (1 Cor. 9:5).

Evidently this illness caused some distress, for "they told Jesus about her" (30, NIV). When guests are coming for dinner after church, it is distressing to have one of the principal helpers in bed with "a high fever" (Luke 4:38, RSV). Perhaps this was the first instance in Christian history when believers felt in their hearts:

> *I must tell Jesus all of my trials,*
> *I cannot bear these burdens alone.*

The response of Jesus, as always, was immediate and compassionate. He went to the sick room, took the afflicted one by the hand, and restored her to the family. It is clear from this story that Jesus was comfortable in a home situation, and that Christian discipleship does not require the repudiation of family relationships.

b. By this time, word of the dramatic deliverances in Capernaum had spread throughout the town. Devout friends of the ill waited for sundown and the close of the Sabbath. They were forbidden to bear burdens across town on the Sabbath (cf. Jer. 17:24). But now that the stars were appearing, the people brought to Jesus "all who were sick or were possessed with demons" (32, RSV).

Mark's excitement is obvious: "the whole town gathered at the door" (33, NIV). Compassionate friends so often were instrumental in bringing the sick and the possessed to Jesus. The compassionate Savior never disappointed them. He healed them all.

2. *The problem of publicity.* Few churches in our time would be concerned about too much publicity, but a twofold problem did develop for Jesus because of the crowds.

a. One problem arose from the fact that the throngs had little if any understanding of His mission on earth. In His compassion for their need, Jesus always responded to their plea. However, increasingly He sought for solitude from the crowds, in order to instruct His disciples and to prepare them for the difficult days ahead.

How many there are who seek for God in a time of crisis or adversity, but who forget Him in more prosperous times! Those who follow Jesus for the "loaves and fishes" will never receive the blessings He really came to bestow.

b. The other problem issued from the incessant struggle between Jesus and the demons. *They knew him* and wanted to scream out that recognition. The Gospels do not tell us why Jesus "would not let the demons speak" (34, NIV). One wonders if modern "gospel hucksters" would not capitalize on such sensational testimony.

It may be that Jesus muzzled the demons because they were not worthy witnesses, or because He did not want His identity revealed by anyone, natural or supernatural (cf. 8:30). Unquestionably Jesus did want to demonstrate His power over Satan and the demonic forces which violate and impair human personality. Whatever the reason may have been, as believers we can claim the promise: "greater is he that is in you, than he that is in the world" (1 John 4:4).

The Prayer Life of Jesus

Mark 1:35-39

> 35 And in the morning, rising up a great while before day, he went out, and departed into a solitary place, and there prayed.
> 36 And Simon and they that were with him followed after him.
> 37 And when they had found him, they said unto him, All men seek for thee.
> 38 And he said unto them, Let us go into the next towns, that I may preach there also: for therefore came I forth.
> 39 And he preached in their synagogues throughout all Galilee, and cast out devils.

It is a moving experience to reflect upon the prayer life of Jesus. He prayed often and at length. Mark reports earnest periods of prayer at the outset, in the midst, and at the close of our Lord's ministry (35; 6:46; 14:32). Luke alone notes that Jesus prayed at His baptism and at the Transfiguration.

From these verses, we may learn something more

about prayer as communion with God, and prayer as a source of divine direction.

1. *Prayer and communion with God.* How can one put into words the sense of need, of dependency, of longing, which impels one to pray and to become oblivious to time?

   a. Jesus felt a longing to pray. This is obvious. He repeatedly turned away from the crowds, even from the disciples, to pray. The present instance is a classic example: *Rising up a great while before day, he . . . departed into a solitary place, and there prayed* (35). He prayed alone, often in the night hours, and in some place apart from the crowds.

   b. Jesus found strength and comfort in prayer. The Gospels do not describe the inner feelings of Jesus, but they do tell us how Jesus returned from the place of prayer renewed in strength and power, and confident of the next step to take. And so it can and should be with us.

> *We kneel, and all around us seems to low'r.*
> *We rise, and all—the distant and the near—*
> *Stands forth in sunny outline, brave and clear.*

To pray in the Spirit, to lift up "holy hands, without wrath and doubting" (1 Tim. 2:8), is to be in touch with the living God. It is to receive from Him comfort (literally, "strength with"), healing, and poise. Prayer as communion with God is a priceless privilege.

2. *Prayer and divine direction.* The previous day's ministry of healing in Capernaum (29-34) had startled the entire community and had brought *all the city . . . together* (33). Evidently the excitement continued into the next day. Surprised and disappointed that Jesus had disappeared, the disciples searched until they found Him. They may have reproached Him a bit, when they exclaimed, "Everyone is looking for you!" (37, NIV).

   Simon and the others may have been taken aback when Jesus showed no interest in returning to Capernaum and the crowds who clamored for Him. The disciples may have puzzled, "This is a strange way for a new Rabbi-Prophet to gain a following!" So often divine direction is unexpected and surprising. The winds of the Spirit blow where they will, and man cannot predict their movement (cf. John 3:8).

In the solitary place of prayer, Jesus had received His "marching orders." He heard the "beat of a drum" inaudible to everyone else. *Let us go into the next towns, that I may preach there also* (38).

His marching orders included two responsibilities: to *preach* the gospel and to *cast out* Satan (39). What other tasks does the Christian Church have today, but to proclaim the good news of God's holy love and to seize the minions of the devil and destroy them!

An Amazing Miracle

Mark 1:40-45

> 40 And there came a leper to him, beseeching him, and kneeling down to him, and saying unto him, If thou wilt, thou canst make me clean.
> 41 And Jesus, moved with compassion, put forth his hand, and touched him, and saith unto him, I will; be thou clean.
> 42 And as soon as he had spoken, immediately the leprosy departed from him, and he was cleansed.
> 43 And he straitly charged him, and forthwith sent him away;
> 44 And saith unto him, See thou say nothing to any man: but go thy way, shew thyself to the priest, and offer for thy cleansing those things which Moses commanded, for a testimony unto them.
> 45 But he went out, and began to publish it much, and to blaze abroad the matter, insomuch that Jesus could no more openly enter into the city, but was without in desert places: and they came to him from every quarter.

The healing of a man "full of leprosy" (Luke 5:12) was an amazing miracle, to say the least. The rabbis of the day believed that it was as easy to cure a leper as to raise the dead.

The unfolding of this story tells us something about the plight of lepers in general, as well as the pluck of this one. We gain an insight into the reaction of Jesus to such need and some understanding concerning His view of established religious authorities.

1. *The plight and pluck of the leper.* The plight of lepers in that day was a sad one. Not only did they suffer a destructive and disfiguring disease, they experienced isolation and humiliation in their society. The experience of lepers must have been crushing and depressing.

a. Chapters 13 and 14 of Leviticus describe the Mosaic legislation concerning leprosy. The following verses depict some of the restrictions on the leper: "The leper who has the disease shall wear torn clothes and let the hair of his head hang loose, and he shall cover his upper lip and cry, 'Unclean, unclean.' He shall remain unclean as long as he has the disease; he is unclean; he shall dwell alone in a habitation outside the camp" (Lev. 13:45-46, RSV).

In addition to these restraints, the rabbis had refined the biblical legislation, imposing further requirements on the lepers. They were not permitted, for example, to enter the city of Jerusalem. All non-lepers feared even a chance contact with lepers, because of the resultant legal contamination.

b. The pluck of this leper is inspiring. He had broken the law in coming close to Jesus and in begging Him for cleansing. He must not have known who Jesus was, but he had faith that Jesus could do what was utterly impossible. "If you are willing, you can make me clean" (40, NIV).

2. *The reactions and feeling of Jesus.* To someone looking on, the response of Jesus would have been shocking: "he stretched out his hand and touched him" (41, RSV). Touch a leper? Never! A person was rendered ceremonially unclean if a leper came near him.

That healing touch was prompted by deep and powerful emotions in the soul of Jesus: He was "filled with compassion" (41, NIV). Completely aware of the ravages of the disease, probably annoyed by the endless rabbinical legalities, Jesus cut through all the ecclesiastical and social regulations to touch the leper, and healed him! *I will: be thou clean* (41).

An interesting textual variant here describes Jesus as

"moved with anger" rather than with compassion. The NEB adopts that reading. William L. Lane agrees and explains its implications: "The anger can be understood as an expression of righteous indignation at the ravages of sin, disease and death which take their toll even upon the living, a toll particularly evident in a leper."

3. *The recognition of religious authorities.* It is instructive to examine the painstaking care with which Jesus sought to follow *those things which Moses commanded* concerning such a healing. The procedures are described in Lev. 14:2-31.

The person who believed he had been cleansed was required to offer certain sacrifices, depending upon his financial ability. The poor presented less expensive offerings. In New Testament times this person would first undergo an examination by the priest nearby and then journey to Jerusalem for final clearance and further sacrifices. Such deliverance was rare (cf. Num. 12:10 ff.; 2 Kings 5:1 ff.).

We may say that, in a certain sense, Jesus worked "within the system." His faithful attendance at the synagogue and regular trips to the Temple in Jerusalem are evidence enough. However, a final comment of Jesus calls for more careful scrutiny: *for a testimony unto them* (44).

This may mean simply that verification was desirable. "So that everyone will have proof that you are well again" (44, TLB). However, the comment may also carry a somber warning and be rendered, "for a testimony against them" (cf. 13:9, where the New Testament words are the same). This would be to say that a new thing has happened in Israel. God's kingdom, with power over disease, demons, and death, is at hand. Would the ecclesiastical authorities recognize and acknowledge that Kingdom? If not, judgment is also near.

We are not told whether the cleansed leper followed the directions Jesus gave him. We do know that he began *to blaze abroad the matter,* contrary to the explicit command of Jesus, so that the Lord's ministry was hindered even more by the masses who *came to him from every quarter* (45).

MARK 2

The Authority of the Son of Man
Mark 2:1-12

> 1 And again he entered into Capernaum after some days; and it was noised that he was in the house.
> 2 And straightway many were gathered together, insomuch that there was no room to receive them, no, not so much as about the door: and he preached the word unto them.
> 3 And they come unto him, bringing one sick of the palsy, which was borne of four.
> 4 And when they could not come nigh unto him for the press, they uncovered the roof where he was: and when they had broken it up, they let down the bed wherein the sick of the palsy lay.
> 5 When Jesus saw their faith, he said unto the sick of the palsy, Son, thy sins be forgiven thee.
> 6 But there were certain of the scribes sitting there, and reasoning in their hearts,
> 7 Why doth this man thus speak blasphemies? who can forgive sins but God only?
> 8 And immediately when Jesus perceived in his spirit that they so reasoned within themselves, he said unto them, Why reason ye these things in your hearts?
> 9 Whether is it easier to say to the sick of the palsy, Thy sins be forgiven thee; or to say, Arise, and take up thy bed, and walk?
> 10 But that ye may know that the Son of man hath power on earth to forgive sins, (he saith to the sick of the palsy,)
> 11 I say unto thee, Arise, and take up thy bed, and go thy way into thine house.
> 12 And immediately he arose, took up the bed, and went forth before them all; insomuch that they were all amazed, and glorified God, saying, We never saw it on this fashion.

We have reached something of a transition at this point. It is already clear what manner of Man Jesus is. His mighty words and deeds confirm the affirmation that He is the "Christ, the Son of God" (1:1). What follows next (2:1—3:6) is the account of a developing conflict with the Pharisees and other leaders of Judaism. Mark reports a series of five controversies in this section. He will later (11:27—12:37) include another series of five such encounters.

In Jesus of Nazareth the "kingdom of God" (1:15) had come near. He had cast out evil spirits, "healed many that were sick of divers diseases" (1:34), and had even cleansed a leper of that loathsome disease. But all of this produced resistance and conflict. "He came unto his own, and his own received him not" (John 1:11). His people neither repented nor believed.

In the first of these conflict narratives, Mark makes it plain that Jesus, now described as *the Son of man* (10), has the authority to forgive sins and the power to prove it. The story involves the visible faith of friends, the hostile thoughts of foes, and the healing words of Jesus.

1. *Visible faith.* It is impressive to discover, in the Gospel story, how often the afflicted and needy found healing and deliverance because friends brought them to Jesus (e.g., 1:32). It was so in this instance. Four faithful friends brought a paralytic to Jesus and surmounted stubborn hurdles to reach Him.

a. They were confident that Jesus could and would heal their friend. From some experience or observation, they were convinced of both the ability and the willingness of Jesus to restore the paralytic to an active life. The leper (1:40) was confident of the ability of Jesus, less sure of His willingness.

b. They were persistent in their purpose, despite serious obstacles. Men with fainter hearts would have given up. They made a way when no way was apparent. The material values represented by the roof and its damage were secondary.

It is startling to consider how many needs are *not* met because no one cared, or prayed, or interceded, when such caring was possible to someone.

> *Do you really care?*
> *Do you know how to share*
> *With people everywhere?*

It was *when Jesus saw their faith* (5), i.e., the faith of

those who accompanied the paralytic, that He responded to their plea: *Son, thy sins be forgiven thee* (5).

2. *Hostile thoughts.* Opposition to Jesus was at first unexpressed. The scribes were *reasoning in their hearts* (6). This hostility soon broke out into criticism of the disciples (2:16) and, of course, ultimately in designs on the life of Jesus (3:6). It is the heart which we must guard "with all diligence, for from it flow the springs of life" (Prov. 4:23, NASB).

a. Inadvertently, the scribes attributed something to Jesus which was true (literally): *Who is able to forgive sins except the one God?* (7). *The Son of man* (10) is also *the Son of God* (1:1). Belief in the two natures of Christ, divine and human, forever united in one Person, is a cornerstone of the Christian faith.

b. Jesus was at once and fully aware of this silent hostility. "Immediately Jesus knew in his spirit that this was what they were thinking" (8, NIV). Mark suggests something more than a natural surmising. And so it was later on. As the tension and antagonism mounted, Jesus knew what to expect, finally, in Jerusalem. Thrice He announced to the bewildered disciples His suffering, death, and resurrection. "I lay down my life. . . . No man taketh it from me" (John 10:17-18).

3. *Healing words.* The Gospels depict Jesus as a master of every situation. He was never surprised or at loss. His total adequacy was never more evident than in this event.

a. As a great Teacher, Jesus knew the value of creating suspense, the importance of motivating learning. He asked questions, probed minds, stimulated thought. In coping with the nonverbal charge of blasphemy (7), Jesus asked a penetrating question: Which is easier: "to say . . . 'Your sins are forgiven,' or to say, 'Get up, take your mat and walk'?" (9, NIV). Without serious reflection, the reply would be, "it's easier to say, 'Your sins are forgiven.'"

But it is not easy to forgive sins. When one has been

wronged—defrauded, misrepresented, betrayed—it is difficult to extend forgiveness. It is not easy for God to forgive sins. But God, in the Person of His Son, has taken into himself the guilt and disgrace of our sins so as to "be just, and the justifier of him which believeth in Jesus" (Rom. 3:25-26). It is not easy to say, *Thy sins be forgiven thee* (9).

Moreover, Jesus may well have been disturbing the doctrine of suffering promoted by these "teachers of the law" (6, NIV). In their view, this man must have been a sinner because he had a serious affliction. To sin greatly was to suffer greatly; therefore, if one suffered greatly he had sinned greatly.

On this view, it would follow that to cure the afflicted person would be the only way to prove he had been forgiven. When Jesus said to the paralytic, *Arise, and take up thy bed, and go thy way* (11), He was piling up evidence that "the Son of man has authority on earth to forgive sins" (10, RSV).

b. In response to His own penetrating question, Jesus had given a powerful reply. The reactions were, as usual, varied and contrasting.

The teachers of the law (the scribes) saw their own doctrine and authority under attack, in danger of demolition. Like everyone else, they may have been amazed, though it is doubtful that they were among those who *glorified God* for what they saw (12). They would soon be plotting with others "how they might destroy him" (3:6).

What thoughts flooded the mind of the one who came to Jesus *borne of four* (3), but who returned home sound in body, mind, and soul? He must have needed the assurance of forgiveness which Jesus communicated to him. It is possible that his affliction was related to some sinful practice. It is also possible that he had needlessly heaped blame and guilt upon himself for his distress. Often good and devout people have an overpowering sense of guilt when disaster strikes them or some member of their family. "What did I do wrong?" they ask.

Elsewhere, Jesus makes it clear that no necessary connection exists between personal misfortune and sinfulness. His disciples once asked Him, concerning a man blind from birth, "Who did sin, this man, or his parents, that he was born blind?" (John 9:2). Their prejudice was obvious. Jesus answered, "Neither hath this man sinned, nor his parents." It was, instead, an occasion for "the works of God [to] be made manifest in him" (John 9:3).

Like all men, the paralytic had sinned and needed divine forgiveness for personal transgressions. Like most of us, he probably also needed the assurance of a compassionate Savior that God accepts us as we are, apart from sin, and that we should accept that fact.

The Son of Man has authority on earth to forgive sins: *Son, thy sins be forgiven thee* (5). He also has power on earth to prove it: *Arise, take up thy bed, and go thy way* (11).

The Call and Response of Levi

Mark 2:13-17

> 13 And he went forth again by the sea side; and all the multitude resorted unto him, and he taught them.
> 14 And as he passed by, he saw Levi the son of Alphaeus sitting at the receipt of custom, and said unto him, Follow me. And he arose and followed him.
> 15 And it came to pass, that, as Jesus sat at meat in his house, many publicans and sinners sat also together with Jesus and his disciples: for there were many, and they followed him.
> 16 And when the scribes and Pharisees saw him eat with publicans and sinners, they said unto his disciples, How is it that he eateth and drinketh with publicans and sinners?
> 17 When Jesus heard it, he saith unto them, They that are whole have no need of the physician, but they that are sick: I came not to call the righteous, but sinners to repentance.

Jesus now takes up again the calling of those who would be among the Twelve. As *he went forth again by the sea side* (13), He saw *Levi the Son of Alphaeus* in the crowd and singled him out: *Follow me* (14). The response of Levi, known also as Matthew (Matt. 9:9), was immediate: *He arose and followed him* (14).

Despite the multitudes which followed, the seaside, like the wilderness and the mountains, probably represented a place of retreat and solitude, where Jesus could ponder His ministry in the face of hostile forces.

Our Lord's sovereign choice of Levi, the tax collector's obedience, and the tragic attitude of the Pharisees are among the issues here.

1. *The Lord's sovereign choice.* Why did Jesus choose Levi? John Henry Jowett speaks of "the possibilities of the unlikely. A disciple from among the publicans!" Jesus did not go first to the schools for His disciples, but to the fishing boats and to "the tax office" (14, RSV). It is in the wilderness that waters shall break out, and streams in the desert (Isa. 35:6).

Divine election to places of responsibility and service is inscrutable. We cannot know the mind of the Lord on such matters. "Ye have not chosen me, but I have chosen you" (John 15:16). We can be confident that however unlikely the prospect may be, the Lord can help him to become what is needed: "I will make you to become" (1:17).

2. *Levi's free and friendly response.* We have already seen how the first disciples (Simon and Andrew, James and John), upon hearing the voice of Jesus, dropped everything and followed Him (1:14-20). It was so also with Levi.

It is likely that Levi's choice was more costly. The fishermen could easily return to their boats and nets, as indeed they later were tempted to do (John 21:3). The possibility of returning to the *receipt of custom* was less probable. But what an exchange Levi made! He turned from a post where he was hated by everyone, to become an immortal apostle, forever remembered as the author of the First Gospel.

3. *The Pharisees' tragic rejection.* Perhaps as a farewell occasion, and with a missionary motive, Levi prepared a dinner for Jesus, the disciples, and "many tax collectors and 'sinners'" (15, NIV). The Pharisees, with their punctilious observances of ceremonial law, criticized Jesus for

His association with "publicans and sinners," the outcasts of their society.

It is worthy of note that new converts, recently redeemed out of the darkness of this present evil world, are often more effective soul winners than established Christians, whose close friends may be largely in church circles. Levi's associations were chiefly with the despised tax collectors and Jews who were careless about the ceremonial law.

The reply of Jesus should give all of us pause. He does not call *the righteous,* the self-sufficient and satisfied, *but sinners* (17), those who are "poor in spirit" and who "mourn" over their spiritual poverty (Matt. 5:3-4).

The Old Vis-à-vis The New

Mark 2:18-22

> 18 And the disciples of John and of the Pharisees used to fast: and they come and say unto him, Why do the disciples of John and of the Pharisees fast, but thy disciples fast not?
> 19 And Jesus said unto them, Can the children of the bridechamber fast, while the bridegroom is with them? as long as they have the bridegroom with them, they cannot fast.
> 20 But the days will come, when the bridegroom shall be taken away from them, and then shall they fast in those days.
> 21 No man also seweth a piece of new cloth on an old garment: else the new piece that filled it up taketh away from the old, and the rent is made worse.
> 22 And no man putteth new wine into old bottles: else the new wine doth burst the bottles, and the wine is spilled, and the bottles will be marred: but new wine must be put into new bottles.

A couple of issues are evident in this passage. The question of fasting had obviously arisen in the Early Church. The practice of the Pharisees and the disciples of John seemed to set a standard. What would be the Christian practice?

Another and more fundamental question was the relationship of the old era to the new. In Christ "the new has come" (2 Cor. 5:17, RSV). What would become of the old form? It will be important to contrast the comfort of the old with the pain of the new, while seeking a way to reconcile the two.

1. *The comfort of the old.* Change is nearly always disturbing, resulting in discomfort. Transition from the old covenant to the new (Jer. 31:31-34; Heb. 8:8-12) created stress.

    a. It was appropriate for John's disciples to fast. Their noble leader had suffered martyrdom at the hands of Herod Antipas. In their view it was no time for rejoicing.

    b. It was traditional for the Pharisees and their disciples to fast. The Pharisees, among others, were the bearers of a distinguished tradition of loyalty to the Jewish law. They represented the Jews who withstood at great personal cost the blasphemies of the Syrian invader nearly two centuries before.

    c. When the young Prophet of Nazareth came into this situation, leading a happy crowd of people who never fasted and who seemed to be careless about other niceties of the ceremonial law, consternation ensued. The question naturally arose: *Why do . . . thy disciples fast not?* (18).

2. *The pain of the new.* Jesus replied with a counter question. It is striking to discover how frequently and effectively Jesus asked questions, both to fend off a foe and to spur the thought of disciples. "Can the wedding guests fast while the bridegroom is with them?" (19, RSV).

It was inappropriate, *at this time,* for the disciples of Jesus to fast. To imagine a service of fasting at a wedding reception would be out of the question. What follows was more sobering, though few would have understood the implications until after the Resurrection. *The days will come, when the bridegroom shall be taken away* (20).

Jesus here obliquely alludes to the dignity of His own Person as the bridegroom (cf. Isa. 54:5) and clearly implies that His own death would be violent. The bridegroom would *be taken away from them* (20). In those tragic days fasting would be appropriate.

But for now gladness and joy are in order: "The blind receive their sight, and the lame walk, the lepers are cleansed" (Matt. 11:5)—and much more! "How can the guests . . . fast?" (19, NIV). No! It is time for the old to give way to the new.

3. *The possibility of reconciliation.* These ideas are surely startling and revolutionary. The old forms of Judaism were brutally destroyed, while the new Christian faith burst into flame. *The new wine* of the kingdom found *new wineskins* (22), new ways of worship, new songs and hymns, new standards of behavior, even a new covenant, and a New Testament.

a. But must the new wine of the Kingdom always burst the old forms? This is a continuing problem in a family, a church, or a society where timeless values are precious. Sooner or later a new generation will hold the reins of power. What will that generation do with the biblical ideals of marriage and the home? With "the faith which was once delivered unto the saints" (Jude 3)? With the treasures of freedom found in the democracies?

b. The possibility of reconciliation between the old and the new must lie in the ability of both to transmit the new wine to each succeeding generation in new forms so that the wine is not spilled nor the wineskins marred (22).

The Master of the Sabbath
Mark 2:23—3:6

> 23 And it came to pass, that he went through the corn fields on the sabbath day; and his disciples began, as they went, to pluck the ears of corn.
> 24 And the Pharisees said unto him, Behold, why do they on the sabbath day that which is not lawful?
> 25 And he said unto them, Have ye never read what David did, when he had need, and was an hungred, he, and they that were with him?
> 26 How he went into the house of God in the days of Abiathar the high priest, and did eat the shewbread, which is not lawful to eat but for the priests, and gave also to them which were with him?
> 27 And he said unto them, The sabbath was made for man, and not man for the sabbath:
> 28 Therefore the Son of man is Lord also of the sabbath.
> 3:1 And he entered again into the synagogue; and there was a man there which had a withered hand.
> 2 And they watched him, whether he would heal him on the sabbath day; that they might accuse him.

> 3 And he saith unto the man which had the withered hand, Stand forth.
> 4 And he saith unto them, Is it lawful to do good on the sabbath days, or to do evil? to save life, or to kill? But they held their peace.
> 5 And when he had looked round about on them with anger, being grieved for the hardness of their hearts, he saith unto the man, Stretch forth thine hand. And he stretched it out: and his hand was restored whole as the other.
> 6 And the Pharisees went forth, and straightway took counsel with the Herodians against him, how they might destroy him.

The Pharisees criticized Jesus with increasing harshness. Their enmity and hostility grew until they were ready, in collusion with the Herodians, to destroy Him (3:6). The issues in this section (2:1—3:6) were the forgiveness of sins, friendship with tax collectors and "sinners," the practice of fasting, the laws of Sabbath observance.

The two conflict stories before us relate to controversy over the Sabbath and disclose the sharp contrast between the qualities of the critics and the qualities of Jesus.

In the first instance (2:23-24), Jesus and the disciples were criticized for plucking heads of grain as they walked along the way. This was perfectly legitimate, as long as a sickle was not used (Deut. 23:25). In the opinion of the critics, the disciples were in violation of the law against "reaping" on the Sabbath.

MARK 3

In the second instance (3:1-6), Jesus was about to heal a man in the synagogue who *had a withered hand* (3:1). The Pharisees grumbled that this was not a matter of life and death and could wait until the Sabbath was over.

1. *The qualities of the critics.* Those who were by profession "teachers of the law" appear in a poor light.

a. *The critics were insensitive to human need.* Once more, Jesus countered with questions. In response to the charge of "reaping" on the Sabbath, Jesus queried, *Have ye never read what David did?* (2:26). He reminded them of what must have been a familiar story that, for the sake of human need, David persuaded the priest to feed his soldiers with holy bread, lawful only for the priests to eat (2:25; cf. 1 Sam. 21:3-6).

In response to the charge that He was "practicing medicine" on the Sabbath, Jesus probed further: *Is it lawful to do good on the sabbath days, or to do evil* (3:4)? The answer is obvious: To do good, to save life, is lawful on the Sabbath. To do evil, to kill life is unlawful.

b. The critics were ignorant of the scriptures. What a sharp question Jesus addressed to men who were reputed to be experts in their Scriptures! *Have you never read* (25)? They had indeed read but without understanding. However careful and thorough one's knowledge of the Scriptures may be, if that learning does not convey meaning, it is deficient.

c. The critics were slaves of the Law. Jesus was no iconoclast. He had not "come to destroy the law, or the prophets . . . but to fulfill" (Matt. 5:17), to bring them to completion, to their full flower. The letter of the law is murderous: "the letter killeth, but the spirit giveth life" (2 Cor. 3:6). In the words of William L. Lane, "Jesus argues that the tradition of the Pharisees is unduly stringent and exceeds the intention of the Law."

2. *The qualities of the Master.* In these two conflict stories the qualities of Jesus appear in bright contrast to those of His critics. We see:

a. His understanding of the Scriptures. That He was familiar with the Scriptures is clear both from His insights and from His facility in using the scrolls (see Luke 4:16-21). Jesus often rebuked His listeners and His critics for their obtuse grasp of their own Scriptures. "Ye do err, not knowing the scriptures, nor the power of God" (Matt. 22:29).

Scholarship must have its rights, but the scholar who

has no fellowship with the Spirit of truth (cf. John 15:26) will not understand the Scriptures as Jesus did.

b. His compassion and caring. Religion is not primarily a matter of ritual, as it was with the Pharisees, but rather a means of serving human need.

On that Sabbath day, as the disciples walked through the grainfields, they took advantage of a compassionate provision in their own law to satisfy their hunger. But that need was less important to the Pharisees than their tradition.

The man in the synagogue with the shriveled right hand had a serious handicap. Legend has it that he was a bricklayer who had lost his means of livelihood. However, the tradition of the Pharisees required that no medical treatment could be given which would improve the condition of a patient. Only emergency measures to prevent a worsening of the problem were allowed.

It is not surprising that Jesus *looked round about on them with anger* before He said to the man, *Stretch forth thine hand* (3:5). This is the only place in the Gospels where Jesus is described as being angry, but one thinks at once of the statement in Hebrews, "Thou hast loved righteousness and hated iniquity" (Heb. 1:9). The antagonism of Jesus to evil was implacable.

c. His self-awareness as Lord. Here is the sum of all issues concerning Sabbath observance: *The sabbath was made for man, not man for the Sabbath. So the Son of Man is Lord even of the sabbath* (2:27-28).

It would be unfair and ungracious not to give the Jewish people due recognition and appreciation for their love of the Sabbath and their steadfast loyalty to the fourth commandment of the Decalogue. In our day, the significance of the Christian Sabbath as the Lord's Day has declined. The consequence is a threat to the Christian elements in our society.

Many a Jew has given his life rather than tarnish his devotion to the Sabbath and its sacred history. The Roman general Pompey beseiged Jerusalem on the Sabbath, knowing that no Jew would defend himself. According to William Barclay, "The Romans, who had compulsory military service, had in the end to exempt the Jews from army service because no strict Jew would fight on the Sabbath."

However, the tradition of the Pharisees had become, as Peter declared, "a yoke . . . which neither our fathers nor we were able to bear" (Acts 15:10). Jesus brought liberty and freedom, not from moral responsibility, but from the dreadful blight of legalism.

In our desire to balance Christian liberty and moral responsibility, how are we to escape the twin evils of legalism and lawlessness? In Christian history, some form of "prescriptive ethics," i.e., the use of "rules," has often been accepted as expedient. This was true of the New Testament church, following the Jerusalem Council, when it seemed wise to draw up and promulgate certain "rules" and request the believers everywhere to "obey these rules" (Acts 16:4, TEV).

It is the judgment of Christian maturity, however, that the only lasting moral guidelines and controls are inward, spiritual. "The acts of the sinful nature are obvious" (Gal. 5:19, NIV). The person filled with the Spirit will recoil from the works of the flesh.

The resolution of this apparent impasse lies in the recognition of Jesus as the Lord of the Sabbath. The control, then, is in the Person of Jesus, and we know what His character and spirit are. All remaining differences of opinion should be left to conscience, where possible, or to group conscience, where necessary.

The Attractiveness of Jesus

Mark 3:7-12

> 7 But Jesus withdrew himself with his disciples to the sea: and a great multitude from Galilee followed him, and from Judaea,
> 8 And from Jerusalem, and from Idumaea, and from beyond Jordan; and they about Tyre and Sidon, a great multitude, when they had heard what great things he did, came unto him.

> 9 And he spake to his disciples, that a small ship should wait on him because of the multitude, lest they should throng him.
>
> 10 For he had healed many; insomuch that they pressed upon him for to touch him, as many as had plagues.
>
> 11 And unclean spirits, when they saw him, fell down before him, and cried, saying, Thou art the Son of God.
>
> 12 And he straitly charged them that they should not make him known.

The mounting opposition of His foes, clearly seen in the conspiracy of the Pharisees and the Herodians (3:6), impelled Jesus to seek a friendlier locale. He *withdrew himself with his disciples to the sea* (7).

Jesus was never reluctant to confront His enemies, but "his hour was not yet come" (John 7:30; 8:20). Until then, He often withdrew for solitude, for fellowship with His disciples, for safety.

Even as He withdrew to the seaside, *a great multitude . . . followed* (7). What drew people to Jesus? The attractiveness of Jesus drew multitudes to Him then and now.

> *Give me a love that knows no ill;*
> *Give me the grace to do Thy will. . . .*
> *Give me a heart like Thine.*
> —JUDSON W. VAN DEVENTER
>
> Copyright 1920 by Homer A. Rodeheaver. © Renewed 1948,
> The Rodeheaver Co. Used by permission.

This attractiveness produced simultaneously a temporary unity among diverse peoples and consternation among the demons. As usual, severe strictures of silence were necessary to quell the tumult.

1. *Unity in the Mideast.* The multitude following Jesus was not only from Galilee, but also "from Judea, Jerusalem, Idumea, and the regions across the Jordan and around Tyre and Sidon" (8, NIV).

   a. In our day, when the peoples of this area are locked in struggle, it is a pity they do not all find unity in the One who once drew them together.

   b. The geographical districts named figure significantly in the subsequent ministry of Jesus. Galilee, Judea, and Jerusalem were segments of Israel proper. The other areas bordered Israel on the south, east, and northwest, respectively. Whether by design or not, Jesus later visited all of them except Idumea. Perhaps He was responding to their expressed hunger for His ministry (see 5:1; 7:24, 31; 10:1; 11:11).

c. The magnetic attraction of Jesus, across national and cultural barriers, anticipated the Great Commission and the task of the Church to "make disciples of all nations" (Matt. 28:19, RSV).

2. *Consternation and conflict.* The teaching-healing ministry of Jesus produced two contrasting results.

a. The throngs *pressed upon him for to touch him* (10) and threatened His safety. Mark only records that Jesus "told his disciples to have a small boat ready for him" (9, NIV) in order to escape the crush. Jesus often touched those whom He healed (e.g., 1:31, 41), so it is evident the feeling of concern was reciprocal.

b. The reaction of the *unclean spirits* (11), as always, was very different. The behavior of the demoniacs suggests consternation and conflict. Strikingly, they knew who Jesus was if the Pharisees did not. *Thou art the Son of God* (11). Why Jesus so strongly resisted them perplexes and challenges our thought: "He gave them strict orders not to tell who he was" (12, NIV).

c. Scholars believe that the demons were in a contest with Jesus and sought to overpower and control Him by means of the use and manipulation of His name. William L. Lane offers this helpful explanation: "These cries of recognition were designed to control and strip him of his power, in accordance with the conception that knowledge of the precise name or quality of a person confers mastery over him."

The Holy Spirit, who was in Jesus, and the unclean spirits, were in irreconcilable conflict. The One who has "all authority in heaven and on earth" (Matt. 28:18, RSV), therefore, rebuked and silenced them. The Father has more appropriate, less aggressive, ways to reveal himself.

An Ordination Service

Mark 3:13-19

> 13 And he goeth up into a mountain, and calleth unto him whom he would: and they came unto him.
> 14 And he ordained twelve, that they should be with him, and that he might send them forth to preach,
> 15 And to have power to heal sicknesses, and to cast out devils:
> 16 And Simon he surnamed Peter;
> 17 And James the son of Zebedee, and John the brother of James; and he surnamed them Boanerges, which is, The sons of thunder:
> 18 And Andrew, and Philip, and Bartholomew, and Matthew, and Thomas, and James the son of Alphaeus, and Thaddaeus, and Simon the Canaanite,
> 19 And Judas Iscariot, which also betrayed him: and they went into an house.

Jesus sensed that the time was short. A growing work and rising hostility must have been factors leading to the call of the Twelve and their "ordination" as apostles. It was evidently one of the Lord's major goals to prepare a small group of disciples for the breathtaking task of discipling all nations. The impression grows that Jesus chose 12 ordinary men to be His disciples. But what an extraordinary Teacher they had!

1. *Twelve ordinary men.* We cannot know why and how Jesus decided upon these men, but we do know that it was after a period of solitude and prayer. Luke tells us that "Jesus went out into a mountain to pray, and continued all night in prayer to God" (Luke 6:12). Perhaps there He found perspective, poise, and wisdom for this momentous decision.

   a. The disciples possessed the strengths and weaknesses of ordinary men. They were unstable, tempestuous, even revolutionary, considerate and thoughtful, skillful in labor, astute in fiscal matters, uncertain, greedy, sceptical, even treacherous. Quite a kaleidescope of characteristics!

   b. They also had the promise of better things to come.

Jesus called these men not so much for what they were as for what He could help them to become.

Ultimately—after the Resurrection and Pentecost—they became rock-like in their dependability, utterly persuaded in their faith, fierce in their loyalty, amazingly fruitful as evangelists, gifted in their testimony (cf. the Gospel of John and 1, 2, Peter), "fishers of men" par excellence, foundation stones of the Church (Eph. 2:20).

Simon is possibly the best example of these changes. Jesus renamed him Peter, which means "rock." But we remember him for his impulsive actions, as when he walked on the water (Matt. 14:28-29), and for his denials of the Lord after his protestations of loyalty (14:29-31). However, Simon did become Peter the Rock: each of the four lists of the Twelve begins with his name (Matt. 10:2-4; Mark 3:16-19; Luke 6:14-16; Acts 1:13). In a real sense, Jesus did build His Church upon Simon Peter and the other apostles, as well as upon their confession of Him as "the Christ, the Son of the living God" (Matt. 16:16). As Augustine said: "Without Him we *cannot.* Without us He *will not.*"

2. *An extraordinary Teacher.* The Lord calls *all* men to salvation, to "take the water of life freely" (Rev. 22:17), but He calls *some* men to positions of special service and responsibility. None seem more surprised by such a call than the persons involved. Moses contended that he lacked eloquence (Exod. 4:10), and Jeremiah felt insecure because of his youth (Jer. 1:6).

a. From the many who followed Him, Jesus very pointedly and deliberately "appointed Twelve—designating them apostles" (14, NIV). Three or four were members of an "inner circle," one (always listed last) *betrayed him* (19), some were not especially colorful, but all became immortal because they freely left all and followed the Master.

All believers have gifts and talents for the building of the Kingdom. A few may be chosen for the crushing responsibility of the foundation stones, but we may all be "living stones . . . built into a spiritual house" (1 Pet. 2:4).

b. The Twelve (something of a technical term in the Early Church) received a commission, involving companionship, proclamation, and healing. They received *authority* (*exousia,* not *dunamis,* power) to carry out their commission. Such authority is moral and spiritual and is not earned or attained but *obtained* from the Head of the Church.

Here are all the elements necessary to the life of the Church in any age: power or authority to preach the gospel and "to drive out demons" (15, NIV). A world heavy-hearted with bad news would be blessed with the hearing of good news. The demons of hate, sensualism, and greed need new exorcists. But such a commission began with companionship: *He ordained twelve, that they should be with him* (14). Fellowship with Jesus is a prerequisite to ministry for Him.

> *O Master, let me walk with Thee*
> . . . .
> *Help me the slow of heart to move*
> *By some clear, winning word of love.*
> *Teach me the wayward feet to stay,*
> *And guide them in the homeward way.*
>
> —WASHINGTON GLADDEN

"Christus Victor!"

Mark 3:20-30

20 And the multitude cometh together again, so that they could not so much as eat bread.
21 And when his friends heard of it, they went out to lay hold on him: for they said, He is beside himself.
22 And the scribes which came down from Jerusalem said, He hath Beelzebub, and by the prince of the devils casteth he out devils.
23 And he called them unto him, and said unto them in parables, How can Satan cast out Satan?
24 And if a kingdom be divided against itself, that kingdom cannot stand.
25 And if a house be divided against itself, that house cannot stand.

26 And if Satan rise up against himself, and be divided, he cannot stand, but hath an end.
27 No man can enter into a strong man's house, and spoil his goods, except he will first bind the strong man; and then he will spoil his house.
28 Verily I say unto you, All sins shall be forgiven unto the sons of men, and blasphemies wherewith soever they shall blaspheme:
29 But he that shall blaspheme against the Holy Ghost hath never forgiveness, but is in danger of eternal damnation:
30 Because they said, He hath an unclean spirit.

The public ministry of Jesus may have been brief, but it was intense, sometimes hectic. The story unfolding is full of suspense. The labors of Jesus quicken, until friends as well as family feel concern for His well-being. Resistance to His ministry likewise grows in power and malignity. Through it all, Mark helps us to see Jesus as He really was: Victor in the maelstrom: "Be of good cheer; I have overcome the world" (John 16:33).

1. *The zeal of Jesus.* Mark never multiplies words, but the evidence is clear that Jesus was almost constantly occupied with crowds. He taught them, gave them His healing touch, listened to their questions, and so expended His energy in giving "his life a ransom for many" (10:45).

a. Jesus was obviously a Man with physical energy. He had toiled most of His life as a carpenter and must have built strong muscles and a sturdy body. He spent most of His time out of doors and travelled everywhere by foot. Having lived without sin (Heb. 4:15), Jesus was surely an example of one who has a "sound mind in a sound body."

b. More than this, Jesus possessed a driving purpose. He had long been aware that the Father had "sanctified, and sent [Him] into the world" (John 10:36). As He preached the gospel of God (1:14), felt compassion for the sick (1:41), cast out demons and bound Satan (27), and prepared His disciples for the days beyond the Cross (3:13-14), He was bringing in the kingdom of God (1:15). How true were His words, "My Father worketh hitherto, and I work" (John 5:17). It is not surprising that His disciples remembered the scripture (Ps. 69:9), "The zeal of thine house hath eaten me up" (John 2:17).

2. *The apprehension of friend and foe.* Two forces are present in this scene: the desire of His friends and family "to take charge of him" (21, NIV), and the desire of His foes to defame Him (22).

a. The anxiety of His friends had reached a fever pitch. They thought He was deranged: *He is beside himself* (21). Whether the expression translated *friends* included His family is debatable. His mother may have been perplexed betimes, but surely never doubted the sanity of her Son.

The delegation from Nazareth was desperate and was ready *to lay hold on him* (21). His ceaseless activity, the crowded days, too full even for rest or meals, the emotional enervation of association with the multitudes, all pointed to imbalance. Someone needed to save Jesus from himself!

Christian history has not infrequently recorded such "madness" in other emissaries of the Cross. When Paul defended himself before King Agrippa and Festus, as a prisoner in Caesarea, the Roman governor "shouted at him, 'You are mad, Paul! Your great learning is driving you mad!'" (Acts 26:24, TEV). And so with many others, including, doubtless, such missionaries as Adoniram Judson of Burma, David Livingston of Africa, and Harmon Schmelzenbach of Swaziland. They all suffered greatly and often laid loved ones to rest far from home.

b. If the friends of Jesus sought to take charge of Him, His foes sought to defame Him: "He is possessed by Beelzebul" (22, RSV).

News of the popularity of Jesus in Galilee had reached and disturbed the authorities in Jerusalem. A body of scribes had come down (literally) to Capernaum to examine the city and the Prophet. Their conclusion: the teaching of Jesus was unlawful. He was possessed by Satan!

Beelzebub (most Greek manuscripts have Beelzeboul) was the name of a pagan god, a rival to the God of Israel (see 2 Kings 1:2). In later Jewish thought the term was synonymous with Satan. As a further slur, the Jews corrupted the label from "lord of the divine abode" to "lord of the flies." The scribes had indeed made a scurrilous, malicious charge in saying of Jesus, *He hath an unclean spirit* (30).

3. *A promise and a warning.* Jesus countered their charge by showing that it was nonsense, and then by adding a marvelous promise and a solemn warning.

a. Their charge that "by the prince of demons he is driving out demons" (22, NIV) was nonsense. Satan does not *rise up against himself, and be divided* (26), for he knows that a *house . . . divided against itself . . . cannot stand* (25). And it should be obvious that Satan is still strong! Moreover, someone external to Satan and stronger than he must "first bind" him before "he can ransack the house" (27, NEB).

It should be noted that this was precisely what Jesus was doing. He was binding *the strong man* and plundering *his house* (27). In Matthew's parallel account (Matt. 12:22-30), the Pharisees had just witnessed such a plundering of Satan's house, when Jesus healed "a demon-possessed man who was blind and dumb" (Matt. 12:22, NASB). No, their charge that by Satan He cast out Satan was nonsense (23)!

b. With this rejoinder, Jesus gave a marvelous promise: *Verily, I say unto you, all sins shall be forgiven unto the sons of men* (28). The expression, *Verily, I say unto you,* is reserved in the New Testament for Jesus alone. It carries with it two implications: that what Jesus is about to say is significant and reliable, and that the One who makes the statement represents the highest Authority. Whatever *the blasphemies wherewith they shall blaspheme,* except against the Holy Spirit, *shall be forgiven* (28). That is amazing.

> *Amazing grace! how sweet the sound!*
> *That saved a wretch like me!*

c. Along with the marvelous promise, Jesus also issued a solemn warning, likewise prefaced by the words, *Verily, I say unto you.* When the scribes "were saying" (imperfect tense, suggesting repetition) that Jesus cast out demons by means of Satan, the prince of demons (22), they were close to blaspheming *against the Holy Ghost,* for which there is *never forgiveness* (29). This is to be "guilty of an eternal sin" (29, NASB). Why?

The Spirit who possessed Jesus was not an *unclean spirit* (30), such as Beelzebul, but the *Holy* Spirit.

If a person were thoroughly persuaded that Jesus was under the control of an evil or unclean spirit, he would not turn to Him for salvation. That person would then forever be separated from Him who is "the way, the truth, and the life" (John 14:6). "Woe unto them that call evil good, and good evil; that put darkness for light, and light for darkness" (Isa. 5:20).

The Lord's Family

Mark 3:31-35

> 31 There came then his brethren and his mother, and, standing without, sent unto him, calling him.
> 32 And the multitude sat about him, and they said unto him, Behold, thy mother and they brethren without seek for thee.
> 33 And he answered them, saying, Who is my mother, or my brethren?
> 34 And he looked round about on them which sat about him, and said, Behold my mother and my brethren!
> 35 For whosoever shall do the will of God, the same is my brother, and my sister, and mother.

This narrative is apparently a continuation of the account in v. 21. There a group of friends, possibly members of His family, tried *to lay hold on him,* fearful of His sanity. In this instance, *his brethren and his mother* (31) had reached the perimeter of the *multitude . . . about him* (32) and were *calling him.*

The story is saturated with deep emotions. Normally, our family ties are the strongest, the most precious and delicate we have in life. The picture of an anxious mother and a cluster of dubious brothers, on the outside looking in

(32), is very touching. How did they receive the apparent rebuff of their loved One: *Who is my mother, or my brethren?* (33).

1. *The perplexity of Mary.* The beloved physician, Luke, very probably had personal contact with Mary, the mother of Jesus (cf. Luke 1:2, *eyewitnesses*). He tells us that from the beginning, Mary lived with a great deal of mystery: "Mary kept all these things, and pondered them in her heart" (Luke 2:19).

a. Scattered through the Gospels are indications that Mary betimes experienced bewilderment, even suffering, as a consequence of her unique natural ties with Jesus. When Mary and Joseph presented their Son as a babe, in the Temple at Jerusalem, Simeon forewarned Mary: "Yea, a sword shall pierce through thy own soul also" (Luke 2:35).

That prophecy was fulfilled at the Crucifixion: "Now there stood by the cross of Jesus his mother" (John 19:25). Has life ever brought anyone a more piercing sword?

b. But now Mary, and her other sons, stood at the doorway of some humble dwelling in Capernaum, some 25 miles from Nazareth, unable to reach Jesus.

The day came, however, when Mary's perplexity and bewilderment vanished. She was among the 120 believers who waited in the Upper Room for the Day of Pentecost (Acts 1:14).

2. *The scepticism of the brothers.* This evaluation is an inference drawn from the fact that the brothers of Jesus, like Mary, did not understand His demanding, massive ministry.

a. In another context, however, John tells us: "neither did his brethren believe in him" (John 7:5). On one occasion, they teased and ridiculed Him for delaying a trip to Jerusalem: "No one who wants to become a public figure acts in secret" (John 7:4, NIV).

b. Like their mother, they finally came to understand

Jesus and to believe in Him. They also were among the believers in the Upper Room at Jerusalem (Acts 1:4). One of them, "James the Lord's brother" (Gal. 1:19), became titular head of the Jerusalem church (cf. Acts 15:13 ff.).

3. *The assurances of our Brother*. The humanity of our Lord reaches out to us in His response to the call of His mother and brothers.

a. At first it may seem that Jesus rebuffed His family with the question, *Who is my mother, or my brethren* (33)? It is true that Jesus expressed some disappointment in their limited understanding of His ministry, but He wanted to make a point: in the Kingdom, spiritual relationships are stronger than family ties.

b. We next see a colorful detail such as an eyewitness would remember: Jesus *looked round about on them which sat about him* (34). Turning in a circle, He looked at each one with startling directness. Matthew adds that "he stretched forth his hand toward his disciples" (Matt. 12:49), as He said, *Behold my mother and my brethren!* (34). Those dear, humble people could scarcely have been an illustrious lot, but they were brothers, sisters, and mothers of the Lord!

Two assurances may be drawn from this pronouncement of Jesus. First, if anyone has been denied a Christian family, for whatever the reason, he may find another family in the household of faith. In times when the Church has suffered severe persecution and ostracism, with resultant broken families, believers have discovered they are members of the "family of God." Jesus warned His disciples that such a disintegration of the family would occur (13:12).

The other assurance is implied in the words *whosoever shall do the will of God* (35). Jesus offers no basis here for the view that sinning and sinfulness are inevitable in the life of the believer. It is both necessary and possible to *do the will of God* if one desires to be a member of the Lord's family.

The Master Storyteller

Mark 4:1-20

1 And he began again to teach by the sea side: and there was gathered unto him a great multitude, so that he entered into a ship, and sat in the sea; and the whole multitude was by the sea on the land.

2 And he taught them many things by parables, and said unto them in his doctrine,

3 Hearken; Behold, there went out a sower to sow:

4 And it came to pass, as he sowed, some fell by the way side, and the fowls of the air came and devoured it up.

5 And some fell on stony ground, where it had not much earth; and immediately it sprang up, because it had no depth of earth:

6 But when the sun was up, it was scorched; and because it had no root, it withered away.

7 And some fell among thorns, and the thorns grew up, and choked it, and it yielded no fruit.

8 And other fell on good ground, and did yield fruit that sprang up and increased; and brought forth, some thirty, and some sixty, and some an hundred.

9 And he said unto them, He that hath ears to hear, let him hear.

10 And when he was alone, they that were about him with the twelve asked of him the parable.

11 And he said unto them, Unto you it is given to know the mystery of the kingdom of God: but unto them that are without, all these things are done in parables:

12 That seeing they may see, and not perceive; and hearing they may hear, and not understand; lest at any time they should be converted, and their sins should be forgiven them.

13 And he said unto them, Know ye not this parable? and how then will ye know all parables?

14 The sower soweth the word.

15 And these are they by the way side, where the word is sown; but when they have heard, Satan cometh immediately, and taketh away the word that was sown in their hearts.

16 And these are they likewise which are sown on stony ground; who, when they have heard the word, immediately receive it with gladness;

17 And have no root in themselves, and so endure but for a time: afterward, when affliction or persecution ariseth for the word's sake, immediately they are offended.

18 And these are they which are sown among thorns; such as hear the word,

19 And the cares of this world, and the deceitfulness of riches, and the lusts of other things entering in, choke the word, and it becometh unfruitful.

20 And these are they which are sown on good ground; such as hear the word, and receive it, and bring forth fruit, some thirtyfold, some sixty, and some an hundred.

Mark gives more attention to the *works* of Jesus than to His *words*. Chapter 4 contains the largest grouping of Jesus' parables in this Gospel.

From a larger collection, Mark selected three representative parables on the growth of the Kingdom—sowing, growing, reaping. The parable of the sower is foundational to an understanding of the other parables, their purpose, paradoxical character, and value.

1. *The parable of the sower.* When one reflects upon typical pulpit delivery—standing, gesticulating, movement— he is amazed that Jesus "got into a boat and sat in it" (1, NIV). He was relaxed and at ease but somehow captured and held the attention of the great multitude on the shore. This was evidently because "His usual method of teaching was to tell the people stories" (2, TLB).

a. The intention of the sower was to broadcast the seed wherever there was hope it would take root. "A farmer went out to sow his seed" (3, NIV). And so the Son of Man "came forth from the Father" (John 16:28) to sow "the good seed [and] . . . the field is the world" (Matt. 13:37-38).

b. The power of the seed is amazing. The Sower has great faith in the vitality of the seed. Wrapped up in a compact little package is all the vigor and quality of life.

c. But the contradictory character of the soil presents both problems and promise. Some of the soil—the hard, the shallow, the crowded soil—offers resistance to the seed. Some of it—the *good ground* (8)—is extremely productive, increasing "thirty, sixty, or even a hundred times" (20, TLB).

2. *The purpose of the parables.* Jesus was alert to the problem of communication. So often He appealed to the listeners, *He that hath ears to hear, let him hear* (9). By conscious design Jesus taught the multitudes *many things by parables* (2), i.e., by stories, similes, allegories, proverbs, and the like—"earthly stories with a heavenly meaning."

a. In addition to arousing interest, the parable involved the listener in the plot. He found himself making judgments, identifying with certain elements in the account, and reaching decisions. In the parables, the Kingdom came near and required a response from the hearer.

b. What follows next (10-13) is a description of the paradoxical nature of the parables.

(1) *The secret of the Kingdom is revealed to believers.* Jesus did not include an explanation of the parables when He taught the crowds "that gathered around him" (1, NIV). This explanation was reserved for "those who were about him with the Twelve" (10, RSV).

The Scriptures elsewhere speak of the *mystery* disclosed only *by revelation.* Paul was grateful for his knowledge, his "insight into the mystery of Christ" (Eph. 3:3-4, NIV). Only to those who are close to Christ, who have the "eyes of faith" is it *given to know the mystery of the kingdom of God* (11).

> *Open my eyes, that I may see*
> *Glimpses of truth Thou hast for me.*

(2) *The secret of the Kingdom is concealed to the outsiders* (but with an evangelistic purpose). The statement of Jesus in vv. 11-12 calls for careful study and interpretation. Did Jesus use parables to screen the truth, to hide the message in order to block salvation? Believe it who will!

Here we must remember the atmosphere of unbelief and growing hostility in which Jesus was teaching (3:6). Temporarily, Jesus veiled who He was (3:12) and screened the full import of His message, by the parabolic method, in order to bring *judgment* to those who rejected Him and *grace* to those who would receive Him. Those who were willfully blind and deaf would reject the parable as meaningless. Those who longed to enter the Kingdom would find the parable perplexing, intriguing, and would attempt to unravel the mystery, to solve the riddle.

In his commentary on Mark, G. Campbell Morgan

summarizes the issues: "Jesus used the parabolic method, not in order to blind them, but in order to make them look again; not in order to prevent them coming to forgiveness, but in order to lure them toward a new attention."

3. *The comfort of this parable.* Turning again to the parable of the sower, we may find it a source of comfort and encouragement.

a. In the parable is an answer to the question, Why does the preaching of the gospel not yield uniform results? The situation of the first-century Church was not essentially different from ours. We lament the presence of instability, shallowness, and defection in the Church today, and so did they.

Defection, falling away from the faith, was especially trying in times of severe persecution. When life and limb were literally at stake, many did deny the faith. There were those who had *no root in themselves* and who would *endure but for a time* (17).

Resistance to the growth of the Word is enormous now as it was then: "The delights of wealth, and the search for success and lure of nice things . . . crowd out God's message" (19, TLB). Here is a harsh realism the Church would do well to acknowledge. Here also is evidence that the plan and will of God can be thwarted, Augustinians to the contrary. Perhaps we should remember the words of the Lord, "Behold, I have told you before" (Matt. 24:25).

b. In the parable is the assurance that some of the seed will fall upon good earth and produce a vast harvest. William Hendriksen classifies the four types of soil as: "unresponsive hearts . . . impulsive hearts . . . preoccupied hearts . . . responsive hearts." Discouragements abound in building the Kingdom, but we may be confident that some of the seed will find the soil of "responsive hearts."

Those described as *good soil* do not respond passively. They hear the word attentively, receive or accept it, and bring forth fruit (20). The paradox of grace is implied here. The good ground does respond to grace actively; nevertheless, it is God who makes the plant grow (cf. 1 Cor. 3:6, TEV).

Another point of assurance and understanding is that the good ground varies in its productivity: thirty, sixty, or a hundredfold. In every case the increase is miraculous, but variety does exist. "Now there are varieities of gifts, but the same Spirit" (1 Cor. 12:4, RSV).

> *They that sow in tears*
> *Shall reap in joy.*
> *He that goeth forth and weepeth,*
> *bearing precious seed,*
> *Shall doubtless come again with rejoicing,*
> *bringing his sheaves with him* (Ps. 126:5-6).

Sage Advice to the Listener

Mark 4:21-25

> 21 And he said unto them, Is a candle brought to be put under a bushel, or under a bed? and not to be set on a candlestick?
> 22 For there is nothing hid, which shall not be manifested; neither was any thing kept secret, but that it should come abroad.
> 23 If any man have ears to hear, let him hear.
> 24 And he said unto them, Take heed what ye hear: with what measure ye mete, it shall be measured to you: and unto you that hear shall more be given.
> 25 For he that hath, to him shall be given: and he that hath not, from him shall be taken even that which he hath.

Repeatedly Jesus cautioned, *If any man has ears to hear, let him hear* (23). He pled with His disciples, goaded and cajoled them to search out meanings, to discover, to understand. For example, before explaining to them the parable of the sower, Jesus queried: "Do you really not understand this parable? Then how are you going to understand all the other parables?" (13, Phillips).

We have already seen that when He spoke to the multitudes, Jesus cloaked *the mystery of the kingdom* (11) by means of parables—not to block understanding, but to capture attention and to lure the casual listener into more thoughtful reflection.

All of these considerations have a general application

in the realm of truth. We shall miss the deeper intention of Jesus and Mark, however, if we fail to see that the real *mystery of the kingdom* (11) is the "messianic secret"— that Jesus is the Messiah, the Son of God, and that in Him "the kingdom of God is at hand" (1:15). The demons knew this, but the Pharisees did not. The witness of the demons was both unworthy and premature.

Two aphorisms sum up the implications of vv. 21-25: "the truth will out," and "the rich get richer."

1. *The truth will out* (21-23). The American Watergate scandals of the 1972 presidential elections are evidence enough that *there is nothing hid, which shall not be manifested* (22). "Be sure your sin will find you out" (Num. 32:23) is a biblical truth and a fact of reality. However, we need to look beneath the surface for a fuller understanding of this passage.

a. The function of light is to reveal, to disclose. Elsewhere Jesus said, "I am the light of the world" (John 8:12), and to the disciples, "Ye are the light of the world" (Matt. 5:14).

Literally, v. 21 may be rendered, "Does the lamp come in order to be put under a bushel and not on a stand?" He who had ears to hear might have picked up the implication: "I am come a light into the world" (John 12:46).

b. The function of mystery is to entice, to lure. It is true that Jesus muzzled the demoniacs (3:12) and commanded those whom He had healed to say nothing (1:44). It is true that He puzzled the multitudes with His parables (11), but it is not true that He came as *a candle . . . to be put under* a bushel, *or under a bed* (21). He came "to be disclosed . . . to be brought out into the open" (22, NIV).

One day before long, Peter would see and declare: "Thou art the Christ" (8:29). Before Mark closes his story, the Roman centurion would also see and declare, "Truly this man was the Son of God" (15:39). These two confessions, from the people of Israel and from the Gentile world, forecast the day when believers the world around would acclaim Jesus as "Christ, the Son of God" (1:1).

2. *The rich get richer* (24-25). Again a truth of reality and a truth of revelation blend together. We need both.

a. The reward of the interested learner. We are to take heed *how* we hear (Luke 8:18) and *what we hear* (24). We are to give heed to the gospel (1:15). We are to be thoughtful, attentive learners. "The measure you use will be the measure you receive—and *more!*"

A smile begets a smile; a scowl begets a scowl. Diligent study enhances learning. A spirit of generosity returns bearing gifts:

> *One man gives freely, yet grows all*
> *the richer;*
> *another withholds what he should*
> *give, and only suffers want* (Prov. 11:24, RSV).

But all of this is common knowledge from everyday experience. The Kingdom has an added factor: *Unto you that hear shall more be given* (24)—a divine largess, an openhandedness. Thus: "I am come that they might have life, and that they might have it more abundantly" (John 10:10).

"And everyone who has left houses or brothers or sisters or father or mother or children or fields for my sake will receive a hundred times as much and will inherit eternal life" (Matt. 19:29, NIV).

b. The judgment on the listless learner. A veteran teacher of New Testament Greek said to a young student, "If you use what you have learned, your facility in the Scriptures will grow. If you neglect it, you will lose what you have." This is true in all fields of learning, as well as in the professions and the skills.

Something more is intended in these verses than intellectual growth, even in Christian truth. Jesus did not come to found an esoteric gnosticism. We are to "grow in grace, and in the knowledge of our Lord and Saviour Jesus

Christ" (2 Pet. 3:18). "We are to grow up in every way into him who is the head, into Christ" (Eph. 4:15, RSV).

Where the growth of the Kingdom is hindered by myopic vision, meager faith, criticism, conflicts—in a word, by cripples in the army of the Lord—could it be that from these who have not, has been taken even that which they had? (25).

The Growth of God's Kingdom

Mark 4:26-29

> 26 And he said, So is the kingdom of God, as if a man should cast seed into the ground;
> 27 And should sleep, and rise night and day, and the seed should spring and grow up, he knoweth not how.
> 28 For the earth bringeth forth fruit of herself; first the blade, then the ear, after that the full corn in the ear.
> 29 But when the fruit is brought forth, immediately he putteth in the sickle, because the harvest is come.

The parable of the seed growing secretly appears only in Mark. All three of the parables in this chapter (c. 4) describe the growth of the Kingdom in terms of the sowing, growing, and reaping of seed. Now the parable is this: "the seed is the word of God" (Luke 8:11).

The parable before us stresses the fact that the seed grows independently of those who sow it. The Kingdom *is* growing. The Kingdom *is* coming. "Thine is the kingdom!" (Matt. 6:13).

1. *The growth of God's kingdom is beyond man's control.* To be sure a man must *cast seed into the ground* (26), and when the harvest time has come, he will put in the sickle (29). The laborer does have a responsibility.

Something more is essential: the seed must germinate, appropriate nutrients in the soil, and produce the plant unique to the seed's inner law of life. "Night and day, whether" the farmer "sleeps or gets up, the seed sprouts and grows, though he does not know how." This happens "all by itself" (27-28, NIV).

How the seed should spring and grow up is a mystery,

even to the agricultural scientist. Likewise with the Kingdom. We do not govern it; we do not understand it.

2. *The growth of God's kingdom is certain, inevitable.* The parable describes an inexorable process: "The earth produces of itself, first the blade, then the ear. Then the full grain in the ear" (28, RSV). Jesus affirmed essentially the same truth in another context: "And I say this to you: . . . I will build my church, and the forces of death shall never overpower it" (Matt. 16:18, NEB).

When we are tempted to despise "the day of small things" (Zech. 4:10), or in a period of ebb and flow, we must repose faith not in our own labor and toil, but in the power of the seed: The Word of our God which shall stand forever (Isa. 40:8).

3. *The growth of God's kingdom implies a final harvest.* When will the grain be ripe and the time of harvest come? (29).

a. A harvest of blessing is available now. The "harvest of the Spirit is love, joy, peace, patience, kindness, goodness, fidelity, gentleness, and self-control" (Gal. 5:22-23, NEB). Not one of these is antisocial or lawless; hence, "against such things there is no law" (Gal. 5:23, NIV).

b. A harvest of judgment and victory is coming. A great many learned people in our society are gloomy about the future of our planet. Problems of dwindling natural resources, pollution, the population explosion, among others, are alarming. The last word will be spoken, however, by Him who is "the Alpha and Omega, the beginning and the ending" (Rev. 1:8) and who has said, "Behold I make all things new" (Rev. 21:5).

> *Jesus shall reign wher-e'er the sun*
> *Does his successive journeys run;*
> *His kingdom spread from shore to shore,*
> *Till moons shall wax and wane no more.*
> — Isaac Watts

The Master Teacher at Work

Mark 4:30-34

> 30 And he said, Whereunto shall we liken the kingdom of God? or with what comparison shall we compare it?
> 31 It is like a grain of mustard seed, which, when it is sown in the earth, is less than all the seeds that be in the earth:
> 32 But when it is sown, it groweth up, and becometh greater than all herbs, and shooteth out great branches; so that the fowls of the air may lodge under the shadow of it.
> 33 And with many such parables spake he the word unto them, as they were able to hear it.
> 34 But without a parable spake he not unto them: and when they were alone, he expounded all things to his disciples.

This section might well be titled "The parable of the mustard seed," and could have been linked with the preceding verses (26-29). However, it should also be instructive and inspiring to study the procedures Jesus used as He taught the Word to His disciples.

If preachers and teachers could learn from the Master Teacher how to communicate the Word more winsomely and fruitfully, it would be great gain.

1. *Jesus involved the disciples in the learning process.* It is fascinating to visualize Jesus in His teaching, almost casting about in His mind for appropriate parables, metaphors, and similes with which to describe the Kingdom: "How shall we picture the kingdom of God, or by what parable shall we describe it?" (30, NEB).

a. He probed their minds with questions. If the reader will look for them, he will find that Jesus used a great many questions in His teaching (cf. 4:13, 21, 30). Questions spur the mind to think, to search, and oftentimes to discover and to be creative.

b. He implied that He was open to a variety of answers. When He raised the question, *Whereunto shall we liken the kingdom of God?* (30), many of His listeners would have had responses in their own minds. In a classroom situation, such a question would prompt replies, discussion, possibly debate. The teaching of Jesus was with a good deal of flexibility and resilience. He was with the multitudes for hours, even days (8:2). We can well imagine something of the interchange which took place under those circumstances—no clocks, no schedules, no walls! (cf. 12:13-34).

2. *Jesus helped them to see, to picture the truth.* Mark says it flatly: *But without a parable spake he not unto them* (34). What priceless gems the parables are! Walter Bowie has described them as "imperishable truth in indestructible form."

a. The parable of the mustard seed is a good example of the pictorial qualities in Jesus' teaching. Suppose He had said: "We are a small and not very imposing group. I am only one and you are few in number and not very sophisticated. But someday we shall be a great movement!" Instead He used a graphic part of their experience: the tiny mustard seed—"the smallest seed you plant—grows and becomes the largest of all garden plants" (31-32, NIV). So with the Kingdom!

b. With our hindsight, it is difficult to appreciate what hope and faith this parable engendered in the first-century Church. The Christian Church *has* become the mightiest movement on earth, but Mark wrote to a fellowship of believers despised and hounded by the Roman authorities, perhaps fearful of total destruction. They needed, as do we, a divine word to hold them true in a day of small beginnings.

3. *Jesus accepted and worked with the capacities of the learners.* One marvels at the insight and patience He manifested in working with His disciples.

a. Jesus began where they were. He spoke *the word unto them, as they were able to hear it* (33), i.e., he told them as much as they could understand.

Jesus maintained what has been called a relationship of mutuality. He stayed with them, neither moving ahead nor falling behind; as He said in another place, *I have yet many things to say unto you, but ye cannot bear them now*. When they could bear them, however, the Spirit of Truth would be with them to guide them into all truth (John 16:12-13).

b. Jesus began where they were, but He also sought to help them advance, to grow in understanding. As we have already seen (10-12), Jesus spoke to the multitudes in parables but reserved an explanation of them for His disciples: *when they were alone, he expounded all things to his disciples* (34).

The teaching-learning process is a demanding one, but when the Master Teacher is present, learning is enhanced. A missionary from New Guinea told of a Bible school student who struggled with a difficult Christian concept. In a flash of insight, he understood and related it to his own culture. (The concept was predestination. The student's example was the pumpkin crop: The grower planned for each pumpkin to do well, but some pumpkins fell short of their destiny.) The missionary explained: "He had heard the Spirit speak through the Word in a language he could understand."

Jesus and the Storms of Life

Mark 4:35-41

> 35 And the same day, when the even was come, he saith unto them, Let us pass over unto the other side.
> 36 And when they had sent away the multitude, they took him even as he was in the ship. And there were also with him other little ships.
> 37 And there arose a great storm of wind, and the waves beat into the ship, so that it was now full.
> 38 And he was in the hinder part of the ship, asleep on a pillow: and they awake him, and say unto him, Master, carest thou not that we perish?
> 39 And he arose, and rebuked the wind, and said unto the sea, Peace, be still. And the wind ceased, and there was a great calm. ·
> 40 And he said unto them, Why are ye so fearful? how is it that ye have no faith?
> 41 And they feared exceedingly, and said one to another, What manner of man is this, that even the wind and the sea obey him?

Mark turns now from a rapid review of the teaching ministry of Jesus to His ministry of mighty works. The foes He confronts are fierce: the storms in nature, in demon possession, and in death. The storms of life are often severe, but Jesus is Lord of all. Mark wants his readers to examine the evidence leading to this unequivocal conviction.

1. *The storm came in the line of duty.* Because the Gospels are not designed to be biographical, many details in the movement of Jesus are not clear. It does seem that Jesus had been teaching the crowds by the seaside, so that when the evening came, He and the disciples were in a position to *pass over unto the other side* (35).

a. The day had been a crowded one. So large were the throngs that gathered around him, it was necessary for Jesus to get into a boat and sit in it out on the lake (1, NIV), as He taught them.

It is certain that the Gospels give us only a sampling of the parables and miracles. Mark tells us that with *many such parables spake he the word unto them* (33). And John records that if the whole story were told, "even the world itself could not contain the books" (John 21:25).

b. Jesus was, therefore, ready to find some solitude and rest. When the disciples *had sent away the multitude, they took him even as he was in the ship* (36). The Twelve included experienced fishermen who were at home on the Sea of Galilee. A few other little boats followed for a while, but Jesus was soon sound asleep, weary from the demands of the day. What followed did indeed come in the line of duty.

2. *The storm was real, the fear genuine.* "A furious squall came up, and the waves broke over the boat, so that it was nearly swamped" (37, NIV).

a. The Sea of Galilee is a relatively small body of water, some 8 miles wide and 13 miles long, heart-shaped, situated in a basin 680 feet below the Mediterranean. Strong winds from the southwest, as well as downdrafts of cold air from the surrounding mountains, are common and often cause storms.

Such violent winds more often come up in the afternoon, rather than at night or in the morning. Fishermen worked at night (Luke 5:5), when storms were less likely but more dangerous.

b. Mark's account is dotted with the colorful detail a participant would recall: the disciples took Jesus *even as he was* (36), with no preparation; *other little ships* (36) followed for a time; the terror of the disciples and their brusqueness in reproaching Jesus: "Master, we are sinking! Do you not care?" (38, NEB). They were in very real danger of drowning, or so they supposed, and were exasperated that Jesus could sleep through their distress. The roughness of this account argues, scholars believe, for its genuineness and proximity to the event.

3. *The storm was subservient to the divine Word.* Jesus responded at once to the cry for help. He *rebuked the wind, and said unto the sea, Peace, be still.* (39).

a. The claim which Mark and the Early Church were making was the highest possible—Jesus is one with the God of Israel, whose word governs the sea and the wind:

Who dost still the roaring of the seas,
   the roaring of their waves,
   the tumult of the peoples (Ps. 65:7, RSV).

His way is in whirlwind and storm,
   and the clouds are the dust of his feet (Nah. 1:3, RSV).

The God of Israel is the God of history and of nature. When it serves His purposes, He speaks and nature responds. So it was at the Exodus from Egypt and the conquest of Canaan:

   What ails you, O sea, that you flee?
   O Jordan, that you turn back? (Ps. 114:5, NASB).

The *creative* Word is also the *ruling* Word (cf. John 1:3; Col. 1:17).

b. All of those events were long ago and far away;

what of the storms each of us encounters in life—the disappointments, bereavement, losses, and heartaches? Jesus has a word for us as well. *When the wind had ceased, and there was a great calm* (39), He turned to the disciples with those unanswerable questions: *Why are ye so fearful? how is it that ye have no faith?* (40).

The disciples were now as terrified of Jesus as they had been of the storm. Who is this? Even the wind and the waves obey Him! The question is adroitly placed and is rhetorical. The question is an invitation to faith. Peter will respond, "Thou art the Christ" (8:29). The centurion will respond, "Truly this man was the Son of God" (15:39). How will the reader respond?

If Jesus, who is the Christ, the Son of God, is with us, He will help us chart a course over the treacherous and stormy seas of life. "Jesus, Saviour, pilot me!"

Be still, my soul; the wind and waves still know
His voice who ruled them while He dwelt below.

MARK 5

A Light for the Gentiles

Mark 5:1-20

> 1 And they came over unto the other side of the sea, into the country of the Gadarenes.
> 2 And when he was come out of the ship, immediately there met him out of the tombs a man with an unclean spirit,
> 3 Who had his dwelling among the tombs; and no man could bind him, no, not with chains:
> 4 Because that he had been often bound with fetters and chains, and the chains had been plucked asunder by him, and the fetters broken in pieces: neither could any man tame him.
> 5 And always, night and day, he was in the mountains, and in the tombs, crying, and cutting himself with stones.
> 6 But when he saw Jesus afar off, he ran and worshipped him,
> 7 And cried with a loud voice, and said, What have I to do with thee, Jesus, thou Son of the most high God? I adjure thee by God, that thou torment me not.
> 8 For he said unto him, Come out of the man, thou unclean spirit.
> 9 And he asked him, What is thy name? And he answered, saying, My name is Legion: for we are many.

10 And he besought him much that he would not send them away out of the country.

11 Now there was there nigh unto the mountains a great herd of swine feeding.

12 And all the devils besought him, saying, Send us into the swine, that we may enter into them.

13 And forthwith Jesus gave them leave. And the unclean spirits went out, and entered into the swine: and the herd ran violently down a steep place into the sea, (they were about two thousand;) and were choked in the sea.

14 And they that fed the swine fled, and told it in the city, and in the country. And they went out to see what it was that was done.

15 And they come to Jesus, and see him that was possessed with the devil, and had the legion, sitting, and clothed, and in his right mind: and they were afraid.

16 And they that saw it told them how it befell to him that was possessed with the devil, and also concerning the swine.

17 And they began to pray him to depart out of their coasts.

18 And when he was come into the ship, he that had been possessed with the devil prayed him that he might be with him.

19 Howbeit Jesus suffered him not, but saith unto him, Go home to thy friends, and tell them how great things the Lord hath done for thee, and hath had compassion on thee.

20 And he departed, and began to publish in Decapolis how great things Jesus had done for him: and all men did marvel.

Jesus now begins a series of withdrawals from the crowds in order to be alone with His disciples. He steps up the task of preparing them for the traumatic events soon to follow in Jerusalem.

The trip across the lake to *the country of the Gadarenes* (1) (or Gerasenes) was actually a foray into Gentile territory. Decapolis (20) was a cluster of 10 cities in a region with strong Gentile influence.

The immediate and sharp encounter of Jesus with the Gerasene demoniac opens our minds to new vistas of gospel truth: we get a heightened understanding of the power of Jesus over Satan; we see the shocking contrast between divine and human priorities; we receive fresh instruction on the character and value of the Christian witness.

1. *The power of Jesus over Satan.* This was not the first encounter of Jesus with a demoniac (cf. 1:21-28; 3:20-30). The circumstances are more dramatic, however, and are heavily weighted with meaning: Satan has power among the Gentiles, but the greater power of Jesus is present there also.

a. The unclean spirit in the man took the initiative in the contest with Jesus: "a man with an evil spirit came from the tombs to meet him" (2, NIV). Jesus had, of course, already taken the initiative, first, by penetrating that region, but also by coming "forth from the Father" (John 16:28). It is worth observing, however, that evil does take the initiative in temptation, and in defiling and besmirching the human person.

b. Mark delineates with particular care the violent, self-destructive forces of evil. The Gerasene demoniac dwelt *among the tombs,* shattered the *chains* and *fetters* used to bind him, and spent his time, *night and day,* roaming the lonely *mountains, . . . crying and cutting himself with stones* (3-5).

It would be difficult to imagine a more pathetic sight. Its import is clear and compelling: the nature of sin and the purpose of Satan is to deface, corrupt, and destroy the image of God in man (Gen. 1:26-27).

c. What followed was an alarmed recognition of Jesus by *Legion* (9), the host of evil spirits tormenting the man. Much about the ensuing conversation lies in the realm of mystery: What is the nature and destiny of the unclean spirits? Why did the demons appeal to Jesus in the name of God? Why did they beg to enter the swine, only to destroy them? The answer to such questions is not essential to our salvation, and revelation has not disclosed that information.

It is obvious, however, that once again the evil spirits recognized who Jesus truly was, when no one else did; that the presence of Jesus, *the Son of the most high God* (7), frightened them into a frenzy of entreaty; and that to possess and destroy the swine was a more desirable alternative (in their view) than to be sent *away out of the country* (10).

The fact of lasting significance is that, out of compassion for the man and with implacable fury for evil, Jesus delivered the demoniac: *Come out of the man, thou unclean spirit* (8). Before Jesus came, "no one was strong enough to subdue him" (4, NIV). The power of Jesus over Satan changed all of that.

2. *Priorities: human and divine.* A good deal of excitement followed the conversation between Jesus and Legion. Aware of the *great herd of swine feeding* (11) nearby, the demons asked Jesus, *Send us into the swine* (12). The result was that "the whole herd of about two thousand stampeded down the cliff into the lake and was drowned" (13, Phillips). A contrast in priorities soon appeared.

a. Divine priorities. No naturalistic explanations will suffice. "The demons begged Jesus," and Jesus "gave them permission" (12-13, NIV). Suddenly the demons left the man and seized the swine.

The Synoptic Gospels give us no defense for the action Jesus took. It is neither a cliché nor rationalization to say, "God moves in mysterious ways His wonders to perform." It is simply true. Perhaps the man of Gerasa needed a visual demonstration of his deliverance. Perhaps the Gerasenes needed a lesson in the relative value of pigs and persons.

William L. Lane has suggested a twofold explanation: first, that Jesus allowed this temporary concession to the demons, because the *eschaton* (the End) is yet to come; second, to demonstrate that the real purpose of Satan and his minions is "the total destruction of their host." Whether men or swine, Satan will destroy whatever, whomever he possesses. Overriding all other considerations was the worth of this one disturbed man.

b. Human priorities. It was not long before word of the event reached the people of the community, including the owners of the swine. The people *in the city, and in the country . . . went out to see what it was that was done* (14).

What they found should have been cause for rejoicing. "They came to Jesus and saw the madman who had been possessed by the legion of devils, sitting there clothed and in his right mind" (15, NEB). Instead, they were alarmed and "began to entreat Him to depart from their region"

(17, NASB). Afraid of sanity! Someone has facetiously said that the Gerasenes were more interested in the price of pork than in the value of a human soul!

> *Is this vile world a friend of grace,*
> *To help me on to God?*

3. *The presence of a witness.* The story of the Gerasene demoniac, and his deliverance, closes with some surprises. Jesus refused the man's offer to leave all and follow Him. Instead, Jesus asked the ex-demoniac *to publish in Decapolis how great things* He *had done for him* (20)—the very thing Jesus had forbidden others to do in Galilee (1:43-44).

a. A firm refusal. The episode is a tender one: as Jesus was getting into the boat to leave that unwelcome region, "the man who had been possessed with demons begged him that he might be with him" (18, RSV).

The earnest plea was understandable. Memories of the hideous past would be unpleasant. Perhaps he felt uncertainty, even insecurity, in returning to the area where people did not understand his healing. Companionship with Jesus and His disciples would have been comforting, reassuring. The Lord's refusal was firm: He *suffered him not* (19).

b. A reversal of policy. As we have seen, Jesus repeatedly and strictly charged those whom He had healed in Galilee to say nothing about it. These happy people seldom followed instructions (1:45), but the intention of Jesus was plain enough.

Now Jesus commands the Gerasene: *Go home to thy friends, and tell them how great things the Lord hath done for thee, and hath had compassion on thee* (19). Why the change in policy?

In all likelihood the difference lay in the expectations of the Jewish people, not shared by the Gentiles. The Jews were eagerly anticipating and promoting the coming of a sensational, miracle-working Messiah, who would return Israel to "a land flowing with milk and honey" (Exod.

3:8) and who would evict with apocalyptic force the Roman invader. Jesus, whose "kingdom is not of this world" (John 18:36), had no wish to inflame those false hopes. The people of the Decapolis did not share these dreams.

Mark's account is crisp and to the point: "The man went off and spread the news in the Ten Towns of all that Jesus had done for him; and they were all amazed" (20, NEB). His testimony was "a light to lighten the Gentiles" (Luke 2:32; Isa. 42:6).

What fresh instruction on the character and value of the Christian witness may be found here? At the very least, that the person with a story of deliverance makes an effective witness; that those who have seen the change will likely be amazed; that Jesus impels such a witness to tell his story as an expression of gratefulness to God.

Twin Foes: Disease and Death

Mark 5:21-43

> 21 And when Jesus was passed over again by ship unto the other side, much people gathered unto him: and he was nigh unto the sea.
> 22 And, behold, there cometh one of the rulers of the synagogue, Jairus by name; and when he saw him, he fell at his feet,
> 23 And besought him greatly, saying, My little daughter lieth at the point of death: I pray thee, come and lay thy hands on her, that she may be healed; and she shall live.
> 24 And Jesus went with him; and much people followed him, and thronged him.
> 25 And a certain woman, which had an issue of blood twelve years,
> 26 And had suffered many things of many physicians, and had spent all that she had, and was nothing bettered, but rather grew worse,
> 27 When she had heard of Jesus, came in the press behind, and touched his garment.
> 28 For she said, If I may touch but his clothes, I shall be whole.
> 29 And straightway the fountain of her blood was dried up; and she felt in her body that she was healed of that plague.
> 30 And Jesus, immediately knowing in himself that virtue had gone out of him, turned him about in the press, and said, Who touched my clothes?
> 31 And his disciples said unto him, Thou seest the multitude thronging thee, and sayest thou, Who touched me?
> 32 And he looked round about to see her that had done this thing.
> 33 But the woman fearing and trembling, knowing what was done in her, came and fell down before him, and told him all the truth.
> 34 And he said unto her, Daughter, thy faith hath made thee whole; go in peace, and be whole of thy plague.

35 While he yet spake, there came from the ruler of the synagogue's house certain which said, Thy daughter is dead: why troublest thou the Master any further?

36 As soon as Jesus heard the word that was spoken, he saith unto the ruler of the synagogue, Be not afraid, only believe.

37 And he suffered no man to follow him, save Peter, and James, and John the brother of James.

38 And he cometh to the house of the ruler of the synagogue, and seeth the tumult, and them that wept and wailed greatly.

39 And when he was come in, he saith unto them, Why make ye this ado, and weep? the damsel is not dead, but sleepeth.

40 And they laughed him to scorn. But when he had put them all out, he taketh the father and the mother of the damsel, and them that were with him, and entereth in where the damsel was lying.

41 And he took the damsel by the hand, and said unto her, Talitha cumi; which is, being interpreted, Damsel, I say unto thee, arise.

42 And straightway the damsel arose, and walked; for she was of the age of twelve years. And they were astonished with a great astonishment.

43 And he charged them straitly that no man should know it; and commanded that something should be given her to eat.

In the two previous sections (4:35-41; 5:1-20), we have seen Jesus as He calmed storms on the Sea of Galilee and in the soul of a demon-possessed Gentile. In each case, the witnesses were amazed beyond words.

In the passage before us, we see Jesus coping with two other hostile foes: disease and death. One senses the intrinsic authority Jesus possessed as He moved from one scene of need to another, as He heard and heeded the pleas of desperation, as He responded with caring compassion.

1. *The presence of disease and death.* The two accounts—Jairus' daughter and the afflicted woman—are interrelated. Disease eventually leads to death, but the restoration of health is the promise of life. The healing of the woman anticipates the raising of the dead girl.

a. The 12-year-old girl. We are not told what her ailment was, but it was serious enough to send her father searching for Jesus. Jairus was a leader in the community and knew enough about Jesus to have faith in Him and His ability to heal the sick.

How relieved Jairus must have been when Jesus agreed to go with him, but how anguished he must have been when Jesus was delayed! When the word came, *Thy daughter is dead* (35), what emotions flooded his mind—grief at the loss, frustration over the delay, perhaps bitterness toward the woman who interrupted Jesus!

b. The 12-year-old distress. The woman who had suffered the loss of blood for over a decade had a wretched existence. Not only was her plague debilitating and costly, it was also a social disgrace. The issue of blood meant that she was ceremonially unclean and would render unclean anyone she touched (Lev. 15:25-30). She would have been accorded treatment nearly as unkind as that given a leper. Her situation was desperate.

Disease and death—twin foes of mankind; consequently, hostile powers for Jesus to confront and overcome. "I am come that they might have life, and that they might have it more abundantly" (John 10:10).

2. *The persistence of desperation.* When Jesus returned to the other side of the lake, perhaps near Capernaum, a large and expectant crowd soon gathered around him (21). This was in contrast to the people on the opposite shore, who had urged him to depart (17).

a. The plea of Jairus. One of the prominent citizens of the region, a ruler of the local synagogue, came to Jesus greatly disturbed over the critical illness of his daughter. He fell at the feet of Jesus and begged Him to come to their home, put His hands on her, so that she would be healed and live (22-23).

Jairus would have had the responsibility, with others, for the management of the synagogue and the planning of the services. He may have known Jesus in that relationship. His plea touched the Master's heart and so He went with him (24).

b. The touch of the woman. With some sense of the mounting tension, the large crowd followed Jesus and Jairus, pressing around them. It was obviously an excited, jostling multitude.

In the midst of that tumult the afflicted woman disregarded all the Levitical laws and the sanctions of her society and reached through the throng to touch the robe of Jesus.

She had heard about Jesus and believed that if she could but touch Him, even by stealth, she would be healed of her scourge. Her faith, like that of Jairus, is challenging. *If I may touch but his clothes, I shall be whole* (28). She had only a fleeting moment, but she seized her opportunity with great longing. How often it is true that "now is the accepted time; behold now is the day of salvation!" (2 Cor. 6:2). Another moment, and it will be too late.

Jairus and the woman shared a feeling of desperation and sought the help of Jesus with unrelenting persistence. And so we should pray in time of crushing need.

Jesus encouraged such praying: "I say unto you, Ask, and it shall be given you; seek, and ye shall find; knock, and it shall be opened unto you" (Luke 11:9). James may disturb us a bit when he writes, "Ye have not, because ye ask not" (Jas. 4:2).

3. *The response of caring compassion.* The lovingkindness of Jesus is one of the qualities that melts the hearts of men and women and draws them to Him. In each of these instances, the consideration, compassion, and thoughtfulness of Jesus challenges His disciples. In the later words of Peter: "it is for you to follow in his steps" (1 Pet. 2:21, NEB).

> *Love lifted me! Love lifted me!*
> *When nothing else could help,*
> *Love lifted me.*

a. *The Lord's solicitude for the woman.* When the woman with the issue of blood succeeded in "stealing a miracle" (A. M. Hunter), she stopped the procession en route to Jairus' house. It is fascinating to examine the reactions of Jesus.

Realizing that "power had gone out from him," Jesus turned and asked what seemed to be an unreasonable question: "Who touched my clothes?" (30, NIV). The comment of the disciples was a bit sharp; with a multitude pressing upon Him, why should He ask, *Who touched me?* (31).

The woman, who knew *that she was healed of that plague* (29), now was frightened and apprehensive. Would the Master be angry with her? Jesus searched the crowd, looking *round about to see her that had done this thing.* The implication is that Jesus knew who she was. Despite her anxiety, the woman *came and fell down before him, and told him all the truth* (33).

With what compassion Jesus replied: *Daughter* (the only instance of this word in the Gospels), *thy faith hath made thee whole* (34). It was important for the woman to know that it was the power of God, in response to her faith, which had made her whole, and not some quasi-magical touch.

Also, Jesus wanted to do something more for her: *Go in* (literally, *into*) *peace, and be whole of thy plague* (34). She could now return home, not only relieved of her dreadful incubus but also free of her fears and sense of guilt. She had been made *whole.* Her secret touch had now become public testimony.

It is not surprising that traditions concerning this woman developed early. She was variously named Bernice or Veronica. The church historian Eusebius located her in Caesarea Philippi and reported that she had erected a statue in recognition of her healing.

A truer, more lasting monument is the fact that in a situation packed with emotion, Jesus had time to heal a distressful person and extend words of kindness, consideration, and compassion.

b. His concern for the family of Jairus. As we have seen, Jesus responded at once to the pleas of the frightened father. After the interruption by the afflicted woman, like a loving pastor, Jesus stayed very close to Jairus as they made their way to the troubled home.

First of all, it was shocking to Jairus to hear the callous report that his daughter had died and that he should not trouble *the Master any further* (35). But at once Jesus, at his elbow, gave Jairus reassurance: *Be not afraid, only believe* (36). If we can but hear Him say that to us, it will calm our fears and dry our tears.

And then, coming *to the house of the ruler of the synagogue* (38), Jesus quelled the commotion of the hired and fickle mourners, who could weep and wail one moment and laugh in scorn the next. A man of Jairus' standing would have had a considerable number of paid mourners, for "even the poorest man was required by common custom to hire a minimum of two flute-players and one professional mourner in the event of his wife's death" (William L. Lane).

In a moment of exquisite tenderness, after putting the mourners outside (a suggestion of some force), Jesus took the father and mother, possibly with the "inner circle" of disciples, into the room where *the damsel was lying* (40).

What a surge of feeling must have convulsed the parents and filled the room, when Jesus took the girl by the hand and said, *"'Talitha koum!'* (which means 'Little girl, I say to you, get up!')" (41, NIV). These were the Aramaic words Jesus had used, words that were prized and preserved from the beginning of the Church.

In this mighty work, Jesus prefigured His own resurrection. It was therefore important that only His closest disciples should witness the event. It was also important "to let no one hear about it" (NEB). But, of course, *they were astonished with a great astonishment* (42).

Mark records still another touch, such as a participant and eyewitness would see and recall: Jesus commanded that something should be given her to eat (cf. 8:3).

Across the centuries, not only Mark, but eyewitnesses like Peter and interpreters like Paul, are telling us that Jesus has in fact "overcome the world" (John 16:33). He has authority over the realm of nature: "even the wind and the sea obey him" (4:41). He has authority over the kingdom of Satan: "even the unclean spirits . . . obey him" (1:27). Now it is evident that the hostile powers of disease and death are subject to His word. "The last enemy that shall be destroyed is death" (1 Cor. 15:26), and Jesus is the Destroyer.

MARK 6

Greatness Incognito

Mark 6:1-6

> 1 And he went out from thence, and came into his own country; and his disciples follow him.
> 2 And when the sabbath day was come, he began to teach in the synagogue: and many hearing him were astonished, saying, From whence hath this man these things? and what wisdom is this which is given unto him, that even such mighty works are wrought by his hands?
> 3 Is not this the carpenter, the son of Mary, the brother of James, and Joses, and of Juda, and Simon? and are not his sisters here with us? And they were offended at him.
> 4 But Jesus said unto them, A prophet is not without honour, but in his own country, and among his own kin, and in his own house.
> 5 And he could there do no mighty work, save that he laid his hands upon a few sick folk, and healed them.
> 6 And he marvelled because of their unbelief. And he went round about the villages, teaching.

Jesus now begins a preaching tour of Galilee. His disciples will receive "in-service" training as they go from village to village, preaching and teaching. The tour began with a trip to Nazareth, where Jesus grew up (Luke 4:16). It was His hometown.

As a lad Jesus had the experience of a loving home and a large family. Mark names four brothers in addition to his sisters. As a carpenter and the Son of a carpenter (Matt. 13:55), He would have been well known in the village. The fact that He was invited to teach in the synagogue on the sabbath day (2) is evidence of His standing in Nazareth. Greatness was among them and they knew it not.

1. *A paradox in the hometown.* This time the reception was disappointing. "He came unto his own, and his own received him not" (John 1:11).

a. The people of Nazareth were amazed at the teaching of Jesus and the *mighty works . . . wrought by his hands* (2). Luke gives us the story in greater detail (Luke 4:16-30). His teaching was from the book of the prophet Isaiah. "The Spirit of the Lord is upon me, because he has anointed me to preach good news to the poor" (Luke 4:18, RSV).

Jesus applied this passage (Isa. 61:1-2) to himself. "Today this scripture has been fulfilled in your hearing" (Luke 4:21, RSV). *And they were offended at him* (3).

John Henry Jowett once spoke of "The deadening familiarity with the sublime," and warned young ministers not to lose the sense of the sacred. The people of Nazareth could not accept the fact that One they knew so well could be a prophet. *Is not this the carpenter, the son of Mary?* (3).

b. But if the people of Nazareth were amazed at Jesus, He was amazed at them. *He marvelled because of their unbelief* (6).

It is possible that we may too easily and superficially read this story, without entering into what the experience meant to Jesus. Criticism stings us; rejection pains us. It was no different with Him.

The officers of the chief priests and Pharisees were once sent to apprehend Jesus and take Him into custody. After listening to Him, they returned empty-handed, with this explanation: "Never man spake like this man" (John 7:45-46).

Even in Nazareth, the long-time friends of Jesus acknowledged His uniqueness: "Where did this man get these things? . . . What's this wisdom that has been given him?" (2, NIV). Nevertheless, they were (literally) scandalized.

The experience of criticism and rejection was painful and incredible for Jesus. The circle of exclusion seemed to close in on Him: "'Only in his home town, among his relatives and in his own house is a prophet without honor'" (4, NIV).

2. *A powerless, impoverished people.* The people of Naz-areth were robbed of the power and riches Jesus could have brought them. Their rejection followed a process of specious reasoning.

a. Their secret questions were weighted with deroga-tory innuendo. *From whence hath this man these things?* (2) sounds somewhat like the scribes when they charged that Jesus was in league with Satan (3:22). His own family had feared for His sanity (3:21). Perhaps, they may have reasoned, Jesus had consorted with some mysterious, sin-ister influence.

And when they asked, *Is not this the carpenter, the son of Mary?* (3), they were reflecting on His social status. How could a working man, without the distinguished background and education of a rabbi, have such wisdom? Reference to His mother only may carry a hint of dis-respect. Some scholars take that reference to be evidence for the truth of the Virgin Birth.

b. In Luke's fuller record, we learn that Jesus rebuked His friends for their blindness and consequent loss. He reminded them that in a time of famine, Elijah was sent to none of the many widows in Israel, but to one in Zare-phath in the region of Sidon; and that Elisha cleansed the leper, Naaman the Syrian, and none of the lepers in Israel (cf. Luke 4:26-27).

This made the people of Nazareth so angry they would have cast Jesus down from a cliff to destroy Him, but He escaped their hands. Greatness had come to the people of Nazareth, and they knew it not. How often have we failed to recognize greatness incognito? The Epistle to the He-brews reminds us that, by their hospitality, some believers have entertained angels without knowing it (Heb. 13:2).

When the immortal Thomas Aquinas was a student, his appearance and behavior led his classmates to call him "the dumb ox." His famous teacher, Albertus Mag-nus, replied, "Yes, and one day the lowing of 'the dumb ox' will fill the world."

An Apprenticeship for the Twelve

Mark 6:7-13

> 7 And he called unto him the twelve, and began to send them forth by two and two; and gave them power over unclean spirits;
> 8 And commanded them that they should take nothing for their journey, save a staff only; no scrip, no bread, no money in their purse:
> 9 But be shod with sandals; and not put on two coats.
> 10 And he said unto them, In what place soever ye enter into an house, there abide till ye depart from that place.
> 11 And whosoever shall not receive you, nor hear you, when ye depart thence, shake off the dust under your feet for a testimony against them. Verily I say unto you, It shall be more tolerable for Sodom and Gomorrha in the day of judgment, than for that city.
> 12 And they went out, and preached that men should repent.
> 13 And they cast out many devils, and anointed with oil many that were sick, and healed them.

Immediately following His rejection in Nazareth, Jesus continued His teaching ministry from place to place in Galilee (6b). Presumably the disciples were with Him. The rebuff He received in the hometown served only to accelerate His missionary travels and work.

It was time for the disciples, who had been called from their secular tasks and commissioned as apostles, to begin their own ministry. The time would soon come when the responsibility for the Christian mission would be in their hands alone.

Although this "tour of duty" was to be temporary and brief, it was a paradigm, a pattern for a lifetime in the Christian ministry. It was an apprenticeship for the Twelve. An apprentice, according to *Webster's New Collegiate Dictionary,* is "one who is learning by practical experience under skilled workers a trade, art, or calling."

1. *The Christian ministry is a calling.* Mark has brought us carefully to this point. We have seen how Jesus called His followers to leave their nets and become fishers of men (1:17).

This initial calling had been reinforced by their appointment as the twelve apostles and by the corresponding promise that He would "send them forth to preach, and to have power [authority] to heal . . . and to cast out devils" (3:14-15).

They subsequently shared and observed the experiences of Jesus as He preached the gospel, healed the sick, cast out demons, and confronted the rising tide of misunderstanding and ill will among the official leaders of Judaism.

What had before been a promise now became a reality: *he called unto him the twelve, and began to send them forth by two and two* (7). Their call would be tested as never before. It is folly to enter the ministry without a divine call.

2. *The Christian ministry requires empowerment.* Not only is the ministry a calling no one should take unto himself, it also is a task no one can carry out in his own strength.

a. The disciples were able to go in the confidence that the Lord had sent them. They went as His delegated representatives. Wherever they went it was as if He were present. This practice was common in Jewish legal circles. Persons so authorized could carry out official responsibilities for another. Paul said it well to the Corinthians: "We are therefore Christ's ambassadors, as though God were making his appeal through us" (2 Cor. 5:20, NIV).

b. The disciples received something more than an official, legal designation as representatives of Jesus. They received *power,* in the sense of authority, both to proclaim a message of repentance and to cast out unclean spirits (7), and heal the sick (13). How was such authority delegated? In what ways were the disciples aware that they possessed such authority? How may those sent out in our day receive this authority?

Mark does not answer these crucial questions. For us who live this side of Pentecost, however, the answer is to be found in the very last words of Jesus: "But you shall receive power when the Holy Spirit has come upon you; and you shall be My witnesses both in Jerusalem, and in all

Judea and Samaria, and even to the remotest part of the earth" (Acts 1:8, NASB). If it is folly to enter the ministry without a divine call, it is equally foolish to attempt the work of the ministry without the power of the Spirit.

3. *The Christian ministry demands self-dedication.* As the disciples went out, two by two (for purposes of mutual encouragement and as valid witnesses; see Deut. 19:15), they were commanded to practice frugality, courtesy, and single-minded loyalty to the message of Jesus.

a. They were to practice frugality. Their instructions were not so much what they *should* take with them as what they *should not* take. They were to take no food, bag, or money. A staff was permitted (if they already had one) but no extras: "Wear sandals but not an extra tunic" (9, NIV). The extra garment was for the chill night air, something they would not need. (See *Beacon Bible Commentary,* 6:107-9, 317-19, for a discussion of details.) They were to learn the lesson of complete dependence upon God and His ability to provide (Gen. 22:8).

b. They were to practice courtesy. When they accepted the hospitality of a home, regularly extended to travellers, they were to remain there for the period of their stay. To move to more comfortable quarters would be discourteous to their hosts.

c. They were to practice single-minded loyalty to the message of Jesus. Just as Jesus had experienced rejection in Nazareth and elsewhere, they could expect resistance and rejection also. In line with the Jewish custom of shaking the dust of a pagan land from their feet, they were to declare in symbolism that the unfriendly place was pagan. The hoped-for result of this prophetic action was repentance. Paul and Barnabas "shook off the dust of their feet against" Antioch in Pisidia (Acts 13:51).

4. Under such conditions, *the Christian ministry will be productive.* A divinely called ministry, totally and unselfishly committed to preaching, deliverance, and healing

will be fruitful. *And they went out, and preached . . . and cast out many [demons], and anointed with oil many that were sick* (12-13).

a. They preached repentance. Repentance has a positive as well as a negative side. It involves not only a renunciation of sin and a break with a sinful past, but also a turning to God in faith and turst. It is, in a sense, conversion. "Repent ye, and believe the gospel" (1:15) is still the message of Jesus.

b. They brought deliverance to the demoniacs. The disciples were not always successful as exorcists (9:18). At that subsequent point of failure, Jesus stressed the necessity of a prayer life which produces genuine faith (9:19, 29).

So many in our society are tormented by fear, guilt, anxiety, and hopelessness. The man of God who can bring deliverance to such harassed souls will have their gratitude.

c. They anointed with oil for the healing of the sick. In biblical times oil was used in a variety of ways: as food, medicine, even cosmetics. However, it symbolized especially the presence and power of the Holy Spirit, the supernatural (Zech. 4:1-6).

The task of the Christian ministry is to seek the healing of the whole person: body, mind, and soul. Such healing is the result of the supernatural power of God. When the disciples *anointed with oil many that were sick, and healed them* (13), they were directing attention away from themselves to the One who sent and empowered them.

> *Jesus calls us. By Thy mercies,*
> *Saviour, may we hear Thy call,*
> *Give our hearts to Thy obedience,*
> *Serve and love Thee best of all.*

> —Cecil F. Alexander

An Alarming Flashback

Mark 6:14-29

14 And king Herod heard of him; (for his name was spread abroad:) and he said, That John the Baptist was risen from the dead, and therefore mighty works do shew forth themselves in him.

15 Others said, That it is Elias. And others said, That it is a prophet, or as one of the prophets.

16 But when Herod heard thereof, he said, It is John, whom I beheaded: he is risen from the dead.

17 For Herod himself had sent forth and laid hold upon John, and bound him in prison for Herodias' sake, his brother Philip's wife: for he had married her.

18 For John had said unto Herod, It is not lawful for thee to have thy brother's wife.

19 Therefore Herodias had a quarrel against him, and would have killed him; but she could not:

20 For Herod feared John, knowing that he was a just man and an holy, and observed him; and when he heard him, he did many things, and heard him gladly.

21 And when a convenient day was come, that Herod on his birthday made a supper to his lords, high captains, and chief estates of Galilee;

22 And when the daughter of the said Herodias came in, and danced, and pleased Herod and them that sat with him, the king said unto the damsel, Ask of me whatsoever thou wilt, and I will give it thee.

23 And he sware unto her, Whatsoever thou shalt ask of me, I will give it thee, unto the half of my kingdom.

24 And she went forth, and said unto her mother, What shall I ask? And she said, The head of John the Baptist.

25 And she came in straightway with haste unto the king, and asked, saying, I will that thou give me by and by in a charger the head of John the Baptist.

26 And the king was exceeding sorry; yet for his oath's sake, and for their sakes which sat with him, he would not reject her.

27 And immediately the king sent an executioner, and commanded his head to be brought: and he went and beheaded him in the prison.

28 And brought his head in a charger, and gave it to the damsel: and the damsel gave it to her mother.

29 And when his disciples heard of it, they came and took up his corpse, and laid it in a tomb.

The preaching tour of Jesus and the disciples (6:6*b*-13) must have created quite a stir in Galilee. Large numbers of people would have heard the messages and witnessed the miracles. The effect could possibly be compared to the impact of the mass meetings Billy Graham has held in some of our cities.

Among those who heard of the campaign was King Herod (14), a son of Herod the Great, and who ruled over Galilee and Perea from 4 B.C. to A.D. 39. This long period encompassed the lifetime of Jesus. Herod Antipas was actually not a king, though he sought the title and lost his position as tetrarch for his ambition. Mark may have used the title with irony, a point the Romans would enjoy.

Herod's "alarming flashback" recalls a grisly event which took place earlier, possibly soon after Jesus began His public ministry. In addition to Herod, the story involves Jesus, John, and Herodias.

1. *Jesus, a disturber of men.* It may help us to visualize what Jesus was like by considering the impression He made on those who saw and heard Him. They likened Him to a distinguished group of men—the prophets of Israel, who were second in public esteem only to the Messiah.

When people looked at Jesus they thought of strong, rugged, fearless, yet tender men: Elijah, Jeremiah, or John the Baptist, the greatest of them all (8:27-28; Matt. 16:13-14).

Herod Antipas instantly made his own evaluation. His seared and tarnished conscience said, *It is John, whom I beheaded: he is risen from the dead* (16).

2. *John, a preacher of righteousness.* As noted above (see on 1:1-8), John the Baptist was one of the truly great men of the Bible, with very considerable influence upon his society.

a. The region where John preached and baptized encroached upon a section of Perea, a province under the control of Herod Antipas. When John preached in Bethany beyond the Jordan (John 1:28), he could have fallen into Herod's hands. It would make fascinating reading if we could complete the story only hinted at in the Gospels. John must have had frequent and personal contact with Herod. Mark reports: "When Herod heard John, he was greatly puzzled; yet he liked to listen to him" (20, NIV).

Leading evangelists and preachers have often had close association with royalty and heads of state. Bishop Matthew Simpson, of the Methodist church, was a spiritual advisor of Abraham Lincoln and often slipped into the White House for prayer with the president.

b. Whatever the details, John the Baptist preached repentance and righteousness to all in his congregation, including Herod Antipas, whose incestuous marriage to Herodias, *his brother Philip's wife* (17), was an offense to common morality. The message must have been repeated: "For John had been saying to Herod, 'It is not lawful for you to have your brother's wife'" (18, NIV).

Herod respected John, for he knew him to be *a just man and . . . holy* (20). He arrested and imprisoned the Baptist, under pressure from Herodias, not to destroy but to silence him. Josephus wrote that John was imprisoned in a fortress-palace-prison known as Machaerus, located in a bleak region northeast of the Dead Sea.

3. *Herodias, a pattern of corruption.* Mark has opened a window for us to look in on the family of Herod the Great, famous for its intricacies of intrigue and corruption. The Herods served the purposes of their Roman overlords by maintaining a degree of peace in a volatile land. Their stock-in-trade was cruelty and brutality.

a. The implications of this story are too complex to rehearse here. In his commentary on Mark, D. Edmond Hiebert has given us an example of the tangled lives of the Herodian family:

> Herodias, the *niece* of Antipas, by her marriage to her uncle Philip became the *sister-in-law* of Antipas, and then became his *wife.* Through the later marriage of her daughter Salome to Philip the Tetrarch, Herodias, his *niece* and *sister-in-law,* became Philip's *mother-in-law.*

The preaching of John the Baptist infuriated Herodias, who "nursed a grudge against John (and) wanted to kill him" (19, NIV). Consumed with ambition to become the wife of a "king" and enjoy the opulent life of oriental royalty, Herodias had been willing to smash two marriages —her own and that of Herod Antipas. The latter caused an international incident, for Herod's wife was the daughter of the Nabatean king Aretas IV. Ultimately, military conflict followed. Such a woman would brook no resistance to her schemes.

b. Unable to satisfy her grudge, because of the protection Herod gave John, Herodias nevertheless discovered "an opportune time" (21, NIV). The dancing of her daughter Salome, at a regal banquet honoring Herod's birthday, turned the king's head. He made a rash vow with bitter ramifications. *The king said unto the damsel, Ask of me whatsoever thou wilt* (22).

It is a sad commentary on the mother-daughter relationship that, after consulting with her mother, the girl made an unbelievable request: "I want you to give me here and now, on a dish, the head of John the Baptist" (24, NEB).

The king was aghast, but peer pressure would not release him from the vow. A soldier was dispatched for the execution. The head was brought to the girl, as requested, who *gave it to her mother* (28). What a trophy! What a party!

4. *Jesus and John, colaborers.* The Gospels communicate a feeling of pathos in the relationship of John and Jesus. In a real sense, they were colaborers.

a. John knew himself to be "the voice of one crying in the wilderness, Prepare ye the way of the Lord" (1:3). He did not know who the Coming One was until it was revealed to him at the baptism of Jesus (John 1:31-34).

When John was arrested and imprisoned, it was the divine signal for Jesus to begin His public ministry. This He did: "Jesus came . . . preaching the gospel of the kingdom of God" (1:14).

b. For a time, in Machaerus, that bleak prison-fortress overlooking the Dead Sea, John experienced a period of doubt. He sent disciples to Jesus with his questions: "Are you he who is to come, or shall we look for another?" (Luke 7:19, RSV). Jesus understood and sent words of reassurance to John. On that occasion, Jesus paid the

Baptist a memorable tribute: "Among them that are born of women there hath not risen a greater than John the Baptist" (Matt. 11:11).

c. When Herodias broke down the defenses of Herod and secured the execution of John, two beautiful actions followed. The disciples of John tenderly "took his body and laid it in a tomb" (29, NIV). And then, according to Matthew, they "went out and told Jesus" (Matt. 14:12). We do not know what the reaction of Jesus was.

When John Wesley, near the close of his own long life, heard that his brother Charles had died, he was overcome with grief and sorrow. Perhaps it was like that with Jesus and John. We do know what the response of Jesus was to the word that His friend Lazarus had died (John 11:35).

And now the preaching and mighty works of Jesus and His disciples haunt the mind of Herod with memories of remorse and guilt. Which world is better—the dark and decaying world of Herod and Herodias, or the bright and shining world of Jesus and John, *workers together* in God's eternal kingdom?

"He Restoreth My Soul"

Mark 6:30-44

> 30 And the apostles gathered themselves together unto Jesus, and told him all things, both what they had done, and what they had taught.
> 31 And he said unto them, Come ye yourselves apart into a desert place, and rest a while: for there were many coming and going, and they had no leisure so much as to eat.
> 32 And they departed into a desert place by ship privately.
> 33 And the people saw them departing, and many knew him, and ran afoot thither out of all cities, and outwent them, and came together unto him.
> 34 And Jesus, when he came out, saw much people, and was moved with compassion toward them, because they were as sheep not having a shepherd: and he began to teach them many things.
> 35 And when the day was now far spent, his disciples came unto him, and said, This is a dessert place, and now the time is far passed:
> 36 Send them away, that they may go into the country round about, and into the villages, and buy themselves bread: for they have nothing to eat.
> 37 He answered and said unto them, Give ye them to eat. And they say unto him, Shall we go and buy two hundred pennyworth of bread, and give them to eat?

38 He saith unto them, How many loaves have ye? go and see. And when they knew, they say, Five, and two fishes.
39 And he commanded them to make all sit down by companies upon the green grass.
40 And they sat down in ranks, by hundreds, and by fifties.
41 And when he had taken the five loaves and the two fishes, he looked up to heaven, and blessed, and brake the loaves, and gave them to his disciples to set before them; and the two fishes divided he among them all.
42 And they did all eat, and were filled.
43 And they took up twelve baskets full of the fragments, and of the fishes.
44 And they that did eat of the loaves were about five thousand men.

The apostles returned from their preaching-healing tour rejoicing in the results (cf. Luke 10:17) and eager to report *both what they had done, and what they had taught* (30). A happy order—deeds, then words!

What follows is a lesson in "practical theology" for all busy people, including Christian workers. The response of Jesus to all the bustle and hurry was: "Come with me by yourselves to a quiet place and get some rest" (31, NIV).

1. *The need for renewal.* The need for solitude, for rest and renewal, is too often ignored by the followers of Jesus. Mark notes nearly a dozen occasions on which Jesus withdrew from the crowds. Are we wiser and stronger than He?

a. It is a bit surprising that Mark records so little about the return of the apostles from their tour of Galilee. This may suggest something about the pressure of the crowds coming and going and the fact that they had *no leisure so much as to eat* (31). It was time to get away.

b. The proximity of the lake and the availability of a boat provided a convenient way to escape for short periods of time. We may easily overlook resources for renewal close at hand. An Englishman showed a friend his attractive garden. "But it's so small!" was the reaction. The Englishman replied, "Did you see how high it is?" "There remaineth therefore a rest to the people of God" (Heb. 4:9).

c. In this case, the respite of Jesus and His companions was short-lived, but not without its value. "The people saw them departing . . . and ran afoot" around the northern edge of the lake, spreading the word in other towns along the way (33). As a consequence, when Jesus landed, a large crowd was there in the wilderness ahead of Him.

d. One might have expected expressions of disappointment, even annoyance. Instead, Jesus was gripped with compassion toward them. He saw them *as sheep not having a shepherd* (34).

2. *The need for bread.* After an extended period of teaching, it was getting late, and the disciples were getting uneasy. Their counsel was to send the people away, "to go into the country and villages round about and buy themselves something to eat" (36, RSV). Jesus startled them with His answer: *Give ye them to eat* (37).

a. We have already observed the presence of the wilderness motif in Mark's Gospel. The biblical writers looked back on Israel's life in the wilderness with nostalgia and longing. God called Israel into the wilderness to give them His law and make them His people. He led them by day and by night. He fed them manna and quail and supplied them with springs of water. And finally, despite failures and reverses, God led Israel out of the wilderness into the Promised Land.

Toward the close of his life, Moses asked the Lord to appoint a successor, who would be a shepherd over the people of God. The Lord instructed Moses to "take Joshua the son of Nun, a man in whom is the spirit" (Num. 27:18, RSV). In the Greek Old Testament (LXX), the word for Joshua is "Jesus."

b. Many interpreters believe that such implications were certainly in the mind of Mark as he compiled his Gospel and in the thought of the early Christians as they read it. The new Joshua is with the people of God again in the wilderness, leading and feeding them. They will no longer be as sheep without a shepherd.

The concern of Jesus for the physical needs of the people is revealing. It is true that "man does not live by bread alone" (Deut. 8:3, RSV), but he does need bread. We are not to be anxious, saying, "'What shall we eat?' or 'What shall we drink?' or 'What shall we wear?'" for our "heavenly Father knows that you need them all" (Matt. 6:31-32, RSV).

c. The symbolism of bread is a recurring theme in Mark. On the Galilean tour, the disciples were forbidden to take bread with them (6:8). But in this instance, and in the feeding of the 4,000 (8:1-10), they were drawn into a miracle of multiplying loaves and fishes. Later, in two episodes on the lake (6:52; 8:21), Jesus upbraided His disciples for their failure to understand the symbolism. They were puzzled, as we may be also.

Did He want them to realize that He is "the bread which came down from heaven" (John 6:41)? Did He want them to remember that as the Son of God, He has control over nature, including the processes that produce bread, as well as the wind and the waves? He chided them. What would He say to us?

3. *The need for a miracle.* When Jesus challenged the disciples to feed the huge crowd, they were dumfounded. It is often noted that their reply was disrespectful. *Two hundred pennyworth* (200 denarii) *of bread* would have represented about a year's wages at 20 cents a day. But Jesus persisted: "How many loaves do you have? Go look!" (38, NASB). What they discovered was not helpful to them— *five, and two fishes* (38). Jesus knew they needed a miracle. He was prepared for them to witness one and participate in it as well.

a. The mechanics of the miracle are of interest. Jesus directed the enormous throng to be seated in an orderly fashion—in groups of *hundreds* and *fifties* upon *the green grass* (39, 40). With their colorful garments, they probably looked like plots of flowers! Someone would have remembered a similar grouping Moses had made in his juridical organization of Israel (Exod. 18:21).

Jesus took the loaves and the fish and prayed a prayer

of blessing, looking *up to heaven* (41), to the Father who provided the bounty. It has been suggested that Jesus prayed: "Blessed be Thou, our Father in heaven, who gives us today our necessary bread" (William L. Lane). He then broke the loaves, divided the fish, and gave the food to the disciples for distribution to the people. The early Christian Church would have seen in these actions a preview of the Eucharist, the sacrament of the Lord's Supper. When all had eaten and were satisfied, each disciple (including Judas!) filled a basket with the fragments. All was to be conserved.

b. The miracle served a humanitarian purpose. Jesus was concerned that the people—tired, hungry, and a long way from home, might faint by the wayside. He was also sending a message to believers, for all time to come, that the Church should also have a concern for the material needs of mankind.

c. The miracle also served as a witness-event. Mark gives us little evidence that the thousands who partook of the loaves and fishes knew what was happening. However, in John's account, the people saw the event as a miraculous sign and wanted to make him king by force (cf. John 6:14-15).

The primary witness was to the disciples. Jesus was patiently leading them to an understanding of His person and of His mission on earth. They were slow to learn. Only after the Resurrection and Pentecost would the veil be taken away.

Nevertheless, when the day was at an end, the disciples must have had some sense of renewal in body and soul, even though their attempt to seek a place of solitude and rest had met with an unexpected turn of events.

Contrary Winds

Mark 6:45-52

> 45 And straightway he constrained his disciples to get into the ship, and to go to the other side before unto Bethsaida, while he sent away the people.

46 And when he had sent them away, he departed into a mountain to pray.
47 And when even was come, the ship was in the midst of the sea, and he alone on the land.
48 And he saw them toiling in rowing; for the wind was contrary unto them: and about the fourth watch of the night he cometh unto them, walking upon the sea, and would have passed by them.
49 But when they saw him walking upon the sea, they supposed it had been a spirit, and cried out:
50 For they all saw him, and were troubled. And immediately he talked with them, and saith unto them, Be of good cheer: it is I; be not afraid.
51 And he went up unto them into the ship; and the wind ceased: and they were sore amazed in themselves beyond measure, and wondered.
52 For they considered not the miracle of the loaves: for their heart was hardened.

It was time for the benediction! The congregation was huge—5,000 men alone. They may have been restless and excited. Why not make this Man their king? (John 6:15). The disciples would have been eager to support the idea. It was time to disperse, so Jesus *constrained his disciples to get into the ship* and head for the home port, *while he sent away the people* (45). One can imagine that the dismissal was affectionate and thoughtful.

For the moment, Jesus and the disciples went in different directions. The disciples left for the western shore of the lake, while Jesus *departed into a mountain to pray.* What followed was a dark night, troubled by contrary winds for Jesus as well as for the disciples.

1. *The prayer vigil of Jesus.* As we have seen (1:35-39), Jesus was a Man of prayer. He prayed often and at length. Special pressures dictated that He should spend much of this night alone with the Father.

a. One of the pressures could be called *the return of the Temptation.* When Jesus encountered Satan in the wilderness (1:12-13), He rejected the invitation to seek the conquest of the world by means of a sensational display of His power or in collusion with Satan, "the prince of this world" (John 14:30). No shortcuts! The only way to the hearts of men would be the way of suffering love, and that meant a cross.

> *I must needs go home by the way of the Cross:*
> *There's no other way but this.*

The restless, excited crowd must have suggested that the easier route was available. We have no evidence that the decision Jesus made involved a struggle, but communion and fellowship with the Father was a felt need.

b. Another source of pressure was *the shadow of impending events.* Jesus had already begun a series of withdrawals from the crowds in Galilee, in order to be alone with the disciples. The training of the Twelve was essential. And soon His steps would take Him to Jerusalem, where He would present himself to Israel and confront the opposition at its center.

These conclusions are inferential, of course, but reasonable. We cannot know what was in the mind of Jesus on that night. He doubtless also prayed for the disciples (cf. Luke 22:32) that their eyes would be opened and that their hearts would not always be hardened.

2. *The dark night of the disciples.* Mark seems to stress the separation of the disciples and Jesus. They were *in the midst of the sea,* perhaps several miles from the shore, while Jesus was *alone on the land* (47), probably on a hillside overlooking the lake.

a. The night was dark because they were making very little headway toward their destination. The wind was against them. It is possible that this was the second evening following the feeding of the 5,000 (cf. vv. 35 and 47). The expression *toiling in rowing* implies "torture." They were "straining at the oars" (NIV), "laboring against a head-wind" (48, NEB).

b. The night was dark because of growing fears. For the disciples it was a vicious cycle. Because it was a dark night, they were fearful, and their fears made the night even darker. Fear paralyzes and robs one of reason and self-control. Under such conditions, the unexpected triggers panic. Thus, when Jesus did come to them, *walking upon the sea* (48), the disciples cried out in terror. The word for "cried out" is used elsewhere to depict the shrieks of the demoniacs.

What the disciples could not have known was that Jesus *saw them toiling* (48) and was on His way to help them. Mark may imply preternatural sight. Even on a moonlit night, it would have been difficult to see the disciples from the vantage point of the mountainside.

3. *The daybreak of deliverance.* It is trite and probably not true to say that "the darkest hour is just before dawn." Nevertheless, that was the experience of the disciples. At about 3 a.m., *the fourth watch of the night,* according to Roman calculation, Jesus "went out to them, walking on the lake" (48, NIV). This was in accordance with an implied promise when He constrained them to "go on ahead of him" (45, NIV). Only Matthew recounts the story of Peter walking on the water and of his floundering (Matt. 14:28-31).

a. The testing of the disciples was not over. Jesus "meant to pass by them" (48, RSV). Would they recognize Him? Would they call to Him and put their trust in Him? They did not do well on that test. No one walks on the water! It had to be a ghost! No subjective phantasm, *they all saw him, and were troubled* (50).

b. Jesus did *not* pass them by. *Immediately he talked with them,* and spoke those blessed words, *Be of good cheer: it is I; be not afraid* (50). With one exception (10:49), Jesus is the only one in the New Testament to issue that heartening command. The struggle was over. Jesus climbed into the boat with them, while *the wind ceased* (51), as did their fears.

> *He giveth more grace when the burdens grow greater;*
>   *He sendeth more strength when the labors increase.*
> *To added affliction He addeth His mercy;*
>   *To multiplied trials, His multiplied peace.*
>   —ANNIE JOHNSON FLINT

c. The story closes with an observation both clear and puzzling. Once more the disciples *were sore amazed . . . beyond measure* (51). That is clear and understandable. But Mark (and the Church) attributes their fear and amazement to the fact that their heart was hardened (52). That is puzzling. The explanation must be that after *the miracle of the loaves* (52), i.e., the feeding of the 5,000 with five loaves and two fishes, the disciples should not have been surprised at anything—not even the Master *walking upon the sea* (49). But that would require great faith, and the disciples were as yet men of little faith (Matt. 8:26). Who among us will cast the first stone?

Outstretched Hands

Mark 6:53-56

> 53 And when they had passed over, they came into the land of Gennesaret, and drew to the shore.
> 54 And when they were come out of the ship, straightway they knew him,
> 55 And ran through that whole region round about, and began to carry about in beds those that were sick, where they heard he was.
> 56 And whithersoever he entered, into villages, or cities, or country, they laid the sick in the streets, and besought him that they might touch if it were but the border of his garment: and as many as touched him were made whole.

The period of withdrawal for rest and solitude ("Come ye . . . apart . . . and rest a while," 6:31) had been a tumultuous one—the feeding of the 5,000, the long night of rowing against contrary winds, and the amazement of Jesus *walking upon the sea* (48).

Jesus and the disciples moored their boat at Gennesaret, a few miles down the coast from Capernaum. The heavy winds on the Sea of Galilee may have blown them off course. *The land,* or Plain, *of Gennesaret* was a remarkably fertile area, densely populated, about three miles in length and a mile and a half in width. Reputedly, "walnuts, palms, figs, olives, and grapes" (William Hendriksen) grew in profusion.

One picture this brief interlude creates is a forest of hands outstretched to touch the Savior as He passes by.

1. *The crowds readily recognized Jesus. Straightway they knew him* (54). Such prompt recognition of Jesus tells us something about His public exposure, as well as the attractiveness of His ministry. If Jesus had taught in the synagogues of Capernaum and of Nazareth (1:21; 6:2), He may well have taught in the synagogues of other towns also. Many would have seen Him there. More especially, the crowds would have known about Him from what appears to be His incessant travels throughout Galilee, preaching, teaching, and healing. Jesus was a public figure.

2. *The crowds responded with compassion and faith.* The word must have spread like wildfire, as it did later in Jericho (10:47), "Jesus of Nazareth is passing by!" The people *ran through that whole region round about* (55) broadcasting the news. Once more we see the compassion so many had for their ailing friends: "the people . . . began to carry about on their beds (mats) those that were sick, where they heard he was" (54-55, ASV). This occurred repeatedly. It is a testimony to their kindness. The people not only had compassion for their afflicted friends, they also had implicit faith in the power and willingness of Jesus to heal the sick.

3. *The crowds evidenced little spiritual understanding.* In the episode of the feeding of the 5,000 (30-44), no mention is made of Jesus healing the sick (perhaps only the able-bodied could make that hurried trip). In this instance, no mention is made of Jesus teaching the people, only His ministry of healing. He may well have healed and taught in both places, but the omissions are of interest.

a. In healing the sick, Jesus often touched them (1:41). The action is now reversed. Wherever Jesus went, "the marketplaces" (56, NIV) were lined with the sick, who "begged him to let them simply touch the edge of his cloak" (56, NEB). Jesus responded with willingness: *as many as touched him were made whole* (56). It was more than something magic, and not by stealth.

What a picture to haunt the soul—a forest of outstretched hands reaching out to Jesus!

b. Mark does not tell us the purpose or route of the trek Jesus took. It was comprehensive—*into villages, or cities, or country* (56) of Gennesaret—and must have been one the people expected He would take. They were waiting. Patiently Jesus ministered to all who came to Him. Not everyone sought Him, and not many understood His real mission.

MARK 7

Defilement: Contrived

Mark 7:1-13

> 1 Then came together unto him the Pharisees, and certain of the scribes, which came from Jerusalem.
> 2 And when they saw some of his disciples eat bread with defiled, that is to say, with unwashen, hands, they found fault.
> 3 For the Pharisees, and all the Jews, except they wash their hands oft, eat not, holding the tradition of the elders.
> 4 And when they come from the market, except they wash, they eat not. And many other things there be, which they have received to hold, as the washing of cups, and pots, brasen vessels, and of tables.
> 5 Then the Pharisees and scribes asked him, Why walk not thy disciples according to the tradition of the elders, but eat bread with unwashen hands?
> 6 He answered and said unto them, Well hath Esaias prophesied of you hypocrites, as it is written, This people honoureth me with their lips, but their heart is far from me.
> 7 Howbeit in vain do they worship me, teaching for doctrines the commandments of men.
> 8 For laying aside the commandment of God, ye hold the tradition of men, as the washing of pots and cups: and many other such like things ye do.
> 9 And he said unto them, Full well ye reject the commandment of God, that ye may keep your own tradition.
> 10 For Moses said, Honour thy father and thy mother; and, Whoso curseth father or mother, let him die the death:
> 11 But ye say, If a man shall say to his father or mother, It is Corban, that is to say, a gift, by whatsoever thou mightest be profited by me; he shall be free.
> 12 And ye suffer him no more to do ought for his father or his mother;
> 13 Making the word of God of none effect through your tradition, which ye have delivered: and many such like things do ye.

The position of this passage, and the one following (14-23), is instructive. They introduce the subject of defilement and serve as a prelude to the account of three miracles among the Gentiles. The association is surely deliberate. The punctilious Jew felt threatened by defilement in any contact with the Gentile world.

Defilement may be contrived or real. Through the teaching of Jesus, Mark wants his readers to learn the difference. Tradition, ritual, and form can all be vain and evil, or rich and valuable, depending upon their relationship to truth and reality. And that relationship depends upon the character and motivation of those who bear the tradition.

The empty, hollow tradition of the Pharisees and scribes frequently led to a contrived defilement. Jesus rejected that. However, as the next passage will show (14-23), moral defilement is a fact of the spiritual life. Its source lies within the soul and not in the lack of conformity to the petty rules of the scribes.

1. *The vanity of empty forms.* Once more a delegation of Pharisees and scribes had come down from Jerusalem to observe the Prophet of Nazareth. They gathered around Jesus and looked on with critical eye. What they saw they did not like. Some of the disciples were eating *bread with defiled, that is to say, with unwashen, hands* (2). The Pharisees found fault (2), not because the disciples were unhygienic, but because they had broken *the tradition of the elders* (3).

a. It is important to have some understanding of that tradition. With a sense of do-or-die loyalty to the law of Moses, the Jews had constructed a vast and complex code and commentary, designed to protect the Law and to help the faithful understand and obey the Law.

b. Our reaction to this legal process should not be altogether negative. The Hebrews, later known as Jews, had a long and tragic history. Time and again an invading power held them captive on their own soil, or uprooted and transported them to an alien culture. Especially during the Babylonian Exile and the Restoration to their homeland, the Jews collected and preserved their Scriptures—the Law, the Prophets, and the Writings (see Luke 24:44). How precious these were, especially the Law, can be seen from expressions in the Psalms: "Blessed is the man that walketh not in the counsel of the ungodly . . . But his delight is in the law of the Lord; and in his law doth he meditate day and night" (Ps. 1:1-2). The original intention of those who framed *the tradition of the elders* (3) was to build a hedge of protection about the law. But this had become vain and empty.

c. This vast legal apparatus—containing thousands of petty rules and tabus—was developed and interpreted by the scribes. Their authority was final. When the disciples failed to observe the detailed and complicated procedure of washing their hands, and when Jesus repudiated the criticism of the Pharisees and scribes, a collision course was set. Official Judaism would not tolerate what they regarded as insubordination.

2. *The evil of empty forms.* When Jesus, in effect, supported the disciples in their neglect of the ceremonial law, He joined the Old Testament prophets in their denunciation of hollow formality and in their plea for reality in religion: "Rightly did Isaiah prophesy of you hypocrites" (6, NASB).

a. The scribes and Pharisees were guilty of hypocrisy. A hypocrite is, literally, an actor, one whose external role is different from his inner nature. One of the dangers of legalism is the substitution of outward conformity for inward reality. This was true in Isaiah's day: "This people honors me with their lips, but their heart is far from me" (6, RSV). They were religious but not moral, externally correct but internally wrong.

It was likewise with the scribes and Pharisees. Their hands were ceremonially clean from numerous ablutions, as were all their "pots and pans," but their spirits were tarnished with criticism and bitterness, their hearts were clouded with envy, malice, hatred, pride, and thoughts of murder. They were competent religious actors, hypocrites.

b. *The scribes and Pharisees were guilty of subversion.* Jesus said: *Full well ye reject the commandment of God, that ye may keep your own tradition* (9). They subverted the Scriptures by using one passage to nullify another. (Some verbal fencing could be noted here. The scribes charged the disciples with ignoring *the tradition of the elders* [3], alluding to the ancient and worthy leaders of Israel. But Jesus responds by describing this oral tradition as *the tradition of men* [8], and then *your own tradition* [9]!)

Among the many examples He could have used, Jesus chose one: the practice of *Corban* (11). In actuality this meant the placing of a ban on property and services to avoid obedience to the fifth commandment. The biblical injunction was clear and carried with it a serious warning: "Honor your father and mother; and, He who speaks evil of father or mother, let him be put to death" (10, NASB; cf. Exod. 20:12; 21:17).

However, the position of the scribes was that, according to Num. 30:1 f., a vow took precedence over all other commands. Thus if a son vowed to devote his property to God, or to the Temple, that property could never be used to assist aging parents. Moreover, any assistance, even in sickness, would not be permitted. It was very literally true, "you no longer permit him to do anything for his father or mother" (12, NASB). A repentant son could not even withdraw his rash vow. Ironically, the property might never be given to God.

The practice of "Corban (that is, a gift devoted to God)" (11, NIV) was socially vicious. It did indeed nullify the word of God. Jesus categorically refused a casuistry that would set one biblical command against another. The Scripture is whole and internally coherent.

3. *The alternative to empty forms.* The choice is not be-

tween hollow formality and reality without form. The latter is not possible. The alternative is form *and* content, ritual *and* reality, tradition *and* the living Word of God.

a. Jesus did not inveigh against form and institutions per se. He only insisted that form and substance should be compatible, that institutions should convey the truth and reality they profess to bear. Thus Jesus supported the family and the state, and never forsook the synagogue nor the Temple. He did bring the kingdom of God to bear upon all institutions, to cleanse, judge, and heal them.

b. Believers should submit all their forms and traditions to the pure Word of God. Will our doctrines and ethics stand such a test? Such statements should receive the closest scrutiny not only of Spirit-filled scholars but also the examination of the Church as a whole. How important it is to hold fast to our proven values—the unity of the Church, its mission of salvation, the joy of its fellowship, the spur of its moral ideals!

It was noted at the outset that the vain traditions of the scribes led to a contrived defilement. In rejecting that, Jesus directed the attention of His listeners to the very real moral defilement which springs from the human heart. Truth and reality must confront and cope with that fact (see 14-23).

Defilement: Real

Mark 7:14-23

> 14 And when he had called all the people unto him, he said unto them, Hearken unto me every one of you, and understand:
> 15 There is nothing from without a man, that entering into him can defile him: but the things which come out of him, those are they that defile the man.
> 16 If any man have ears to hear, let him hear.
> 17 And when he was entered into the house from the people, his disciples asked him concerning the parable.
> 18 And he saith unto them, Are ye so without understanding also? Do ye not perceive, that whatsoever thing from without entereth into the man, it cannot defile him;
> 19 Because it entereth not into his heart, but into the belly, and goeth out into the draught, purging all meats?

20 And he said, That which cometh out of the man, that defileth the man.
21 For from within, out of the heart of men, proceed evil thoughts, adulteries, fornications, murders,
22 Thefts, covetousness, wickedness, deceit, lasciviousness, an evil eye, blasphemy, pride, foolishness:
23 All these evil things come from within, and defile the man.

Ceremonial defilement is not moral defilement! This is the principle Jesus hammers home throughout this entire section (1-23). Moral defilement is real, but it springs from the inner being of man and not from the conformity or lack of conformity to the maze of detail in the tradition of the elders.

In the present passage, we see the carping critics at work, the hard-hitting Prophet responding, and the tender Teacher leading the disciples to a deeper understanding.

1. *The carping critics.* The charge made by the Pharisees and scribes, who came from Jerusalem, was a serious one. They charged that the disciples ignored the tradition of the elders and that Jesus gave His tacit approval.

a. In a sense, the tradition was the "law of the land." It was generally regarded highly and sometimes followed at severe personal cost. William Barclay tells of a loyal Jew, imprisoned by the Romans, who nearly perished for lack of water. He had used his meagre ration of water to wash his hands in the manner prescribed by the scribes.

The traditions developed in the Jewish schools were transmitted orally but eventually culminated in the Mishnah and the Talmuds. According to the Mishnah, it was a serious offence to disregard the ceremonial washing of hands.

b. In the view of the scribes, something more than a ceremonial defilement was at stake. To eat with unwashed hands was to be unclean before God. The problem of kosher food was thereby introduced; to eat with unrinsed hands would render unclean the food and the person eating it.

2. *The hard-hitting Prophet.* At this point, Jesus *called*

all the people unto him (14). It may be that out of deference to the official delegation from Jerusalem, they had moved back a respectful distance. Perhaps the Pharisees and scribes had now gone.

a. With the friendlier crowd of people around Him again, Jesus began to teach them with words that have a sternness and seriousness about them: "'Listen to me, everyone, and understand this. Nothing outside a man can make him "unclean" by going into him. Rather, it is what comes out of a man that makes him "unclean."'" (14-15, NIV).

It is not what *enters* the human body but what *proceeds from* the human spirit which defiles the person. The numerous scribal regulations dealt only with external matters—the washing of hands before and during a meal, the ablutions of "pots and pans," and the observance of dietary regulations. Moral defilement is real, Jesus presently affirms, but its source is within the human soul.

b. The first-century Christian Church was plagued with the same problem. The vision of Peter in Joppa (Acts 10:9-23) and Paul's correspondence with the Corinthians (1 Cor. 8:1—11:1) are examples. With Gentiles en route from the household of Cornelius to the home of Simon the tanner, Peter needed a change of attitude quickly. The repeated vision of creatures Peter regarded as "common or unclean" along with the divine command, "Rise, Peter; kill and eat" (Acts 10:13-14), at last persuaded the apostle that association with Gentiles would not render him ceremonially unclean. The implications were far-reaching.

The young Christians in Corinth were troubled over the question of meat which had been offered to idols. The more scrupulous, once devotees of the idols, believed it was wrong to eat such meat. Those more broadminded in their views knew that the idols were nothing and felt free to consume such meat. The Church was divided.

The solution which Paul offered is not relevant to the present passage but the problem is. The early Christian Church, like the Jews, faced the issue of ceremonial defilement. Mark must have been aware of these questions when he chose to include in this Gospel the teaching of Jesus on real and imagined defilement.

3. *The tender Teacher.* Another division of the group now takes place. The crowd dispersed, and Jesus with the disciples went into the house. As before (4:10), *his disciples asked him concerning the parable* (17).

a. The response of Jesus to this question should cause all believers to reflect upon their personal Christian growth. Jesus seemed to be exasperated. "Are you too so uncomprehending?" (18, NASB). The NIV renders the question, "Are you so dull?" The disciples had seen, heard, and witnessed so much, Jesus expected more from them. He clearly wants His followers to think, to reflect, to ponder, and to develop understanding of His teachings. The disciples would do better after the Spirit of truth (John 16:13) had come to them.

b. After explaining more carefully what He meant by the statement, "nothing that goes into a man from the outside can defile him" (15, NEB; see vv. 18-19), Jesus went on to instruct the disciples in some basics of Christian doctrine. This instruction (vv. 20-23) gathers around the doctrine of *indwelling sin* or *depravity.*

c. Jesus very clearly taught that the real defiling forces come *from within, out of the heart of man* (21). We are at once reminded of passages from both the Old and New Testaments: "The heart is deceitful above all things, and desperately wicked: Who can know it?" (Jer. 17:9), and "Now if I do what I do not want, it is no longer I that do it, but sin which dwells within me" (Rom. 7:20, RSV).

The Christian Church generally believes and teaches that indwelling sin is the result of the original sin of Adam. In the language of Thomas Aquinas, In Adam, sin *penetrated* the race; in his posterity, sin *permeated* the race. *Indwelling sin* and *inherited depravity* are, therefore, interchangeable terms. The sin which we inherit from the race has a corrupting effect. *All these evils come from within, and defile the man* (23).

As we shall see, inherited depravity has a cumulative or "snowball" effect. The acts of depravity increase the stain of guilt and moral uncleanness. The sinner needs cleansing from *acquired* as well as *inherited* depravity. He needs the work of sanctification, both initial and entire. Paul's words are helpful here: "He saved us through the washing of rebirth and renewal by the Holy Spirit" (Titus 3:5, NIV).

d. Jesus delineates, representatively more than exhaustively, *all these evil things* that *defile.* Mark's account lists 12 terms, all expressions of *evil thoughts* (in the Greek, six are in the plural, six in the singular).

William Hendriksen summarizes and translates them well: "For it is from inside, from men's hearts that the evil schemes arise: sexual sins, thefts, murders, adulteries, covetings, malicious acts, deceit, lewdness, envy, abusive speech, arrogance, folly" (21-22).

e. The great folly of all forms of legalism, including "the tradition of the elders," is that the outside may be clean, while the inside is unclean. As Jesus said to the Pharisees and scribes: "You are like white-washed tombs, which look fine on the outside but inside are full of dead men's bones and all kinds of rottenness" (Matt. 23:27, Phillips).

An Appropriate Sequel

Mark 7:24-30

> 24 And from thence he arose, and went into the borders of Tyre and Sidon, and entered into an house, and would have no man know it, but he could not be hid.
> 25 For a certain woman, whose young daughter had an unclean spirit, heard of him, and came and fell at his feet:
> 26 The woman was a Greek, a Syrophenician by nation; and she besought him that he would cast forth the devil out of her daughter.
> 27 But Jesus said unto her, Let the children first be filled: for it is not meet to take the children's bread, and to cast it unto the dogs.
> 28 And she answered and said unto him, Yes, Lord: yet the dogs under the table eat of the children's crumbs.

29 And he said unto her, For this saying go thy way; the devil is gone out of thy daughter.
30 And when she was come to her house, she found the devil gone out, and her daughter laid upon the bed.

As we have seen (1-23), Jesus repudiated the tradition of the elders, with its habit of making "clean the outside of the cup and of the dish (while) inside they are full of robbery and self-indulgence" (Matt. 23:25, NASB). This oral tradition, perpetuated by the scribes, placed a heavy burden upon the people of Israel and robbed them of the reality of their historic faith.

It was therefore appropriate that Jesus should at once withdraw from the region of Capernaum, enter the land of Phoenicia, and even find lodging in a Gentile home. In a sense this was an action-parable, showing that *nothing from without a man . . . can defile him* (15).

That this was a continuing problem, even among the Christian Jews, may be seen from episodes in the Book of Acts; e.g., when Peter was criticized for entering the home of Cornelius (Acts 11:1-3). How marvelous that Jesus cracked that shell, even before Pentecost! "Salvation is of the Jews," as Jesus said (John 4:22), but it didn't stop there. And as Paul wrote to the church at Rome, the gospel is "to the Jew first," but "also to the Greek" (Rom. 1:16)!

1. *"To the Jew first."* In His continuing series of withdrawals, Jesus left the region of Capernaum and entered Gentile territory, "the vicinity of Tyre" (24, NIV). Tyre and Sidon, some 40-60 miles north of Capernaum, were independent cities, located in Phoenicia, a province of Syria.

   a. This withdrawal of Jesus and His disciples served a variety of purposes. *It prefigured the Great Commission.* With His sense of direction and priorities, Jesus concentrated on "the lost sheep of the house of Israel" (Matt. 15:24) and resisted every attempt to deflect Him from that mission (cf. John 12:20-24). Nevertheless, He kept the whole world in His purview (see Matt. 13:38) and would one day send His disciples to the ends of the earth (Matt. 28:19-20).

b. A further purpose served by this withdrawal was *the need for rest and renewal.* Jesus had previously commanded the disciples to seek solitude and rest and had given them His own example: "Come with me . . . to a quiet place and get some rest" (6:31, NIV). The fact that the effort was sometimes frustrated (cf. 6:34), did not eliminate the need.

At the same time, Mark underscores the availability of Jesus: Even though some anonymous friend had opened his home as a possible retreat, Jesus was available, as in other instances (2:1-5; 3:20).

c. Jesus "would have liked to remain unrecognized, but this was impossible" (24, NEB). One wonders how, before the days of newspaper and electronic communication, news could travel so fast. Word of mouth was effective: *He could not be hid* (24). It may escape attention that word of the healing ministry of Jesus preceded His visit. Among the crowds who came to Him in Galilee were people from *about Tyre and Sidon* (3:8). They would have listened to His teaching and witnessed His mighty works.

Upon hearing of Him, a Gentile woman came and with great entreaty implored Jesus to heal her little daughter. She "kept asking Him to cast the demon out of her daughter" (26, NASB). Matthew's account has greater detail. At first Jesus did not answer her. The disciples asked Him to send her away, so persistent were her cries (Matt. 15:23). Coming from Jesus, the rebuff of this anguished mother seems strange indeed.

2. *"But also to the Greek"* (Gentiles). The conversation which followed is one of the most delightful in the entire Bible. The lessons to be drawn from it are among the most important for the Christian life.

a. Jesus put the faith of the Syrophoenician woman to a very severe test: "Let the children first be fed, for it is not right to take the children's bread and throw it to the dogs"

(27, RSV). How are we to interpret this startling reply? Many attempts have been made to soften the words by noting that "the dogs" were household pets, not the vicious street scavenger dogs. That is a legitimate interpretation, and perhaps the way the woman understood the words of Jesus: "It is unappropriate to interrupt the meal and allow the household dogs to carry off the children's bread" (William L. Lane). The words nevertheless seem harsh. The message Mark communicates is clearly that Jesus restricted His ministry to Israel and only later would send emissaries of the gospel to the Gentiles.

b. The wit, good humor, faith, and persistence of the woman have commanded the admiration of the centuries: *Yes, Lord* (28). This is the only place in the Gospel of Mark where someone addresses Jesus in this manner. The Pharisees said that Jesus was in league with Beelzebul, but this Gentile woman confessed Jesus as Lord (cf. 1 Cor. 12:3).

William Hendriksen comments that Jesus extended a finger, and the woman took the entire hand. She must have had some understanding of the theological situation, as if to say, "If these blessings are yet to come to the Gentiles, I shall claim them today."

Jesus was greatly touched by her reply and the faith it represented. He sent her on her way with the promise of healing for her daughter. With what joy did the woman return home to find the child set free of her plague? With what delays and apparent rebuffs is the Lord testing our faith and the integrity of our prayers? Like the Syrophoenician woman, will we have the faith and persistence to seek until we find (Luke 11:9)?

The Return from "Exile"

Mark 7:31-37

> 31 And again, departing from the coasts of Tyre and Sidon, he came unto the sea of Galilee, through the midst of the coasts of Decapolis.
> 32 And they bring unto him one that was deaf, and had an impediment in his speech; and they beseech him to put his hand upon him.

33 And he took him aside from the multitude, and put his fingers into his ears, and he spit, and touched his tongue;
34 And looking up to heaven, he sighed, and saith unto him, Ephphatha, that is, Be opened.
35 And straightway his ears were opened, and the string of his tongue was loosed, and he spake plain.
36 And he charged them that they should tell no man: but the more he charged them, so much the more a great deal they published it;
37 And were beyond measure astonished, saying, He hath done all things well: he maketh both the deaf to hear, and the dumb to speak.

Jesus continued His travels in Gentile territory. Leaving the vicinity of Tyre, He "went through Sidon to the Sea of Galilee, through the region of the Decapolis" (31, RSV). Thus He journeyed northward to Sidon and then east and south to the vicinity of the Ten Cities, skirting the land of the hostile Herod Antipas.

Both by precept and example, Jesus repudiated the oral tradition of the scribes, which He called *the commandments of men* (7). He had no fear of ceremonial defilement. He touched the leper (1:41), accepted the touch of the woman with an issue of blood (5:25), and entered the house of a Gentile friend (7:24). Now He moves farther into Gentile regions with His healing and helping touch.

It will be recalled that Jesus was expelled from the general area of the Decapolis, following the deliverance of the Gerasene demoniac (5:17, 20). In a sense, Jesus now returns from "exile."

1. *The deaf hear; the dumb speak.* Somewhere in the land of the Decapolis, where Gentile influence was strong, some people brought to Jesus a man who was deaf and partially mute—he "could hardly talk" (32, NIV). Their subsequent surprise, and their request to put His hand upon him, suggests that they may have expected a blessing rather than healing.

a. Again the reader is impressed by the compassion of friends. Over and over in the Gospels the afflicted came to Jesus because *someone cared enough to get involved.* They not only *brought* the sick to Jesus; they usually "entreated" (NASB), "begged" (NIV) Him to touch and heal their friends.

b. In this instance, Mark gives a more detailed account of the healing than is usual. The personal relationships of Jesus with the person to be healed were always important to Him. Communication with this man, so isolated from fellowship, would be especially needed.

Jesus first of all took the man aside from the multitude. The deaf-mute could not hear the noise of the crowd but would have been affected by the commotion and distractions. The instrumental actions Jesus used were significant: "Jesus put his fingers into the man's ears (and) touched the man's tongue with spittle" (33, NIV). "He stretched open his ears and made it clear to him that he wished to make his tongue alive with his own life" (William L. Lane). This was nonverbal communication *par excellence!*

The next step was ineffable in its beauty: *Jesus prayed for him!* Looking up to heaven, Jesus sighed as He spoke the word of deliverance. The Gospels give us evidence of the deep emotion Jesus felt as He encountered the powers of darkness in sickness, disease, and death. At the grave of Lazarus, Jesus not only wept but "groaned in spirit, and was troubled" (John 11:33).

Then came the command of faith: *Be opened!* (34). (*Ephphathah* was the Aramaic expression Jesus used, preserved like a priceless gem by the Early Church). Jesus called not only for the opening of the man's ears but of his whole being to God. Release was immediate. Hearing and speech returned.

2. *"Behold, it was very good."* The effect upon the people was dramatic. "Their astonishment knew no bounds: 'All that he does, he does well'" (37, NEB). These words echo the divine approval of Creation week in Gen. 1:31. Mark intends something more. Obliquely, he is saying that the messianic prophecy of Isaiah 35:5 ff. is fulfilled in Jesus:

Then the eyes of the blind will be opened,
And the ears of the deaf unstopped.
Then the lame will leap like a deer,
And the tongue of the dumb will shout for joy (NASB).

The rabbis taught that this promise would become a reality in the age of the Messiah. Mark and the Early Church are saying: *Messiah has come!*

With typical disregard for the wishes of Jesus, the witnesses proclaimed the amazing news everywhere. "But the more he charged them, the more zealously they proclaimed it" (36, RSV). The word Mark used for *proclaim* or *publish* was a favorite word in the New Testament for *preach.* The exuberant crowd in the region of the Decapolis was (literally) "preaching the good news."

If this was a "return from exile," Jesus experienced an entirely different reception!

MARK 8

"My God Shall Supply All Your Need"

Mark 8:1-10

> 1 In those days the multitude being very great, and having nothing to eat, Jesus called his disciples unto him, and saith unto them,
> 2 I have compassion on the multitude, because they have now been with me three days, and have nothing to eat:
> 3 And if I send them away fasting to their own houses, they will faint by the way: for divers of them came from far.
> 4 And his disciples answered him, From whence can a man satisfy these men with bread here in the wilderness?
> 5 And he asked them, How many loaves have ye? And they said, Seven.
> 6 And he commanded the people to sit down on the ground: and he took the seven loaves, and gave thanks, and brake, and gave to his disciples to set before them; and they did set them before the people.
> 7 And they had a few small fishes: and he blessed, and commanded to set them also before them.
> 8 So they did eat, and were filled: and they took up of the broken meat that was left seven baskets.
> 9 And they that had eaten were about four thousand: and he sent them away.
> 10 And straightway he entered into a ship with his disciples, and came into the parts of Dalmanutha.

The differences between the two miraculous feedings of the multitudes are significant. Jesus himself noted some of them (8:19 f.). The account of the feeding of the 4,000 is not simply another version of the feeding of the 5,000.

In the first instance, the hungry crowd was from Galilee and was largely Jewish. The feeding of the 4,000 evidently took place in the region of the Decapolis. The multitude would have been largely Gentile. The immediate need of the first group was the teaching of Jesus (6:34). The pressing need of the second group was food.

In the feeding of the 4,000 Jesus showed His ability not only to *perform* such mighty works, but also *to repeat* them (William Hendriksen). He also made it clear that the new covenant would include Gentiles as well as Jews. The Church would be made up of all peoples.

Once again Mark records the concern of Jesus for human need and His confidence that God has an adequate supply.

1. *The concern of Jesus for physical needs.* The absence of detail in the gospel narrative is often tantalizing. "Another large crowd had gathered" (1, NIV), sometime after the healing of the deaf-mute (7:31-37), and had been with Jesus three days (2)! What went on all that time there in the wilderness? (4). That was a camp meeting.

a. Did the Gerasene ex-demoniac influence the gathering of the crowd? After his amazing deliverance (5:1-20), the man begged Jesus to go with Him. Jesus firmly refused and gave him a missionary assignment. The Gerasene was evidently an effective witness: "he went off and began to proclaim in Decapolis what great things Jesus had done for him; and everyone marveled" (5:20, NASB).

Now in that rather remote region, Jesus found the way prepared for Him.

b. After three days the supply of food was consumed, and the people faced the prospect of a long walk home without nourishment. The region of the Decapolis was a very large one, perhaps 60 miles in length and 30 miles in width. Moreover, it is possible that people had come, as before, from even greater distances (cf. 3:8). The concern of Jesus was well founded: *they will faint* (literally, "collapse") *by the way* (3).

c. Another aspect of the compassion of Jesus may not be so obvious; He wanted the disciples to share in His concern. When Jesus described the problem, (2-3), it was as if to say, Have you a suggestion? When the disciples replied (4), less brusquely than before (6:37), it was as if to say, What do you intend?

2. *The confidence of Jesus in an adequate supply.* How fascinating are the conversations the Evangelists have recorded for us in the Gospels! The reader begins to relive the experiences of Jesus and His followers.

a. Jesus then asked an interesting question: "How many loaves do you have?" (5, NASB). Two inferences may be drawn. He may well have wanted the disciples to fix the miracle in their minds. *They said, Seven* (5). Previously, they had found five, and two fishes (6:38). But also, it was as if He were saying, I know what I plan to do. With respect to the feeding of the 5,000, John tells us that was His thought: "He himself knew what he would do" (John 6:6).

b. Once more Jesus had the people *sit down on the ground* (6). Nothing is said this time about groupings nor about "the green grass" (cf. 6:39-40). Perhaps in that remote wilderness no such cushion was available. Mention is made of the blessing (7), with the upward look implied (6:41). The breaking and blessing of both the loaves and the fishes would suggest the Lord's Supper to the Early Church (cf. Luke 24:30-31). The action also carries the message that gratitude for the daily bread is in order.

c. When everyone had eaten *and were filled* (8), the disciples, who distributed the food, gathered up "seven basketfuls of broken pieces that were left over" (8, NIV).

After the feeding of the 5,000, the disciples "took up twelve baskets full of fragments" (6:43). The baskets used on the two occasions were not the same size. The seven baskets were larger, hamper-like. The apostle Paul escaped in one of that type over the wall at Damascus (see Acts 9:25).

d. In each case the amount of food left over was greater than the supply with which they all began. The truth comes through with great power: the grace of God is inexhaustible! "My God will supply all your wants out of the magnificence of his riches in Christ Jesus" (Phil. 4:19, NEB). "Jesus said unto them, I am the bread of life: he that cometh to me shall never hunger; and he that believeth on me shall never thirst" (John 6:35).

Closed Minds Versus Inquiring Minds

Mark 8:11-21

> 11 And the Pharisees came forth, and began to question with him, seeking of him a sign from heaven, tempting him.
> 12 And he sighed deeply in his spirit, and saith, Why doth this generation seek after a sign? verily I say unto you, There shall no sign be given unto this generation.
> 13 And he left them, and entering into the ship again departed to the other side.
> 14 Now the disciples had forgotten to take bread, neither had they in the ship with them more than one loaf.
> 15 And he charged them, saying, Take heed, beware of the leaven of the Pharisees, and of the leaven of Herod.
> 16 And they reasoned among themselves, saying, It is because we have no bread.
> 17 And when Jesus knew it, he saith unto them, Why reason ye, because ye have no bread? perceive ye not yet, neither understand? have ye your heart yet hardened?
> 18 Having eyes, see ye not? and having ears, hear ye not? and do ye not remember?
> 19 When I brake the five loaves among five thousand, how many baskets full of fragments took ye up? They say unto him, Twelve.
> 20 And when the seven among four thousand, how many baskets full of fragments took ye up? And they said, Seven.
> 21 And he said unto them, How is it that ye do not understand?

Jesus and the disciples had returned from their travels east of the Sea of Galilee to the more familiar western shore. The site of Dalmanutha has not yet been identified with certainty. Greeting them on this occasion was a group of Pharisees. They came like prosecuting attorneys—questioning, testing, seeking proof—empirical, concrete, coercive. The response of Jesus is chilling, as we shall see.

By contrast, the conversation which followed, between Jesus and the disciples, was heartening, albeit not without tension. The first group had closed minds. The second group was composed of inquiring minds, open to growth in understanding.

1. *Closed minds: the Pharisees.* Mark is probably linking this encounter with 3:22-30, where the Pharisees charged that Jesus cast out demons and did His mighty works by the power of Satan.

a. The sceptical demand for proof. When the Pharisees questioned Jesus, demanding *a sign from heaven* (11), they were setting a trap. The clue is to be found in the expression "tempting him"; i.e., they were *testing* Him. This was in accord with an Old Testament provision for distinguishing false prophets from true (Deut. 13:1-5). However, according to that scripture, a false prophet may perform signs and wonders. The test of a true prophet is the quality of his faith. But the Pharisees had already passed judgment on Jesus: "He hath Beelzebub" (3:22, ASV). If Jesus had taken their bait, the Pharisees would have sprung their trap. The request for a sign from heaven was an expression of fixed unbelief.

b. The divine reply of silence. As noted above, the response of Jesus was chilling. It was both "uttered and unexpressed." He sighed deeply in his spirit (12). The sighs and groans of Jesus (7:34; John 11:38) bring to mind the inarticulate intercession of the Spirit (Rom. 8:26). Then Jesus said, "Why does this generation seek a sign? . . . No sign shall be given" (8:12, RSV). Matthew enlarges a bit on the reply: "'An evil and adulterous generation seeks after a sign; and a sign will not be given it, except the sign of Jonah'" (16:4, NASB), i.e., His own life, death, and resurrection.

Emil Brunner, the influential German theologian,

once said that the only appropriate reply to the question, "Does God exist?" is silence.

The Pharisees wanted Jesus to submit to their categories of evaluation and judgment. Their question was in essence identical with one addressed to Him later in Jerusalem: "By what authority are you doing these things?" (11:28, NIV). Jesus did not answer their question then; He did not answer it now.

"The word of God is not bound" (2 Tim. 2:9) by any of the neat, trim schemes of men. The mighty disclosure of the Word of God calls for one primary response—a radical faith and trust. The Pharisees had all the proof necessary. The divine reply was silence.

2. *Inquiring minds: the disciples.* Immediately after the confrontation with the Pharisees, Jesus and the disciples got back into the boat and crossed to the other side, evidently to Bethsaida (13, 22-26).

a. Their stay on the western shore had been so brief and tense, "they had forgotten to take bread with them (and) had no more than one loaf in the boat" (14, NEB). That little evidence of hurry set off a chain reaction of discussion: a warning, a reminder, and a plea.

b. As the disciples pondered and debated the short supply of bread, Jesus issued a warning wrapped up in a riddle: *Take heed,* beware of the leaven of the Pharisees, and of the leaven of Herod (15).

Leaven (yeast) had become a symbol for the active, pervasive power of evil. The priests of Israel had been forbidden to use it in the sacrificial offerings of the Tabernacle (Lev. 2:11). Leaven could not be used during the Passover. The "leaven of the Pharisees" was hypocrisy. They were not what they appeared or professed to be.

The "leaven of Herod" was worldliness. The family of Herod loved this present age—its pomp and ceremony, sensualism and power. Jesus once referred to Herod Antipas as "that fox" (Luke 13:32).

Twin dangers—hypocrisy and worldliness. They were

in league with each other (3:6) to destroy Jesus and have destroyed not a few of His followers.

c. The disciples missed the point altogether. They were still wondering how to feed a dozen hungry men with one thin loaf of bread. Their problem was not that they were short of bread, but that they had a short memory and very little faith.

In no other place do the Gospels record such a long series of questions, each carrying a rebuke. Among the eight or more questions, these carried the sharpest barbs:

"Why do you discuss the fact that you have no bread? . . .

"Are your hearts hardened? . . .

"And do you not remember?" (17-18, RSV).

Yes they did remember, the 12 baskets of fragments, after the feeding of the 5,000. Yes, they did remember the 7 baskets of fragments, after the feeding of the 4,000. How, then, could they be worried about their present plight? But who else has a short memory and a limited supply of faith?

d. Jesus never gave up on the disciples. He may have left the Pharisees on the shore with unanswered questions, but He toiled endlessly with the Twelve. "He said to them, 'Do you still not understand?'" (21, NIV).

These words often remind one of the earnest plea in Proverbs: "Wisdom is the principal thing; therefore get wisdom: And with all thy getting get understanding" (4:7).

Jesus was seeking for a deeper level of understanding in His followers. Would they come to understand who He was, that He was more than "a prophet mighty in deed and word" (Luke 24:19)?

Yes, indeed, they would understand and would proclaim it to the world. Their minds were not closed. They were *disciples*—interested, inquiring learners.

"Twice He Touched My Blinded Eyes"

Mark 8:22-26

> 22 And he cometh to Bethsaida: and they bring a blind man unto him, and besought him to touch him.

23 And he took the blind man by the hand, and led him out of the town; and when he had spit on his eyes, and put his hands upon him, he asked him if he saw ought.
24 And he looked up, and said, I see men as trees, walking.
25 After that he put his hands again upon his eyes, and made him look up: and he was restored, and saw every man clearly.
26 And he sent him away to his house, saying, Neither go into the town, nor tell it to any in the town.

At this point, Jesus and the disciples are moving in the direction of Caesarea Philippi, where the Great Confession of Peter took place (8:29). En route they came to Bethsaida, located near the mouth of the Jordan River. Herod Philip had elevated the village to the rank of a city and had renamed it Bethsaida-Julias, in honor of his daughter.

This story has an interesting parallel in the healing of the deaf-mute (7:31-37). In each case Jesus led the man aside and took special care in the ministry of healing. Both are in fulfilment of such Old Testament passages as Isa. 29:18: "In that day shall the deaf hear the words of the book, and the eyes of the blind shall see out of obscurity, and out of darkness."

1. *A two-stage miracle.* Once more, the intercession of compassionate friends was a key factor in a healing miracle: "And some people brought to him a blind man, and begged him to touch him" (22, RSV).

Such friends were sensitive to the struggles of the blind—their helplessness, dependence, and temptation to a feeling of hopelessness. What a responsibility those who are whole have to bring sick ones to Jesus (2:17)!

a. As in the case of the deaf-mute in the Decapolis, Jesus took steps to evoke faith in the heart of the blind man: He took the man by the hand, led him out of the village, "spat upon his eyes, and laid His hands over them" (23, TLB). Jesus then inquired, "Do you see anything?" (23, NASB). Thus in five separate steps, Jesus sought to strengthen ties of personal trust and confidence between him and the afflicted one.

b. Something unusual followed: the miracle seemed to be incomplete. The man could see, but not clearly. *And he looked up* (a beautiful symbolism), *and said, I see men as trees, walking* (24). The man had evidently not been born blind. A second time Jesus laid His hands upon the defective eyes, *and he was restored, and saw every man clearly* (25).

2. *A twofold need.* Mark does not tell us why it was necessary for Jesus to touch the blinded eyes a second time. The Man who raised the dead, healed the leper, and cast out demons, could certainly have restored sight with a single touch. Perhaps the further need was in the man's perception or understanding of what he saw. Perhaps the Lord was communicating a message, by means of this symbolism, to His followers.

a. The blind man may have been symbolic of the blindness in Israel. According to Paul, in Romans chapters 10 and 11, Israel will come to see the light of the gospel in two stages: first, the Gentiles will be brought into the fold, and then "all Israel shall be saved" (Rom. 11:26; see *Beacon Bible Commentary,* 8:227).

b. The symbolism may also extend to the disciples. Jesus had already charged them with being blind and deaf: *Having eyes, see ye not? and having ears, hear ye not?* (18).

They, too, were beginning to see and understand, but not clearly. This much we do know—after Pentecost, when the disciples were all filled with the Holy Spirit (Acts 2:4), they did see and understand with clarity and in truth. "The things of the Spirit of God . . . are spiritually discerned (1 Cor. 2:14). We do not see clearly until we are filled with the light of the Spirit of truth.

> *Light, perfect light shines on this holy way;*
> *Twice He touch'd my blinded eyes.*
> *Sight, perfect sight my vision has today,*
> *Healed by Blood that sanctifies.*
> —F. E. HILL

Patient Teacher; Plodding Learners

Mark 8:27-30

> 27 And Jesus went out, and his disciples, into the towns of Caesarea Philippi: and by the way he asked his disciples, saying unto them, Whom do men say that I am?
> 28 And they answered, John the Baptist: but some say, Elias; and others, One of the prophets.
> 29 And he saith unto them, But whom say ye that I am? And Peter answereth and saith unto him, Thou art the Christ.
> 30 And he charged them that they should tell no man of him.

Once more Jesus leads the disciples away from the crowds and the cynics to a locale where they could be alone. At this midpoint in Mark, Jesus turns increasingly away from the multitudes in order to nurture the Twelve and prepare them for the trying days ahead.

1. *The classroom: a pagan culture.* As a patient Teacher, Jesus has been leading His plodding learners to a clearer and truer understanding of His Person. The school had not been the walls of a building, and the campus had not been a restricted area. The classroom had been the great out-of-doors, and the campus had been far and wide: Galilee, the Decapolis, the vicinity of Tyre and Sidon, and now *the towns of Caesarea Philippi* (27).

Caesarea Philippi was a significant city. D. Edmond Hiebert describes its color:

> Located in an area of great natural beauty, this city was situated at the easternmost of the four sources of the Jordan, where a big spring gushes from a wide and lofty cavern at the foot of Mt. Hermon. The place had long been associated with the worship of the Greek god Pan, whence it was known as Paneas. Herod the Great had erected there a magnificent temple in honor of the Roman emperor Augustus. . . . It was a Roman city, dominated by the spirit of paganism.

Herod Philip, one of the nobler members of that family, had recently enlarged the city and renamed it in honor of the emperor and himself. He resided there. It was a pagan city in a Gentile territory.

It is noteworthy that even Jesus and His disciples

lived in a culture dominated by rulers indifferent to, perhaps oblivious of, spiritual values. Nevertheless, in that culture powerful redemptive forces were at work.

2. *The examination: "Who am I?"* At the outset of his Gospel, Mark tells us who Jesus is: "Christ, the Son of God" (1:1). But not until this point (29) does the word "Christ" (Messiah) appear again. The mighty works and words of Jesus all pointed toward this conclusion, but the disciples came to understand the evidence only slowly.

a. The time had come for Jesus to elicit from the Twelve their own confession of faith, but Jesus began indirectly: "Who do men say that I am?" (27, ASV).

The replies are revealing: "Some say John the Baptist; others say Elijah; and still others, one of the prophets" (NIV). Two inferences may be drawn: when the people looked at Jesus, they thought of strong men. However, they did not understand who Jesus really was. The Baptist, Elijah, and the prophets were all forerunners of the coming One (cf. Luke 7:19), not the Anointed One himself.

b. The second question was more personal: "But who say ye that I am?" (29, ASV). If the reader will remember all that has gone before—the calling of the disciples, the amazing miracles of healing and deliverance, the power of the parables—he will wait almost breathlessly for the response of the Twelve. Would Jesus still have to say, "Do you still not understand" (21, NIV)?

c. For the first time in Mark's Gospel, Peter acts as the spokesman for the rest: *Thou art the Christ* (29). Matthew records the joyous response of Jesus: "Blessed are you, Simon Bar-Jona! For flesh and blood has not revealed this to you, but my Father who is in heaven" (Matt. 16:17, RSV). Peter, at least, had passed that examination with high marks!

As William L. Lane has shown persuasively, this is one of two key passages in Mark's "witness-document." In 8:29, as a representative of Israel, Peter confesses that Jesus is the Messiah. In 15:39, as a representative of the

Gentile world, the Roman centurion confesses that Jesus is the Son of God. This dual witness presages the day when every knee shall bow and every tongue shall confess that Jesus Christ is Lord (Phil. 2:10-11).

3. *The report: further study needed.* What follows seems, on the surface, surprising: Jesus charged them that they should tell no man of him (30).

a. Nowhere are we told explicitly why Jesus guarded the "messianic secret" so carefully, but the explanation is clear. For one thing, the people of Israel had a gross misconception of what the Messiah would be like. They looked for a sensational miracle-worker, who would also be a powerful military leader, another David. Steadfastly Jesus refused to play this role and consistently warned those who had been healed to say nothing of their deliverance.

b. The disciples had indeed been blessed with a revelation that Jesus is the Christ, but they likewise expected the Messiah to be a wonder-worker and a political foe of the Romans. They were not yet ready to proclaim the message. Not until after the Resurrection and Pentecost would they understand the concept of a suffering Messiah (see Luke 24:25-26). Further study was indicated. The tedious teaching-learning process would continue as Jesus turned His face toward Jerusalem and the Cross (8:31—9:1).

The First Prediction of the Cross

Mark 8:31—9:1

> 31 And he began to teach them, that the Son of man must suffer many things, and be rejected of the elders, and of the chief priests, and scribes, and be killed, and after three days rise again.
> 32 And he spake that saying openly. And Peter took him, and began to rebuke him.
> 33 But when he had turned about and looked on his disciples, he rebuked Peter, saying, Get thee behind me, Satan: for thou savourest not the things that be of God, but the things that be of men.
> 34 And when he had called the people unto him with his disciples also, he said unto them, Whosoever will come after me, let him deny himself, and take up his cross, and follow me.

35 For whosoever will save his life shall lose it; but whosoever shall lose his life for my sake and the gospel's, the same shall save it.
36 For what shall it profit a man, if he shall gain the whole world, and lose his own soul?
37 Or what shall a man give in exchange for his soul?
38 Whosoever therefore shall be ashamed of me and of my words in this adulterous and sinful generation; of him also shall the Son of man be ashamed, when he cometh in the glory of his Father with the holy angels.
9:1 And he said unto them, Verily I say unto you, That there be some of them that stand here, which shall not taste of death, till they have seen the kingdom of God come with power.

It is clear that Jesus knew He would experience suffering and death, and that He would rise again from the dead. The disciples did not yet understand this prediction of Jesus, nor do the liberal critics, who seem unable to accept the supernatural substance of the gospel.

1. *The true understanding of Messiahship.* From this point onward, Jesus referred to himself more often as the Son of Man. With that title, He blended another figure—that of the Suffering Servant.

a. The Son of Man was an Old Testament figure associated with messianic glory. Daniel saw Him in an overpowering vision:

I kept looking in the night visions,
And behold, with the clouds of heaven
One like a Son of Man was coming,
And He came up to the Ancient of Days
And was presented before Him.
And to Him was given dominion,
Glory and a kingdom,
That all the peoples, nations, and men of every language
Might serve him.
His dominion is an everlasting dominion
Which will not pass away;
And His kingdom is one
Which will not be destroyed (Dan. 7:13-14, NASB).

The messianic glory of the Son of Man was concealed during the days of His flesh. It was anticipated in the Transfiguration, the Resurrection, and at Pentecost, and will be fully disclosed in the *parousia,* the Second Coming.

It should be noted, however, that the Epistle to the Hebrews adds a beautiful touch in its interpretation of the sufferings of Christ as a crown of glory: "We see Jesus, who was made a little lower than the angels for the suffering of death, crowned with glory and honour" (Heb. 2:9).

b. The Suffering Servant of the Old Testament was not properly understood by Israel, nor by the Twelve. When Jesus began to teach them that the Son of Man must suffer, the disciples were offended. "Peter took him aside and began to rebuke him" (32, NIV).

The reaction of Jesus was instantaneous and fierce. Looking around at the disciples, Jesus rebuked Peter: "Out of my sight, Satan! . . . You do not have in mind the things of God, but the things of men" (33, NIV). Peter and the others should have known better, for they had read the Servant Songs of Isaiah: "But he was wounded for our transgressions, he was bruised for our iniquities" (Isa. 53:5). In His own person, Jesus fused the Old Testament prophecies of the Son of Man and the Suffering Servant. Few, if any, understood at the time.

2. *The true understanding of discipleship.* The call to Christian discipleship is terse and breathtaking: *Whosoever will come after me, let him deny himself, and take up his cross, and follow me* (34). The response must be voluntary, and the commitment must be total. Jesus offered several reasons for His imperious, unqualified demands (each of the four verses, 35-38, properly begins with the word *for*):

a. To save one's life is to lose it. The common life teaches us this fact. The married couple which shuns the pain of childbirth and the struggle of family life may be lonely in middle and old age. The person who spares himself and refuses to invest his energies in serving humanity will not know the joy of gratitude and appreciation. "For whoever wishes to save his life shall lose it; and whoever loses his life for My sake and the gospel's shall save it" (35, NASB).

b. To barter one's soul for the treasures of the world is to ensure the ultimate loss. This present *adulterous and sinful generation* (38) can slake the thirst for sinful pleasures, but the price is too high, the cost too great. When one has forfeited his soul for these baubles, he has nothing with which to buy it back. His resources are irretrievably exhausted. "For what does it profit a man to gain the whole world, and forfeit his soul? For what shall a man give in exchange for his soul?" (36-37, NASB).

c. To refuse identification with Christ before men is to invite contempt before the Father. These words are alarming. A future glory is coming: *the glory of the Father with the holy angels* (38) . . . *the kingdom of God . . . with power* (9:1). What can this be? No man can say. It will mean fulfilment and joy ineffable. Of a sudden, the "cost of discipleship" will be seen as nothing when compared with the cost of spurning discipleship.

"For whoever is ashamed of Me and My words in this adulterous and sinful generation, the Son of Man will also be ashamed of him when He comes in the glory of His Father with the holy angels" (38, NASB).

MARK 9

The Message from the Mount

Mark 9:2-13

> 2 And after six days Jesus taketh with him Peter, and James, and John, and leadeth them up into an high mountain apart by themselves: and he was transfigured before them.
> 3 And his raiment became shining, exceeding white as snow; so as no fuller on earth can white them.
> 4 And there appeared unto them Elias with Moses: and they were talking with Jesus.
> 5 And Peter answered and said to Jesus, Master, it is good for us to be here: and let us make three tabernacles; one for thee, and one for Moses, and one for Elias.
> 6 For he wist not what to say; for they were sore afraid.
> 7 And there was a cloud that overshadowed them: and a voice came out of the cloud, saying, This is my beloved Son: hear him.
> 8 And suddenly, when they had looked around about, they saw no man any more, save Jesus only with themselves.

9 And as they came down from the mountain, he charged them that they should tell no man what things they had seen, till the Son of man were risen from the dead.
10 And they kept that saying with themselves, questioning one with another what the rising from the dead should mean.
11 And they asked him, saying, Why say the scribes that Elias must first come?
12 And he answered and told them, Elias verily cometh first, and restoreth all things; and how it is written of the Son of man, that he must suffer many things, and be set at nought.
13 But I say unto you, That Elias is indeed come, and they have done unto him whatsoever they listed, as it is written of him.

Jesus now takes the inner circle of disciples with Him to a place where they could be alone—an unidentified high mountain (2) (see Exod. 24:16). Peter, James, and John were to become pillars of the Church. The Lord's sovereign choice set them apart from the rest of the Twelve as leaders. Such divine election to service is a fact in the Church today. It is unwise and futile to quarrel with or to resist that choice.

Privilege always entails responsibility. It would not be long before these three men would bear the burden of leadership in the young Church. They would suffer persecution, ridicule, and imprisonment. James early became one of the first Christian martyrs (Acts 12:1-2).

At this point in their learning, Peter, James, and John very much needed a confirmation of the Great Confession, "Thou art the Christ" (8:29). They also needed to learn what it meant for Jesus to be the Christ; it meant suffering, mistreatment, and death, but resurrection also! The fledgling Church would soon need capable, strong witnesses. The Lord was preparing them for that day.

Among the words which stand out in a consideration of the Transfiguration are: *promise, Passion, proclamation, and perplexity.*

1. *The fulfillment of a promise.* Immediately after describing what true discipleship involves (8:34-35), Jesus lifted the veil screening the future and described the *parousia,* the Second Coming (8:38). One day the concealment of the present will come to an end, and the glory of the Son of Man will burst forth.

a. Jesus then surprised His disciples and puzzled many scholars yet to come by declaring that "some who are standing here will not taste death before they see the kingdom of God come with power" (1, NIV). Too many have mistakenly presumed that Jesus expected the Parousia within the lifetime of His followers.

b. The Transfiguration was the fulfillment of that promise. The coming of the kingdom of God with power is synonymous in thought with the presence of Jesus. When He came preaching the gospel, He announced: "The kingdom of God is at hand" (1:14-15). In Him the Kingdom had come near.

c. In the Transfiguration, the brilliance of the Son's eternal glory was released for a short time, and the disciples witnessed a preview of the Second Coming. Further anticipation of that glorious event would appear in the Resurrection and at Pentecost. *The kingdom of God* (had) *come with power* (1).

2. *Consultation on the Passion.* In the midst of that glorious scene, when Jesus *was transfigured before them* (2), two great Old Testament personages appeared: Elijah and Moses. It is important to note the two expressions, "before them" and "unto them." These amazing events took place, to a large extent, for the benefit of the disciples!

a. Elijah and Moses were talking with Jesus. Luke reports that they "spoke of his departure, the destiny he was to fulfill in Jerusalem" (Luke 9:31, NEB). Literally, they talked with Jesus about His exodus. We are not told how the disciples identified the two men. Perhaps Jesus told them (cf. Matt. 17:7).

b. In a sense, both Elijah and Moses were prophets. The Lord had promised Moses that someday He would raise up a Prophet like him (Deut. 18:15). That day had come.

c. Like Jesus, both men were associated with the wilderness, and both had experiences of God's glory on a holy mountain—Moses at Mount Sinai (Exodus 24) and Elijah at Mount Horeb (1 Kings 19).

d. But, more importantly, here the Law and the Prophets were in consultation with Jesus, comforting and strengthening Him for the Second Exodus (Luke 9:31). In this fact we have mighty proof that the Old and New Testaments comprise *one book.* All of the writers of the New Testament would have agreed with Paul that "the gospel of God [was] promised beforehand through his prophets in the holy scriptures" (Rom. 1:1-2, RSV).

3. *The renewal of a proclamation.* The reaction of the disciples to the heavenly scene was one of fright and bewilderment. Not really knowing what to say, Peter responded, "Rabbi, it is good for us to be here: and let us make three tabernacles" (5, ASV). What Peter said for the group was well-intentioned but misguided. The new era of the Messiah's kingdom and sanctuary had not yet come. The journey through the wilderness was not over.

a. Another significant event then took place. A cloud enveloped Jesus, Moses, and Elijah. A cloud was often an Old Testament symbol of God's presence: "It came to pass, as Aaron spake . . . behold, the glory of the Lord appeared in a cloud" (Exod. 16:10). How precious to be enclosed in God's glory!

b. Then, as at the outset of Jesus' ministry, the Father spoke *out of the cloud, saying, This is my beloved Son: hear him* (7). At the baptism, the voice was addressed to Jesus (1:11). Here the voice spoke to the disciples. Two inferences should be drawn from this renewal of the Father's proclamation:

First, the heavenly pronouncement was an affirmation of the Person of Christ. He is God's unique Son. No other Christology will do. Jesus is God's only Son. What theology has attempted to say in abstract terms, that the Son is eternally one with the Father, is practically and devotionally a necessity. He is "Immanuel, God with us" (Matt. 1:23).

Second, it therefore follows that all men should heed the Father's command: "Hear ye him" (7, ASV). This injunction applies to all that Jesus said and taught, but perhaps especially to what He was soon to say concerning His resurrection from the dead (9).

4. *The continuation of perplexity.* The light had begun to dawn, in the minds of the disciples concerning the identity of Jesus, but a good deal remained unclear. They had witnessed the Transfiguration and wondered if the consummation of all things was at hand. Had not Jesus only recently said that "the Son of man [would come] in the glory of his Father with the holy angels" (8:38, ASV)? The cross, the tomb, and the Resurrection were now incomprehensible to them. Three questions appear in quick succession:

a. What does the rising from the dead mean? (10) Many times Jesus had commanded His followers to say nothing about some great event, such as a miracle. But this time He set a time limit. He had given "them orders not to tell anyone what they had seen until the Son of Man had risen from the dead" (9, NIV). The disciples could not understand what rising again from the dead meant, because they could not fathom the possibility of the cross.

b. Why do the scribes say that Elijah must come first? (11) It was commonly understood, on the basis of Mal. 4:5-6, that the prophet Elijah would return and "set things straight" before the coming of the Messiah. It was also commonly taught that Elijah had not returned. Consequently, the opponents of Jesus argued that He was not the Messiah. But "Elijah" had returned, in the ministry of John the Baptist (Matt. 11:14). His preaching of repentance had stirred the nation. The disciples probably raised the question as a veiled objection to the trend of Jesus' thought.

c. The rejoinder of Jesus was in the form of another question: "How is it written of the Son of man, that he should suffer many things and be set at nought?" (12, ASV).

Each day the shadow of the cross fell more heavily upon the path of Jesus. The Transfiguration was not an escape. It was a source of strength to bear that cross. Like Paul, Jesus pressed on *as unknown* [to man], *and yet well known* [to God]. The present existence is a time of suffering. The glory is yet to be revealed. "Beloved, . . . it doth not yet appear what we shall be: but we know that, when he shall appear, we shall be like him" (1 John 3:2).

Despair and Deliverance in the Valley

Mark 9:14-29

> 14 And when he came to his disciples, he saw a great multitude about them, and the scribes questioning with them.
> 15 And straightway all the people, when they beheld him, were greatly amazed, and running to him saluted him.
> 16 And he asked the scribes, What question ye with them?
> 17 And one of the multitude answered and said, Master, I have brought unto thee my son, which hath a dumb spirit;
> 18 And wheresoever he taketh him, he teareth him: and he foameth, and gnasheth with his teeth, and pineth away: and I spake to thy disciples that they should cast him out; and they could not.
> 19 He answereth him, and saith, O faithless generation, how long shall I be with you? how long shall I suffer you? bring him unto me.
> 20 And they brought him unto him: and when he saw him, straightway the spirit tare him; and he fell on the ground, and wallowed foaming.
> 21 And he asked his father, How long is it ago since this came unto him? And he said, Of a child.
> 22 And ofttimes it hath cast him into the fire, and into the waters, to destroy him: but if thou canst do any thing, have compassion on us, and help us.
> 23 Jesus said unto him, If thou canst believe, all things are possible to him that believeth.
> 24 And straightway the father of the child cried out, and said with tears, Lord, I believe; help thou mine unbelief.
> 25 When Jesus saw that the people came running together, he rebuked the foul spirit, saying unto him, Thou dumb and deaf spirit, I charge thee, come out of him, and enter no more into him.
> 26 And the spirit cried, and rent him sore, and came out of him: and he was as one dead; insomuch that many said, He is dead.
> 27 But Jesus took him by the hand, and lifted him up; and he arose.
> 28 And when he was come into the house, his disciples asked him privately, Why could not we cast him out?
> 29 And he said unto them, This kind can come forth by nothing, but by prayer and fasting.

Jesus and the inner circle of disciples now come down from the mount of transfiguration, with all its glory, to the gloom of the valley. On the mount, they were engaged in *worship*. In the valley they will be involved in *work*. Glory and gloom, worship and work, inspiration and struggle are paradoxes characteristic of discipleship.

In the valley they found a despairing father and a group of defeated disciples, greatly in need of a dramatic deliverance and divine directions for coping with demonic situations.

1. *A despairing father.* Mark records an arresting statement by this man: *Master, I have brought unto thee my son* (17). Luke adds that the boy was an only child (Luke 9:38). In the absence of Jesus, who was on the mount, the father had come with his afflicted child, only to find the disciples alone without their Teacher.

The father had come with *hope*. He had heard of Jesus and had sought Him out. He had found the disciples of Jesus but not their Master. The man who had come with high hopes was now filled with *disappointment*. "I spake to thy disciples that they should cast him out; and they could not" (18). Everything reported about the father suggests dejection, despair. It was as if he said to Jesus: "I came with my troubled son, but You were not here. I implored Your followers to help, but they were powerless. Look at the child—how convulsed he is!"

2. *Defeated disciples.* The nine disciples, at the foot of the mountain, were undergoing a severe trial. During the preaching tour of Galilee, they had been successful in casting out demons and in healing the sick (6:7-13). Now they were unsuccessful and defeated.

a. They were *lacking in experience.* When they set out on the tour of Galilee, they had gone with special authority from Jesus: "He gave them authority over the unclean spirits" (6:7, ASV). It was needful for them to learn that such power and authority must be maintained and renewed by a continuous relationship with its Source.

Somehow, in that scene of frustration, the disciples had become embroiled in conflict with the scribes. When

Jesus and His companions returned from the mount, they found "the teachers of the law arguing with them" (14, NIV).

The Twelve had often witnessed the developing conflict between Jesus and the various Jewish groups, such as the scribes and Pharisees. Now the disciples were on their own and were not getting along well. Jesus broke in on them with the question, "What are you arguing with them about?" (16, NIV). He apparently came to their rescue. The nine defeated and discouraged disciples are a picture of a church which feels powerless in the absence of the Lord.

b. They were also *lacking in faith.* This is clear from the response of Jesus to the report of the father that the disciples could not cast out the demon. *He answereth him, and saith, O faithless generation* (19)!

Later in the story, when the disciples asked him privately about their failure, Jesus talked to them about the relationship of faith and prayer. Here He simply charges them with a lack of faith. In Matthew's account, Jesus elaborates on this point: "If ye have faith as a grain of mustard seed, ye shall say unto this mountain, remove hence to yonder place; and it shall remove" (Matt. 17:20).

3. *A dramatic deliverance.* With the rising excitement and the gathering crowd (25), Jesus moved at once to deliver the possessed epileptic (see Matt. 17:15).

a. The exasperation of Jesus was obvious: "What an unbelieving and perverse generation! . . . How long must I endure you?" (19, NEB). That faithless generation included the father, whose faith was faltering; it included the scribes, who were evidently gloating over the defeat of the disciples (14), as well as the nine disciples, "because of their failure to exercise their faith by putting their whole heart into persevering prayer" (William Hendriksen). It probably also included the crowd, which was often neutral, even selfish (John 6:26). The cry of Jesus voiced "the loneliness and the anguish of the one authentic believer in a world which expresses only unbelief" (William L. Lane).

b. The inquiry of Jesus was revealing. Like a compassionate physician, He asked the father, "How long has this been happening to him?" (Hendriksen). The question caused the father to recall the years of travail and possibly was an aid to his faith as he sensed the concern of Jesus. The reply indicates once again that the demons seek the destruction of man, who is created in the image of God: "Oft-times it hath cast him both into the fire and into the waters, to destroy him" (22, ASV).

This inquiry of Jesus drew out the father's fading hopes: *but if thou canst do anything, have compassion on us, and help us* (22). The plea ("help *us*") is not for the child alone, but for the child *and* the father, whose life was intertwined with that of his son.

c. The exchange which followed is challenging. "'What do you mean, "If you can"?' said Jesus. 'Everything is possible for him who believes'" (23, NIV). At this, the distressed father broke down and said with tears, "'I do have faith; oh, help me to have *more!*'" (24, TLB). Who among us could not also pray that prayer?

d. There followed almost at once a stern command and a tender touch. Jesus rebuked the malevolent spirit with a dual command: "Thou dumb and deaf spirit, I command thee, come out of him, and enter no more into him" (25, ASV). Characteristically, Luke recalls a touch of tenderness: Jesus "healed the boy, and gave him back to his father" (Luke 9:42, ASV).

The double command—*come out . . . enter no more*—expresses the implacable fury Jesus had for the realm of Satan. (Thou hast loved righteousness, and hated iniquity."—Heb. 1:9.) The foul spirit responded with one last fling of malice, tearing the boy and leaving him on the ground as one dead. In fact, many said he was dead.

But the lad was not dead. *Jesus took him by the hand, and lifted him up; and he arose* (27).

From sinking sand He lifted me;
With tender hand He lifted me.
   From shades of night to planes of light,
Oh, praise His name, He lifted me!
—CHARLES H. GABRIEL

4. *Divine direction.* As on other occasions (4:10; 7:17; 10:10), when the crowds had dispersed, and Jesus was alone with the Twelve, they asked the plaintive question, "Why, Lord?" *Why could not we cast him out?* (28). How many times, during the intervening centuries, have discouraged, defeated workers in the Lord's vineyard gone to a solitary place with the same cry, "Why, Lord?" The Lord's reply should both challenge and inspire us.

   a. So little faith—was a part of that reply. As we have seen, Jesus had already startled the father of the epileptic boy with the promise, *All things are possible to him that believeth* (23). Now He startles the disciples with the confident assurance that if they had as much faith as a tiny but vital seed of mustard, they could say to the nearby hill, "'"Up you get and mover over there!"' . . . you will find nothing is impossible'" (Matt. 17:20, Phillips).

   Staggering words! But how does one find such faith? The rest of Jesus' response suggests the answer.

   b. So little prayer—completes the Lord's reply. "This kind can come out by nothing, save by prayer" (29, ASV).

   The implication is clear: this quality of faith is the "fallout" of persevering prayer. Earnest prayer often leads to periods of fasting. It is not surprising, therefore, that early in the transmission of the Greek text, the words *and fasting* (29) were added. The great majority of the Greek manuscripts include these words. However, the oldest and most reliable do not, hence, the more recent versions omit them. For certain, the faith which makes *all things . . . possible* (23) is a faith that prays.

   Jesus was a Man of much prayer and of great faith. Jesus prodded His followers to discover the power of a faith born of persevering prayer. Again, William L. Lane has said it well: "When faith confronts the demonic, God's omnipotence is its sole assurance, and God's sovereignty is its only restriction. This is the faith which experiences the miracle of deliverance." This is the faith that prays.

In the Classroom with Jesus

Mark 9:30-32

> 30 And they departed thence, and passed through Galilee; and he would not that any man should know it.
> 31 For he taught his disciples, and said unto them, The Son of man is delivered into the hands of men, and they shall kill him; and after that he is killed, he shall rise the third day.
> 32 But they understood not that saying, and were afraid to ask him.

In this passage we are told explicitly what we have previously inferred—that increasingly Jesus avoided the crowds in order to be alone with the Twelve. "Jesus did not want anyone to know where they were, because He was teaching His disciples" (30, NIV).

Once again, Jesus drew His followers into a "classroom," far from buildings and people, where He could teach them the meaning of what was soon to transpire. It is instructive to observe Jesus toiling with "students" who were slow to learn.

1. *A place of solitude and separation.* Mark has told his readers repeatedly of the withdrawals of Jesus and His disciples—sometimes for rest and renewal (6:31), sometimes for fellowship and learning (cf 7:24).

Jesus counsels all His disciples to follow this practice. "But when you pray, go away by yourself, all alone, and shut the door behind you and pray to your Father secretly, and your Father, who knows your secrets, will reward you" (Matt. 6:6, TLB).

> *Take time to be holy. The world rushes on;*
> *Spend much time in secret with Jesus alone.*

2. *A curriculum of mystery.* In that place of solitude and separation Jesus sought to communicate certain facts to

His disciples. He also wanted them to understand their meaning.

a. The facts were that very shortly, in the city of Jerusalem, someone would betray Him into the hands of those who had power to kill Him, but that after three days He would *rise again* (31). This was the second of three such predictions (see 8:31-33 and 10:32-34 for the others).

b. If the disciples failed to understand these facts, neither did they grasp their meaning. *The Son of man* (31) is also the Suffering Servant of the Old Testament. They either could not or would not accept the import of this teaching. But neither did Israel as a whole, then or now. It was a mystery. Perhaps these realities triggered the action of Judas Iscariot.

3. *A tedious learning process.* It must have been a source of distress to Jesus that the Twelve were so slow to learn. He persisted in His teaching, nevertheless.

This should hearten all who teach—whatever the school, whatever the level. The learning process is a tedious one. The disciples, who were at this point even afraid to ask Jesus about the matter (32), finally did come to understand what Jesus had long and patiently taught them. But that did not come until after Calvary, the Resurrection, and Pentecost.

A Surprising Recipe for Greatness

Mark 9:33-37

> 33 And he came to Capernaum: and being in the house he asked them, What was it that ye disputed among yourselves by the way?
> 34 But they held their peace: for by the way they had disputed among themselves, who should be the greatest.
> 35 And he sat down, and called the twelve, and saith unto them, If any man desire to be first, the same shall be last of all, and servant of all.
> 36 And he took a child, and set him in the midst of them: and when he had taken him in his arms, he said unto them,
> 37 Whosoever shall receive one of such children in my name, receiveth me: and whosoever shall receive me, receiveth not me, but him that sent me.

The heart of everyone cries out for recognition, for fulfillment, for achievement. When the disciples, en route to Capernaum, were disputing "one with another on the way, who was the greatest" (34, ASV), they were pursuing a natural desire in a misguided manner.

Jesus seemed to acknowledge the naturalness of such a desire while quietly rebuking the method they used. *What was it that ye disputed among yourselves by the way?* (33). The disciples were sheepish and silent. Jesus offered a recipe for greatness cleansed of destructive selfishness.

1. *The ugly scramble for greatness.* It is clear enough from the passage before us that the world has turned true values upside down. The bitter competition to be the greatest is everywhere and often infects the community of believers.

a. The competition among the disciples for first place was characteristic of their culture. Of the scribes and Pharisees, Jesus said, "They do all their deeds to be seen by men . . . they love the place of honor at feasts and the best seats in the synagogues" (Matt. 23:5-6, RSV).

In warning the disciples against place-seeking, by implication Jesus described how deep-seated the practice was in their culture. "'When you are invited by any one to a marriage feast, do not sit down in a place of honor, lest a more eminent man than you be invited by him . . . But when you are invited, go and sit in the lowest place, so that when your host comes he may say to you, "Friend, go up higher"'" (Luke 14:8, 10, RSV). The disciples had become imbued with the self-centered spirit prevalent in their society.

b. This unpleasant spirit is characteristic of our culture also. It is common knowledge that in the world of business, entertainment, politics, the professions, competition is often sharp, cutting, unethical.

The observations Jesus made of His world could be made of ours: "You know that in the world, rulers lord it over their subjects, and their great men make them feel the weight of authority; but it shall not be so with you" (Matt. 20:25, NEB).

2. *The undiscovered path to greatness.* Jesus seemed to understand and accept the strong natural desire for recognition. However, His way to greatness is surprising and largely undiscovered.

   a. It is the way of *servanthood. If any man desire to be first, the same shall be last of all, and servant of all* (35). It is the way of *self-denial* (8:34-35). When the relationship among believers is that of mutual service motivated by love unfeigned, all occasion for bickering and struggle for recognition evaporates.

   It is also the way of *vicarious sacrifice.* The larger context of the present passage is the account of Jesus on His way to Jerusalem and the Cross. It was important for the disciples, squabbling over greatness, to understand that even Jesus came not to be served, but to serve others, and "to give his life a ransom for many" (10:45).

   b. It is the way of *childlikeness.* To illustrate His point, Jesus called a child and, before them all, put His arms around the little one. His words were profound: to welcome a child in Jesus' name is to welcome both the Lord and the Father who sent Him.

   Normally a child is trustful, unpretentious, responsive to love. When we welcome a little child in Jesus' name, we do so without thought of recognition or reward. But this is the spirit in which we should render all our service. Surprisingly and unexpectedly, in that unselfish, unpretentious action, we receive a great reward.

   If our praise is from men, we shall never have enough, and we shall always be in competition with others. If our praise is from God, we shall be content and never competitive, for we are all equally loved, recognized, and appreciated.

A Divine Rebuke of Sectarianism

Mark 9:38-41

> 38 And John answered him, saying, Master, we saw one casting out devils in thy name, and he followeth not us: and we forbad him, because he followeth not us.
> 39 But Jesus said, Forbid him not: for there is no man which shall do a miracle in my name, that can lightly speak evil of me.
> 40 For he that is not against us is on our part.
> 41 For whosoever shall give you a cup of water to drink in my name, because ye belong to Christ, verily I say unto you, he shall not lose his reward.

Sectarianism is a party spirit, blind to the virtues and strengths of other Christian groups. It is self-centered, provincial, unchristlike. Jesus rebuked it sharply, as did Paul when that spirit divided the Corinthian church (1 Cor. 1:13).

Sectarianism is not to be confused with loyalty to the cause of Christ. Jesus required loyalty and severely condemned those who opposed the Kingdom. Repeatedly Jesus pronounced judgment upon the unjust, who were also religious: "Woe unto you, scribes and Pharisees, hypocrites!" (Matt. 23:13; repeated in vv. 14, 15, 16). But there is no place for sectarianism among the followers of the Lord.

At this point in their Christian walk, John and the other disciples thought otherwise. Observing someone doing mighty works in Jesus' name, they *forbade him* (38), because he was not one of the Twelve. "Unofficial" miracles performed in His name by "unauthorized" persons received the Lord's blessing.

1. *An "unauthorized" miracle.* Once more, John was living up to the nickname Jesus had given him and his brother James—Boanerges, "sons of thunder" (Mark 3:17). Perhaps with an air of contented self-righteousness, John reported seeing a nameless exorcist, who was casting out demons in Jesus' name. "And as he was not one of us, we tried to stop him" (38, NEB). Not long before this, the disciples had unsuccessfully attempted to cast out a demon (9:18). Were they now attempting to compensate?

2. *An unqualified approval.* Jesus corrected them: *Forbid him not* (39). Upon another occasion, when the Twelve received an unfriendly reception in Samaria, James and John were ready to retaliate: "Lord, do you want us to call fire down from heaven to destroy them?" (Luke 9:54, NIV). Jesus frowned upon such an attitude. "Ye know not what manner of spirit ye are of" (Luke 9:55).

Who was the nameless exorcist? How did he come to have such faith in Jesus? Did he give up his work when John commanded him to stop? We have answers to none of these questions. We may surmise that the impulsive words of the disciples caused damage.

We do know how Jesus felt about the matter. "Do not stop him," Jesus said. . . . "Whoever is not against us is for us" (39-40, NIV).

3. *An unrestricted blessing.* Jesus did not stop with the rebuke of narrow sectarianism among His disciples. He went on to proclaim an expansive blessing upon all who do a good work in His name.

Jesus dissolved the differences between trivial and important acts of service in the Kingdom. An otherwise insignificant cup of water (41) would become the gift of life itself to someone whose tongue was parched under the searing sun of an Eastern desert.

Jesus restricted the blessing of His reward only to those who would render service in His name. The unknown exorcist was a man of faith and obedience. It was not required that he be a follower of James and John.

The Causes and Cost of Sinning

Mark 9:42-50

42 And whosoever shall offend one of these little ones that believe in me, it is better for him that a millstone were hanged about his neck, and he were cast into the sea.
43 And if thy hand offend thee, cut it off: it is better for thee to enter into life maimed, than having two hands to go into hell, into the fire that never shall be quenched:
44 Where their worm dieth not, and the fire is not quenched.
45 And if thy foot offend thee, cut it off: it is better for thee to enter

halt into life, than having two feet to be cast into hell, into the fire that
never shall be quenched:

46 Where their worm dieth not, and the fire is not quenched.

47 And if thine eye offend thee, pluck it out: it is better for thee to
enter into the kingdom of God with one eye, than having two eyes to
be cast into hell fire:

48 Where their worm dieth not, and the fire is not quenched.

49 For every one shall be salted with fire, and every sacrifice shall
be salted with salt.

50 Salt is good: but if the salt have lost his saltness, wherewith will
ye season it? Have salt in yourselves, and have peace one with another.

It is possible to group these verses in a variety of ways.
Some commentators include v. 42 with the previous section. Others treat vv. 49-50 separately. We shall include
them all with this unit.

The import of this passage is clear and powerful—to
enter the Kingdom is the highest possible human value; to
lose the Kingdom is the greatest possible human loss. The
causes of stumbling, or sinning, are many. The cost is unspeakable—the loss of one's soul.

1. *The causes of sinning.* Promise and warning are inter-
woven in this chapter. A blessing is promised to those who
welcome "little children" (37, ASV) in Jesus' name. A
curse is pronounced upon those who cause even "one of
these little ones . . . to stumble" (42, ASV).

a. The influence of others is often a cause of stumbling. Examples are left to our imagination, observation,
and experience. One's interpretation of who "these little
ones" are will color that judgment. Jesus sometimes addressed His disciples as little children (John 13:33). In
this warning He could have had in mind the nameless
exorcist, whom John and the others discouraged (38).

Whether thought of in literal or figurative terms, it is
a grievous evil to cause a believer to sin. It would be better
for such a tempter "to be thrown into the sea with a large
millstone tied around his neck" (42, NIV). This gruesome
act was a form of capital punishment practiced by the
Romans and familiar to the disciples.

b. One's own capacities and desires are often a cause
of stumbling, i.e., of sinning. The word translated *offend*

in the KJV is also translated "cause to sin" (NIV) or "cause to stumble" (ASV). Transliterated it would be *scandalize.* The noun form (translated "offenses" in Matt. 18:7 and Luke 17:1) is *skandalon* and refers to the bait-stick of a trap—the device that springs the trap or snare. An *offense, a skandalon,* then, is the bait, the lure, the temptation or enticement.

In vv. 43, 45, and 47, three key members of the body are cited as possible agents in stumbling or sinning. The hand, the foot, or the eye may offend one, i.e., cause him to stumble, to sin. It is, of course, the person who employs these members of his body in the acts of sin, but the symbolism is clear. (It should be noted that vv. 44 and 46 contain a refrain borrowed from v. 48 and are generally not included in recent versions.)

The hand may steal, the foot may walk in sinful ways, the eye may gaze on uncleanness. Symbolically, the remedy is radical surgery. In the words of William Hendriksen:

> Right at this very moment and without any vacillation the obscene book should be burned, the scandalous picture destroyed, the soul-destroying film condemned, the sinister yet very intimate social tie broken, and the baneful habit discarded. . . . Of course, these destructive . . . actions will never succeed apart from the powerful sanctifying and transforming operation of God's Spirit in heart and life.

The alternatives are fixed: "It is better for you to enter life maimed than . . . to go into hell, where the fire never goes out" (43, NIV).

2. *The cost of sinning* is immeasurable. It brings the ultimate penalty: *to go into hell* (43); *to be cast into hell* (45, 47).

   a. The word translated *hell* is *Gehenna,* and refers to the Valley of Hinnom, south of Jerusalem, a place desecrated by human sacrifice and declared unclean (2 Kings 23:10). It became a depository of the city's waste, where fires burned and worms gnawed endlessly.

b. The language is from the Old Testament, the last verse of Isaiah: "And they shall go forth and look on the dead bodies of the men that have rebelled against me; for their worm shall not die, their fire shall not be quenched, and they shall be an abhorrence to all flesh" (Isa. 66:24, RSV).

Let it be noted that these dreadful words describe the men who have rebelled against God, and that we believe it is the finally impenitent who are cast into hell. This passage does not open the doors to legalism. The sin of which the Holy Spirit convicts the world is not this or that act of transgression, but the sin of unbelief. As Jesus said, when the Holy Spirit has come, "he will reprove the world of sin . . . because they believe not on me" (John 16:8-9). Paul teaches that unbelief leads to rebellion, idolatry, and moral corruption (Rom. 1:21-24).

c. It is proper to say no more than Jesus did about the state of the finally impenitent. The loss is total and final. "Shall not the Judge of all the earth do right?" (Gen. 18:25).

In this context, it is important to stress the positive side: *It is better for thee to enter into life* (43). *The kingdom of God* (47) is better than the kingdom of Satan. The fruit of the Spirit is better than the works of the flesh. Love, joy, peace are better than adultery, fornication, uncleanness (Gal. 5:19, 22). That's the choice—life rather than death!

d. The three "salt sayings" of vv. 49, 50*a*, 50*b* are saying to the believer, in substance: A fiery trial is coming to test you; maintain those qualities of character and spirit which make you the salt of the earth (Matt. 5:13); remember especially the word, "Blessed are the peacemakers" (Matt. 5:9).

The Ministry in Jerusalem and Judea

Mark 10:1—13:37

MARK 10

Jesus and the Pangs of Divorce

Mark 10:1-12

1 And he arose from thence, and cometh into the coasts of Judaea by the farther side of Jordan: and the people resort unto him again; and, as he was wont, he taught them again.
2 And the Pharisees came to him, and asked him, Is it lawful for a man to put away his wife? tempting him.
3 And he answered and said unto them, What did Moses command you?
4 And they said, Moses suffered to write a bill of divorcement, and to put her away.
5 And Jesus answered and said unto them, For the hardness of your heart he wrote you this precept.
6 But from the beginning of the creation God made them male and female.
7 For this cause shall a man leave his father and mother, and cleave to his wife;
8 And they twain shall be one flesh: so then they are no more twain, but one flesh.
9 What therefore God hath joined together, let not man put asunder.
10 And in the house his disciples asked him again of the same matter.
11 And he saith unto them, Whosoever shall put away his wife, and marry another, committeth adultery against her.
12 And if a woman shall put away her husband, and be married to another, she committeth adultery.

In this day of multiple marriages, the church must proceed with caution. The holiness of the divine commandment must never be compromised. At the same time, the compassion and gentleness of the divine nature must never be violated.

En route to Jerusalem for the last time, Jesus and the Twelve were accosted by a cluster of Pharisees, unfriendly as usual. They raised a provocative question concerning divorce. In response, Jesus rebuked them for their blindness and hardness of heart. For those who would see, He disclosed the compassion of Moses, as well as His own firmness and flexibility. Jesus held in delicate balance the divine ideal and the human reality.

1. *The motivation of the Pharisees.* Jesus has left Galilee for the last time. The thought is chilling. He is traversing the circuitous route down the Jordan Cleft, touching Judea and Perea on either side, as He goes *up to* (literally) Jerusalem.

a. Among the multitudes who gathered around Him was a group of suspicious Pharisees. They sought to embarrass Jesus with the authorities, political and ecclesiastical. This encounter anticipated controversies soon to develop between Jesus and His enemies in the Temple area of Jerusalem, controversies that would lead to the arrest and execution of Jesus.

b. The Pharisees posed a question thinly veiling a dilemma. *Is it lawful for a man to put away his wife? tempting him* (2). Every listener would call to mind the fact that both Herod Antipas and Herodias had divorced their spouses in order to remarry. The tragedy of John the Baptist, who had condemned that marriage, was still fresh in memory. Likewise, all parties knew that the Sanhedrin, the nominal defenders of the law of Moses, would also be listening. The horns of the dilemma were sharp.

2. *The compassion of Moses.* Jesus parried their question with another. *What did Moses command you?* (3). He referred them back to their own primary authority, the Torah. One wonders what response the Pharisees expected, certainly not to be put on the defensive.

a. Rather lamely, they replied, "Moses permitted a man to divorce his wife by a note of dismissal" (4, NEB). This was not a license for carelessness but a curb on insensitivity. The husband was required to show cause. D. Edmond Hiebert writes: "The requirement restrained the rash and heartless dismissal of a wife, and served to give the wife so treated at least some character and protection."

Jesus set the record straight: "It was a concession to your hardhearted wickedness" (5, TLB). In Judaism the wife had no such recourse. At best it was a "man's world."

b. Here we have an instance of how God, in His mercy, adjusts the perfect ideal to the harsh realities of man's existence. Paul declared that principle on Mars' Hill: "And the times of this ignorance God winked at." The ideal was not repealed, however, for now God "commandeth all men every where to repent" (Acts 17:30). The concession allowed by Moses was, as F. C. Grant states, "consonant with the idea of God's adaptation of His general purpose to immediate circumstances and needs." Nevertheless, the ideal is never abrogated and stands in judgment on the real.

3. *The firmness and flexibility of Jesus.* In the present passage, Jesus sets forth the divine ideal with firmness and without equivocation. Elsewhere in the New Testament His flexibility is just as evident.

a. Firmness was mandatory as Jesus talked with the Pharisees, who so often kept the letter of the law while blaspheming its spirit. One school of Jewish thought, the followers of Hillel, allowed a man to divorce his wife (never the reverse) on trivial grounds, such as the desire for a more attractive woman, or if his wife had burned the food or seasoned it unpleasantly!

b. In recalling the divine ideal of monogamous marriage, Jesus stressed several points:

(1) When man was created in the image of God, he was not a solitary person. "But from the beginning of the creation, Male and female made he them" (6, ASV; cf. Gen. 1:27). Each was made for the other.

(2) Consequently a man shall leave, or abandon his father and his mother (the language is strong) and *cleave to* his wife (literally, "to glue to").

(3) The result of such a union is a fusion not to be dissolved at will. "The two shall become one flesh" (8, ASV; cf. Gen. 2:24).

(4) A man and his wife become "yokefellows," drawing burdens together. The divine intention was that marriage should be indissoluble. "What God has joined together, man must not separate" (9, NEB).

c. The flexibility of Jesus is to be seen not only in His understanding of the compassion of Moses but also in the exception to these binding words found elsewhere in the New Testament.

Matthew and Paul both cite exceptions: fornication (Matt. 19:9) and desertion (1 Cor. 7:15). Exceptions are inevitable, as the church presently recognizes. However, divorce is never painless. Suffering is always involved. Notwithstanding, divorce is sometimes the lesser of two evils. It is right that the church extend its arms of compassion and understanding to receive the wounded, the bleeding, the crushed.

d. Something of a blend of the firmness and flexibility of Jesus may be present in the conversation of Jesus and the Twelve, later. As Matthew records the discussion (Matt. 19:10-12), the disciples were astonished at the firmness of Jesus' teaching and expressed the feeling that it would be better to remain single than to incur the risk of possible divorce. Jesus replied that risk is involved in marriage, therefore some do remain unmarried, for a variety of reasons. However, His closing words are beautiful and encouraging: "He that is able to receive [this high standard for marriage] let him receive it."

"Jesus Loves the Little Children of the World"

Mark 10:13-16

13 And they brought young children to him, that he should touch them: and his disciples rebuked those that brought them.
14 But when Jesus saw it, he was much displeased, and said unto them, Suffer the little children to come unto me, and forbid them not: for of such is the kingdom of God.

> 15 Verily I say unto you, Whosoever shall not receive the kingdom of God as a little child, he shall not enter therein.
> 16 And he took them up in his arms, put his hands upon them, and blessed them.

It is appropriate that the story of Jesus and the children should follow His teaching on divorce. Children are often among the first casualties of a broken home.

The story is meaningful for other reasons as well. It tells us something about the personality of Jesus, especially His attractiveness. The story also reveals a good deal about the Kingdom—its nature and the qualities of spirit required for entering it.

1. *The attractiveness of Jesus.* Why did so many children gather around Jesus? It says something about His personal winsomeness. Parents wanted to bring their children to Jesus. Quite possibly it was the fathers who brought them. Whoever brought them it is obvious that they were attracted to Jesus. The children likewise must have felt the warmth of His welcome. They are sensitive to moods. The image they perceive draws or repels. The love Jesus had for children was genuine.

2. *The wrong-headedness of the disciples.* The parents or friends, who "were bringing unto Jesus little children, that He should touch them" (13, ASV), must have been startled and hurt when they found the way blocked. "The disciples shooed them away, telling them not to bother Him" (13, TLB).

Once again, as when they rebuked the unknown exorcist (9:39), the disciples had abused and exceeded their authority. Their frame of reference, their standard of judgment, was faulty. Perhaps the disciples were well-intentioned, hoping to shield and protect Jesus from the crowds. Perhaps they shared the view of so many, then and now, who classify children as not very important.

Contemporary evidence abounds that cruelty to children was commonplace. The early Christians were soon discovered to be unique in their refusal to destroy children by exposure to the elements.

3. *The only way into the Kingdom.* Seeing what the disciples had done, Jesus "was indignant" (14, NIV). Then followed those beautiful, now classic words: "Let the children come to me . . . I tell you, whoever does not accept the kingdom of God like a child will never enter it" (14-15, NEB). It is true that a child is unsullied, trustful, unpretentious. However, something more is implied in childlikeness as a requisite for entering the Kingdom. "The Kingdom may be entered only by one who knows he is helpless and small, without claim or merit" (William L. Lane).

The closing scene will be etched upon the human mind forever—Jesus enfolding little children in His arms, placing His hands upon them with blessing and prayer for all their future life!

> *Jesus loves the little children,*
> *All the children of the world.*

The Difficulty and Delight of Discipleship

Mark 10:17-31

> 17 And when he was gone forth into the way, there came one running, and kneeled to him, and asked him, Good Master, what shall I do that I may inherit eternal life?
> 18 And Jesus said unto him, Why callest thou me good? there is none good but one, that is, God.
> 19 Thou knowest the commandments, Do not commit adultery, Do not kill, Do not steal, Do not bear false witness, Defraud not, Honour thy father and mother.
> 20 And he answered and said unto him, Master, all these have I observed from my youth.
> 21 Then Jesus beholding him loved him, and said unto him, One thing thou lackest: go thy way, sell whatsoever thou hast, and give to the poor, and thou shalt have treasure in heaven: and come, take up the cross, and follow me.
> 22 And he was sad at that saying, and went away grieved: for he had great possessions.
> 23 And Jesus looked round about, and saith unto his disciples, How hardly shall they that have riches enter into the kingdom of God!
> 24 And the disciples were astonished at his words. But Jesus answereth again, and saith unto them, Children, how hard is it for them that trust in riches to enter into the kingdom of God!
> 25 It is easier for a camel to go through the eye of a needle, than for a rich man to enter into the kingdom of God.
> 26 And they were astonished out of measure, saying among themselves, Who then can be saved?

27 And Jesus looking upon them saith, With men it is impossible, but not with God: for with God all things are possible.
28 Then Peter began to say unto him, Lo, we have left all, and have followed thee.
29 And Jesus answered and said, Verily I say unto you, There is no man that hath left house, or brethren, or sisters, or father, or mother, or wife, or children, or lands, for my sake, and the gospel's,
30 But he shall receive an hundredfold now in this time, houses, and brethren, and sisters, and mothers, and children, and lands, with persecutions; and in the world to come eternal life.
31 But many that are first shall be last; and the last first.

The story of the rich young ruler (cf. Matt. 19:22; Luke 18:18) fires the imagination. The average person, including believers, is generally awed and impressed by those who have wealth and power. There may be no "respect of persons" (1 Pet. 1:17) with God, but there is with man. This man who came running to Jesus lacked nothing which men generally seek with a passion—the vitality of youth, the security of riches, the prestige of influence. In language that sounds severe, Jesus gave him a lesson on the cost of discipleship. The rich man turned away in poverty. The disciples remained to receive the promise of immeasurable riches.

1. *The commendable qualities of the rich young ruler.* The positive qualities in this story should not be overlooked. Jesus felt deep affection for this one who had come running, kneeling, and asking, *Good Master, what shall I do to inherit eternal life?* (17).

a. He confessed a deep spiritual hunger. Matthew records his significant question: "What lack I yet?" (Matt. 19:20). Affluent in every material way, he was aware of a need and confessed it to Jesus.

b. He had lived a good moral life. After reminding him that "no one is good—except God alone" (18, NIV), Jesus referred the man to the Scriptures. "You know the commandments" (19, NIV). Jesus was sinless (Heb. 4:15), but He always related himself to the Father, who alone is good in the absolute sense. That "the Lord is good" (Ps. 100:5) is a cornerstone of our biblical faith.

Jesus summarized the second table of the Law (19; cf.

Exod. 20:12-16). The man's response was touching: "Teacher, all these I have kept since I was a boy" (20, NIV). He had come to Jesus asking what he should do to inherit eternal life. But he had discovered in experience what Paul later taught in his epistles: "Therefore by the deeds of the law there shall no flesh be justified in his sight" (Rom. 3:20).

c. He was a responsible custodian of his wealth. The Scriptures never condone laziness and wastefulness. Qualities of spirit which the Hebrew-Christian faith inculcate tend to produce wealth—diligence, frugality, a sense of responsibility and stewardship: "Abraham the faithful, Job the righteous, Solomon the wise were all men of wealth" (BBC). This man's fault was that his love of wealth and self violated the first table of the Law: "Thou shalt have no other gods before me" (Exod. 20:3).

2. *The startling cost of discipleship.* The words of Jesus astonished everyone—the rich man and the disciples alike: "Jesus felt genuine love for this man as he looked at him. 'You lack only one thing,' he told him; 'go and sell all you have and give the money to the poor—and you shall have treasure in heaven—and come follow me'" (21, TLB).

a. It is appropriate to ask whether Jesus has made the same stringent requirement of all His followers. Many have left all, quite literally, to follow Him—Peter and Andrew, James and John left their nets and their boats; Levi left the tax-collector's table. Presumably the rest of the Twelve did likewise. It is said that Francis of Assisi relinquished a fortune to follow the Master. Dietrich Bonhoeffer laid everything aside to return from the safety of America to work for the Kingdom in Hitler's Germany. In the end, he laid down his life on a Nazi scaffold. Has Jesus altered His requirements for entering the Kingdom?

b. It is appropriate to ask whether the disciples of Jesus now respond to this call of Jesus in spirit, if not in fact. It is still costly to enter the ministry, whether at home or abroad, whether as a pastor, evangelist, missionary, or whatever calling. Substantial sacrifices are still being made; substantial contributions are still being invested in the Kingdom. But perhaps all this misses the point.

c. The real point of the story is that no man can enter the Kingdom unless he leaves all to follow Jesus. The disciples had already heard Jesus say: "Whosoever will come after me, let him deny himself, and take up his cross, and follow me" (8:34). That means everything!

In another context, Jesus taught that the Kingdom was like a merchant man who, finding "one pearl of great price, went and sold all that he had, and bought it" (Matt. 13:45-46). That means everything!

Yes, Jesus does even now make the same stringent requirement of all His followers: *Sell whatsoever thou hast . . . and follow me* (21).

3. *The immeasurable rewards of obedience.* This surprising incident required the disciples to rethink some of their values.

a. The rich young ruler went away sorrowfully, unwilling to become a disciple on the terms Jesus laid down. As he left, Jesus made an observation which astonished the Twelve. "'How hard it will be for those who are wealthy to enter the kingdom of God!'" (23, NASB).

Who then can be saved? (26). If the rich, who do so much good with their wealth and gain so much merit, cannot be saved, who can? So ran the thought of the disciples. Jesus pressed the matter further: "'Children, how hard it is to enter the kingdom of God!'" (24, RSV). The preferred reading of v. 24 puts the issues in baldest terms. It is costly for anyone, rich or poor, to enter the Kingdom!

b. However, what is impossible, even absurd, with men is possible with God. It is impossible for a camel (the largest animal of the land) to go through the eye of a needle (the smallest opening). Indeed, it is absurd even to contemplate that possibility. And so it is with entrance into the Kingdom. But salvation is "entirely the work of

God, His rescue of helpless men" (IOC). *With God all things are possible* (27).

"For it is by grace you have been saved, through faith —and this not from yourselves, it is the gift of God—not by works, so that no one can boast. For we are God's workmanship, created in Christ Jesus to do good works" (Eph. 2:8-10, NIV).

c. Now, all of a sudden it dawns upon Peter that he and his companions have actually done what the rich man refused to do. "Then Peter burst out, 'But look, we have left everything and followed you!'" (28, Phillips). Jesus apparently agreed with Peter. He responded with a promise that is simply staggering: *The rewards of discipleship are far greater than the cost!* The promise was tempered with a word of warning and caution.

A disciple may be called upon to leave his house, or brothers, or sisters, or father and mother, or wife and children, or lands for the sake of Jesus and the gospel. However, the Lord promises that no one will make such a sacrifice "without getting back a hundred times over, now in this present life, homes and brothers and sisters, mothers and children and land . . . and in the next world eternal life" (30, Phillips). Contrast the words *and* here and *or* above. Has any faithful follower of the Lord found these words to be untrue? The fellowship of believers in the body of Christ has fulfilled this promise times without number.

The word of *warning* was that in the midst of this bounty, persecutions will also come. The word of *caution* was possibly for the Twelve. *But many that are first shall be last; and the last first* (31). Their unique position gave them no special claim on God's providence.

The Final Passion Prediction

Mark 10:32-34

> 32 And they were in the way going up to Jerusalem; and Jesus went before them: and they were amazed; and as they followed, they were afraid. And he took again the twelve, and began to tell them what things should happen unto him,
> 33 Saying, Behold, we go up to Jerusalem; and the Son of man shall

> be delivered unto the chief priests, and unto the scribes; and they
> shall condemn him to death, and shall deliver him to the Gentiles:
> 34 And they shall mock him, and shall scourge him, and shall spit
> upon him, and shall kill him: and the third day he shall rise again.

We have in this passage a priceless glimpse of a party of Jewish pilgrims going up to Jerusalem for the exciting Feast of the Passover. Jesus leads the way, with the disciples following, probably in strict order of seniority. The party included other pilgrims as well.

An air of amazement and fear permeates the group. Jesus strides ahead with almost a fierce determination. The disciples do not understand His words or His spirit.

1. *The determination of Jesus.* The suspense and tension mount as one reads Mark's story. Slowly Jesus turns from the crowds of Galilee to be alone with the Twelve. On two previous occasions (8:31-33; 9:30-32) Jesus had predicted His sufferings in Jerusalem—that they were necessary and certain. Now He moves with sure tread toward the city where "the Lamb of God" will be slain for "the sin of the world" (John 1:29). Nothing will deter Him (8:33).

2. *The denseness of the disciples.* Luke spells it out: "The disciples did not understand any of this. Its meaning was hidden from them, and they did not know what He was talking about" (Luke 18:34, NIV).

a. The denseness of the disciples is perplexing. As William Hendriksen points out, Jesus predicted seven items of His passion which were in fact fulfilled: (1) He would be handed over to the Sanhedrin, (2) who would condemn Him to death, and (3) hand Him over to the Gentiles. (4) They would mock and mistreat Him, (5) scourge and (6) kill Him, but (7) three days later He would rise from the dead.

b. Anyone who has tried to communicate spiritual truth to the natural or even the immature mind can appreciate the problem. However, as a good Teacher, Jesus in love led the disciples step by step to deeper levels of understanding, which increasingly overwhelmed Him with sorrow as He contemplated the Cross (Luke 12:50).

The Struggle for Recognition

Mark 10:35-45

> 35 And James and John, the sons of Zebedee, come unto him, saying, Master, we would that thou shouldest do for us whatsoever we shall desire.
> 36 And he said unto them, What would ye that I should do for you?
> 37 They said unto him, Grant unto us that we may sit, one on thy right hand, and the other on thy left hand, in thy glory.
> 38 But Jesus said unto them, Ye know not what ye ask: can ye drink of the cup that I drink of? and be baptized with the baptism that I am baptized with?
> 39 And they said unto him, We can. And Jesus said unto them, Ye shall indeed drink of the cup that I drink of; and with the baptism that I am baptized withal shall ye be baptized:
> 40 But to sit on my right hand and on my left hand is not mine to give; but it shall be given to them for whom it is prepared.
> 41 And when the ten heard it, they began to be much displeased with James and John.
> 42 But Jesus called them to him, and saith unto them, Ye know that they which are accounted to rule over the Gentiles exercise lordship over them; and their great ones exercise authority upon them.
> 43 But so shall it not be among you: but whosoever will be great among you, shall be your minister:
> 44 And whosoever of you will be the chiefest, shall be servant of all.
> 45 For even the Son of man came not to be ministered unto, but to minister, and to give his life a ransom for many.

Once more the contest for position among the Twelve emerges. It is not a pretty sight. James and John, as well as their mother (Matt. 20:20-21), may appear in a poor light, but so do the other disciples, who resented the self-seeking of the "Sons of Thunder" (3:17).

With incredible patience, Jesus in reality accepted the ambition of the disciples and gently probed their minds to lead them to an improved understanding of themselves and of the facts of life. Indeed, He offered guidelines for personal fulfillment, for the way to greatness.

1. *The perennial contest for position.* The present passage sounds like a continued story. The dispute over "who was the greatest" (9:34, NIV) was not over.

a. The plea of James and John is secretive. Apparently somewhat by stealth, "James and John, the sons of Zebedee, came over and spoke to Him in a low voice. 'Master', they said, 'we want You to do us a favor'" (35, TLB). A favor indeed! They were seeking the positions of greatest authority and power in the government they believed Jesus would soon establish. While they were reaching, they reached for the stars!

b. The reaction of the Ten is explosive. The report soon circulated that James and John were seeking unfair advantage. The rest of the disciples exploded. "When the ten heard about this, they became indignant" (41, NIV). Their response was due not so much to a wounded humility as to envy. The request was, after all, a good idea, but they had not thought of it first!

As noted earlier, if our praise is from men, we shall never have enough, and we shall always be in competition with others. If our praise is from God, we shall be content and never competitive, for we are all equally loved, recognized, and appreciated.

2. *The gentle probing of the Teacher.* It is noteworthy that Jesus did not scold James and John for their ambition. He did probe their minds with questions and observations. In substance, He said three things:

a. "Your request is natural but naive." Jesus said to them, "'You do not understand what you are asking'" (38, NEB). This was a gentle rebuke, of course, but it carried no hint of exasperation or anger. He seemed to understand that young men, vigorous and imaginative, would be ambitious. At the moment, they simply did not know what would be involved in bearing heavy burdens for the Kingdom.

b. "The honor of position involves the pain of responsibility." Jesus pursued the issue with a double question: "'Are you able to drink from the bitter cup of sorrow I must drink from? Or to be baptized with the baptism of suffering I must be baptized with?'" (38, TLB).

The figure of taking the cup of sorrow and submitting

to the baptism of suffering was a familiar one. William L. Lane comments, "In the Old Testament the cup of wine is a common metaphor for the wrath of God's judgment upon human sin and rebellion" (Isa. 51:17). The cup which Jesus came to drink of was the divine judgment upon human sin. In His vicarious atonement, Jesus tasted death for every man (Heb. 2:9).

As Jesus approached Jerusalem, more and more His passion and death loomed like a flood of distress. "There is a terrible baptism ahead of me, and how I am pent up until it is accomplished!" (Luke 12:50, TLB). It was as if He said with the Psalmist: "All thy waves and thy billows are gone over me" (Ps. 42:7).

When Jesus asked James and John the question, *Are ye able?* the expected reply was *No.* Jesus' cup and baptism were linked with His messianic mission. In a real sense, Jesus went to Golgotha alone. Their reply is astonishing. "We are able" (Matt. 20:22). Perhaps the response of Jesus is just as astonishing: *Ye shall indeed drink . . . and . . . be baptized* (39). We know that James suffered martyrdom (Acts 12:2) and that John may have also (Rev. 1:9). They did share His travail.

However, many who might desire certain positions of honor and responsibility in the Kingdom would relinquish them quickly, if they could taste the cup of sorrow and undergo the baptism of suffering those positions entail.

c. "Divine providence governs position and promotion." Jesus taught the Twelve a sobering lesson in the facts of divine election: "To sit at my right or left is not for me to grant. These places belong to those for whom they have been prepared" (40, NIV).

Divine election to salvation is universal and conditional. "Whosoever shall call on the name of the Lord shall be saved" (Acts 2:21). Divine election to service is quite another matter; it is selective and, in a sense, unconditional. Positions on the right hand and the left of the Lord are by appointment!

> *For promotion cometh neither from the east,*
> *Nor from the west, nor from the south.*
> *But God is the judge;*
> *He putteth down one, and setteth up another*
>   (Ps. 75:6-7).

Is it not important, therefore, to find what our talents are and then prepare for our appointments? But we cannot really know what our appointments are beforehand. We can, however, get ready.

3. *The sure path to greatness.* It is reassuring to discover that the deepest needs and longings of the human spirit may find satisfaction in the Father's will. "Your heavenly Father knows that you need them all" (Matt. 6:32, RSV). Everyone has a longing to be great, to live a meaningful, significant life, to have some "claim to fame." Jesus has guidelines for "whoever wants to become great" (43, NIV). To live by them is to find a sure path to greatness.

a. The ways of the world are alien to the believer. The disciples knew all too well that "in the world the recognized rulers lord it over their subjects" (42, NEB). The coins they carried bore the image of Tiberius Caesar and the inscription that he was worthy of worship. Oppressive taxation was an expression of this authority. But it is "not so with you" (43, NIV). This spirit is foreign to the community of believers, where the prevailing purpose is to serve one another in love. In such a setting questions of rank evaporate.

b. The model for the believer is the sacrifice of Jesus. The example of Jesus was the severest condemnation of rivalry among the Twelve. "For even the Son of Man did not come to be served, but to serve, and to give His life a ransom for many" (45, NIV). This verse becomes at once a cornerstone of the New Testament doctrine of atonement and a directive for the practice of the Christian life. Isa. 53:10 shines through: "Thou shalt make his soul an offering for sin." "Christ is God's action to rescue men helpless in the power of sin" (IOC).

How tawdry, how shameful is the scramble for recognition among the disciples of the Son of Man! He came among us as one who serves. Who will follow in His steps?

Blindness Then and Now

Mark 10:46-52

> 46 And they came to Jericho: and as he went out of Jericho with his disciples and a great number of people, blind Bartimaeus, the son of Timaeus, sat by the highway side begging.
> 47 And when he heard that it was Jesus of Nazareth, he began to cry out, and say, Jesus, thou son of David, have mercy on me.
> 48 And many charged him that he should hold his peace: but he cried the more a great deal, Thou son of David, have mercy on me.
> 49 And Jesus stood still, and commanded him to be called. And they call the blind man, saying unto him, Be of good comfort, rise; he calleth thee.
> 50 And he, casting away his garment, rose, and came to Jesus.
> 51 And Jesus answered and said unto him, What wilt thou that I should do unto thee? The blind man said unto him, Lord, that I might receive my sight.
> 52 And Jesus said unto him, Go thy way; thy faith hath made thee whole. And immediately he received his sight, and followed Jesus in the way.

The story of blind Bartimaeus is moving and meaningful. Sightlessness is a dreadful affliction. The restoration of sight is a priceless blessing. Bartimaeus experienced both the affliction and the blessing.

The story has timeless meaning. Spiritual blindness is more dreadful than sightlessness. The disciples were spiritually blind. They did not understand Jesus—His person, message, or mission. The multitudes, and the leaders, were also blind. As Paul wrote later: "But we speak the wisdom of God in a mystery . . . which none of the princes of this world knew: for had they known it, they would not have crucified the Lord of glory" (1 Cor. 2:8).

But Jesus offered the precious gift of sight to Bartimaeus. Through the traumatic events in Jerusalem, climaxing in the Resurrection and Pentecost, Jesus opened the eyes of His disciples. What He did in Jericho and Jerusalem He can do today.

1. *Blindness is a dreadful affliction.* The implications of

the biblical account are clear. *Blind Bartimaeus . . . sat by the highway side begging* (46). He was immobile, dependent, forlorn.

Bob was on a sensitive mission in Viet Nam. He picked up an innocent-looking board and triggered a hand grenade. The blast destroyed his sight and wounded him severely. Until Christ came into his life, scattering the shades of night, Bob was bitter, drank heavily, and toyed with thoughts of self-destruction.

A prominent businessman said to his Sunday school teacher, "I pick up the Bible, try to read it, and lay it down." Blindness, literal and spiritual, is to be dreaded.

2. *Restoration of sight is an unspeakable blessing.* The events on the road leading from Jericho were dramatic.

a. Learning that Jesus of Nazareth was passing by, Bartimaeus cried out in language that suggests some understanding of the messianic secret: *Jesus, thou Son of David, have mercy on me* (47). Attempts to silence him came from the crowd but not from Jesus. "Jesus stood still, and said, Call ye him" (49, ASV). Bartimaeus seized that precious moment. Throwing off his garment, so valuable to beggars in a chilly clime, he came to Jesus, full of faith.

b. The question Jesus asked may at first seem superfluous. *What wilt thou that I should do unto thee?* (51). In fact, it was searching. Disability does offer escape from the battle. Did Bartimaeus *really* want to see—the ugly as well as the beautiful? Did he want to become more responsible for his own needs?

The question was also an aid to faith. To verbalize our requests and burdens is to take a step toward finding a solution. "Have no anxiety about anything, but in everything by prayer and supplication with thanksgiving let your requests be made known to God" (Phil. 4:6, RSV).

Bartimaeus knew what he wanted and was willing to accept the implications. *Lord, that I might receive my sight* (51). Jesus spoke the healing word (literally), *Thy faith hath saved thee* (52).

> *One sat alone beside the highway begging,*
> *His eyes were blind, the light he could not see;*
> *He clutched his rags and shivered in the shadows,*
> *Then Jesus came and bade his darkness flee.*
> —OSWALD J. SMITH

Copyright 1940 by the Rodeheaver Co. International copyright secured.
Used by permission.

3. *Such a miracle is by divine intervention alone.* The persistent, insistent cry of Bartimaeus and the loving response of Jesus combined to bring about a mighty miracle. This is the last miracle of healing recorded in Mark's Gospel. It took place on the last stage of the last and fateful journey of Jesus to Jerusalem. Unlike most of the other miracles, the Gospels give us in this case the name of the one healed. Perhaps he became well known in the early Jerusalem church.

What was remembered by the first-century Church was that Jesus of Nazareth, a Prophet mighty in word and deed, the Eternal Son incarnate, proved by another heavenly sign that He is the Son of God and worthy of the worship and service of all mankind.

Bartimaeus at once sensed the call of discipleship *and followed Jesus in the way* (52). He may well have been an eyewitness of the disturbing and surprising events that soon transpired in the city of David.

MARK 11

The Triumphal Entry and Its Meaning

Mark 11:1-11

> 1 And when they came nigh to Jerusalem, unto Bethphage and Bethany, at the mount of Olives, he sendeth forth two of his disciples,
> 2 And saith unto them, Go your way into the village over against you: and as soon as ye be entered into it, ye shall find a colt tied, whereon never man sat; loose him, and bring him.

3 And if any man say unto you, Why do ye this? say ye that the Lord hath need of him; and straightway he will send him hither.

4 And they went their way, and found the colt tied by the door without in a place where two ways met; and they loose him.

5 And certain of them that stood there said unto them, What do ye, loosing the colt?

6 And they said unto them even as Jesus had commanded: and they let them go.

7 And they brought the colt to Jesus, and cast their garments on him; and he sat upon him.

8 And many spread their garments in the way: and others cut down branches off the trees, and strawed them in the way.

9 And they that went before, and they that followed, cried, saying, Hosanna; Blessed is he that cometh in the name of the Lord:

10 Blessed be the kingdom of our father David, that cometh in the name of the Lord: Hosanna in the highest.

11 And Jesus entered into Jerusalem, and into the temple: and when he had looked round about upon all things, and now the eventide was come, he went out unto Bethany with the twelve.

What we see in the Triumphal Entry is in sharp contrast to what we observed throughout the ministry of Jesus in Galilee. During that period Jesus made every effort to keep His Messiahship secret. For example, He repeatedly commanded those whom He had healed to say nothing. He increasingly avoided the crowds and did everything possible not to inflame their nationalistic hopes, as when He quashed their attempt to make Him king by force (John 6:15).

But now Jesus approaches the city of Jerusalem, openly asserting His Messiahship, albeit with biblical symbolism. How awesome that approach must have been, even to Jesus! The question persists—why did He choose to enter the city in such a dramatic fashion? The people really did not understand His mission. The leaders of Judaism feared and hated Him. The Roman authorities would scarcely have known who He was. John has a clue for us. "He came unto his own, and his own received him not" (John 1:11).

1. *Jesus and His destination.* It had somehow become clear to Jesus that His hour had finally come (cf. John 2:4). He was prepared to present himself to Israel as a whole, in the city of David.

a. Jesus took deliberate steps to enter Jerusalem in a

manner to suggest His messianic mission. However, all of His actions were veiled by the symbolism He used. It was not until later, as John plainly states (12:16), that even the disciples understood the Triumphal Entry. When Jesus sent for the *colt tied, whereon never man sat,* He was fulfilling the Oracle of Judah in Gen. 49:8-12. He was also heeding the biblical requirement that an animal used for sacred purposes must be fresh, one "which has never been worked" (Deut. 21:3, RSV).

b. Even more specifically, Jesus fulfilled details of the famous messianic prophecy of Zech. 9:9:

> Rejoice greatly, O daughter of Zion;
> Shout, O daughter of Jerusalem:
> Behold, thy King cometh unto thee:
> He is just, and having salvation;
> Lowly, and riding upon an ass,
> And upon a colt the foal of an ass.

As William L. Lane has noted, "The great messianic oracle, Zech. 9:9, already contained the three essential elements of the Marcan account: the entry . . . , the messianic animal . . . , and the jubilation of the people." For those who had eyes to see, Jesus came as the Messiah of Old Testament prophecy. He came in humility and peace, however, not with threats of political revolution and bloodshed. The Son of Man (Dan. 7:13) was also the Suffering Servant (Isa. 53).

2. *The followers and their welcome.* However unclear the crowds may have been, they sensed that Jesus was approaching Jerusalem on some prophetic mission. *Many spread their garments in the way; and others cut down branches off the trees, and strawed them in the way* (8).

a. Pilgrims normally came to Jerusalem with great exultation and excitement. The sight of the city from the Mount of Olives was impressive—the towering walls, the grandeur of the Temple, the recollection of centuries of sacred history, the throngs of devoted believers gathering for the Passover and other feasts. Little wonder they broke into song, while the Levites responded antiphonally as they received the pilgrims at the gate. "Blessed be he that cometh in the name of the Lord: we have blessed you out of the house of the Lord" (Ps. 118:26).

b. And now the pilgrims did break forth into singing, quite possibly in some antiphonal form:

> *Hosanna!*
> *Blessed is he who comes in the name of the Lord!*
> *Blessed is the coming kingdom of our father David!*
> *Hosanna in the highest!* (9-10, NIV).

The word "Hosanna" is a prayer meaning literally "save us," but with the force of a shout of praise, comparable to "Hallelujah."

c. In addition to the observation of John (12:16) that the disciples did not understand these events until later, two other factors may help us to keep disclosure and restraint in balance: (1) Luke records (19:41-42) that Jesus wept as He approached the city, "Saying, If thou hadst known, even thou, at least in this thy day, the things which belong unto thy peace! but now they are hid from thine eyes." (2) The crowds soon dispersed as they reached the city. The Roman authorities were not aware of any disturbance.

3. *The Lord and His Temple.* The crowds, which had welcomed Jesus with such acclaim, soon melted in with the Passover pilgrims, leaving Jesus to go His own way.

a. It is thought-provoking that Jesus went first to the Temple area. The words of Malachi found a special fulfillment: "the Lord, whom ye seek, will suddenly come to His temple" (Mal. 3:1, ASV). The whole apparatus of official Judaism—the scribes, Pharisees, the chief priests, and others—centered its power in the citadel of the Temple. The Prophet of Nazareth would challenge that power structure at the very seat of its authority.

b. By now the hour was late. After Jesus *had looked*

round about upon all things (11), evidently noting the abuses He would set about to correct, He and the Twleve left the city for the home of friends in nearby Bethany.

c. The following is an outline of Mark's chronology for the week following Sunday and the Triumphal Entry:

Monday: Cursing of the fig tree and cleansing of the Temple (11:12-19)

Tuesday: Parables, controversy stories, and other teachings (11:20—13:37)

Wednesday: Anointing at Bethany and the treachery of Judas (14:1-11)

Thursday: Passover preparation, Last Supper, Gethsemane, arrest, and ecclesiastical trial (14:12-72)

Friday: Trial before Pilate, condemnation, crucifixion, burial (15:1-47)

Saturday: Jesus in the grave

Sunday (Easter): Resurrection (16:1-20) (from BBC).

The Reality and Sternness of Divine Judgment

Mark 11:12-19

> 12 And on the morrow, when they were come from Bethany, he was hungry:
> 13 And seeing a fig tree afar off having leaves, he came, if haply he might find anything thereon: and when he came to it, he found nothing but leaves; for the time of figs was not yet.
> 14 And Jesus answered and said unto it, No man eat fruit of thee hereafter for ever. And his disciples heard it.
> 15 And they come to Jerusalem: and Jesus went into the temple, and began to cast out them that sold and bought in the temple, and overthrew the tables of the moneychangers, and the seats of them that sold doves;
> 16 And would not suffer that any man should carry any vessel through the temple.
> 17 And he taught, saying unto them, Is it not written, My house shall be called of all nations the house of prayer? but ye have made it a den of thieves.
> 18 And the scribes and chief priests heard it, and sought how they might destroy him: for they feared him, because all the people was astonished at his doctrine.
> 19 And when even was come, he went out of the city.

Jesus returned to the city on Monday morning with a sense of purpose and destiny. He had taken stock of the Temple area on the previous evening and must have come with a plan.

The circumstances leading to the withering of the fig tree are puzzling until the event is seen as a prophetic parable in action. A knowledge of the Old Testament background is essential to an understanding of the symbolism. The cleansing of the Temple likewise has Old Testament overtones. The reaction of the authorities was what Jesus expected and had predicted all along. The situation was ominous.

1. *The fig tree and its lesson.* Jesus and the disciples must have left Bethany for Jerusalem before breakfast! Mark reports that *he was hungry* (12). William Hendriksen recalls the touching lines: "Hast thou been hungry, child of mine? / I, too, have needed bread."

a. However, the circumstances that followed are puzzling. "Seeing in the distance a fig tree in leaf, he went to see if he could find anything on it" (13, RSV). The presence of leaves implied the promise of fruit. Jesus expressed disappointment when *he found nothing but leaves* (13).

b. It is essential that we see in the action of Jesus, a prophetic parable of the sort characteristic of Isaiah (20:1-6), Jeremiah (13:1-11), and Ezekiel (4:1-15). In the land of Babylon, for example, Ezekiel staged a mock battle to describe the impending seige of Jerusalem. The "action parables" of the prophets were often dramatic, even shocking, as when Isaiah "walked naked and barefoot three years for a sign" (Isa. 20:3).

A fig tree on the sheltered side of the Mount of Olives might well produce leaves and early immature fruit by the Passover season, but we should probably look for deeper meaning in the words and action of Jesus. Sadly and tragically, Israel was like the fig tree. The magnificence and grandeur of the Temple was a symbol. There Jesus also found nothing but leaves (cf. Jer. 8:13).

2. *The Temple and its subversion.* The disciples must have gone into the city with the words of Jesus still ringing in their ears: *No man eat fruit of thee hereafter for ever.* That charge made quite an impression: *And his disciples heard it* (14).

a. The "vastness and beauty" of the Temple, to use William Hendriksen's words, must have been awesome, especially as a devout pilgrim viewed the entire complex from the Mount of Olives. The Temple area was perhaps a thousand feet square, enclosed by massive walls lined with parallel columns of white marble. Entrance was by means of heavy gates, one or more located on each wall. The sanctuary, or Temple proper, was surrounded by the huge Court of the Gentiles. Its marble and gold glistened in the sun, betimes almost blinding the worshippers.

b. The Court of the Gentiles, paved with marble, had become a marketplace. This was improper, unnecessary, and spiteful. The Sanhedrin controlled four markets on the nearby Mount of Olives, where pilgrims could purchase animals for the sacrifices and also exchange their money for the official Temple coin. However, the greedy high priest, Caiaphas, had opened a marketplace in the Court of the Gentiles. The resultant competition and conflict was bitter.

c. Jesus was angry for several reasons. Not only was it unlawful for these hucksters to peddle their wares in the Temple precincts, it was also an offense to the sincere pilgrim. A wistful, spiritually-hungry Gentile could enter the Temple grounds but not the sanctuary. If he ventured beyond the Court of the Gentiles into the Temple proper, he would lose his life (cf. Acts 21:26-28).

When Jesus had *cast out them that sold and bought in the temple* (15) and stopped the flow of commercial traffic through the Temple grounds (16), He cried out in the language of the prophet Isaiah: "'Is it not written, "My house shall be called a house of prayer for all the nations"? But you have made it a den of robbers'" (17, RSV; cf. Isa. 56:7;

Jer. 7:11). His compassion and love were not for Israel alone, but for the whole world.

3. *The religious leaders and their malice.* The report of what the young Prophet from Nazareth had done soon reached the ears of those who controlled the Temple and its huge revenues. The response of these religious leaders, who were especially powerful in the Sanhedrin, was to be expected, Jesus had announced in advance what their attitude would be. The question was no longer *whether* but *how* to destroy Him. Nevertheless, fearing Jesus, they bided their time.

The response of the people was in sharp contrast to the reaction of their leaders. "All the multitude was astonished at His teaching" (18, RSV). Whether in Galilee or Jerusalem, the country or the city, the teaching of Jesus "never lost its freshness and power" (D. Edmond Hiebert).

A Helpful Lesson from a Helpless Tree

Mark 11:20-26

> 20 And in the morning, as they passed by, they saw the fig tree dried up from the roots.
> 21 And Peter calling to remembrance saith unto him, Master, behold, the fig tree which thou cursedst is withered away.
> 22 And Jesus answering saith unto them, Have faith in God.
> 23 For verily I say unto you, That whosoever shall say unto this mountain, Be thou removed, and be thou cast into the sea; and shall not doubt in his heart, but shall believe that those things which he saith shall come to pass; he shall have whatsoever he saith.
> 24 Therefore I say unto you, What things soever ye desire, when ye pray, believe that ye receive them, and ye shall have them.
> 25 And when ye stand praying, forgive, if ye have ought against any: that your Father also which is in heaven may forgive you your trespasses.
> 26 But if ye do not forgive, neither will your Father which is in heaven forgive your trespasses.

According to Mark's chronology of the Passion Week, it was now Tuesday morning when Jesus and the Twelve returned to Jerusalem from their haven in Bethany. The disciples were startled when they saw the fig tree which Jesus had rebuked the day before. As usual, Peter was the spokesman: "'Rabbi, look! The fig tree you cursed has withered!'" (21, NIV). This startling result became the occasion for a startling promise.

1. *A startling result of an unexpected rebuke.* On successive mornings, the hapless fig tree was conspicuous, but each time for different reasons. On Monday morning, it was conspicuous because of its leaves. On the following morning, it was conspicuous because it was *dried up from the roots* (20). It was dead.

Why would Jesus rebuke and destroy a helpless albeit fruitless tree? This event can only be understood as a prophetic parable (see on vv. 12-14). *Fruitlessness leads to death.* Within a generation Jerusalem and its magnificent Temple would lie in ruins—stark fulfillment of the parable of the fruitless fig tree which promised much but had *nothing but leaves* (13).

However, it should be noted that evidently lower forms of life, in the divine plan, are designed to serve the higher values of humanity.

2. *A startling promise of limitless possibilities.* Jesus responded to the surprise of the disciples with a summons to the faith that rests in the faithfulness of God. In His discussion of the faith that prays, Jesus voiced a command, a promise, and a condition.

a. The command galvanizes the hearer: Have faith in God (22). A significant alternate reading has been translated, "If you only have faith in God" (22, TLB). It is noteworthy that Jesus offered no explanation for the withering of the fig tree nor any interpretation of the symbolism. It is obvious from the immediate response, however, that the miraculous event sprang out of His fellowship with the Father.

b. The command took on increased significance with the addition of a promise which simply boggles the mind: "'I tell you this: if anyone says to this mountain, "Be lifted from your place and hurled into the sea," and has no inward doubts, . . . it will be done for him'" (23, NEB).

The disciples could see the Dead Sea from the Mount of Olives and must have been speechless when they felt the force of Jesus' words. They would have recalled that a rabbi who could explain difficult passages of scripture was called "a mover of mountains." They possibly would have remembered the prophetic word of Zechariah:

> *And in that day His feet will stand on the Mount of Olives, which is in front of Jerusalem on the east; and the Mount of Olives will be split in its middle from east to west by a very large valley, so that half of the mountain will move toward the north and the other half toward the south. . . . And the Lord will be king over all the earth; in that day the Lord will be the only one, and His name the only one* (Zech. 14:4-9, NASB).

But there was more: "Therefore I tell you, whatever you ask for in prayer, believe that you will receive it, and it will be yours" (24, NIV). William L. Lane has a helpful word here: "What is affirmed is God's absolute readiness to respond to the resolute faith that prays (cf. Isa. 65:24)." Jesus set no limits to the possibilities of prayer. The faith that prays rests in the God who can cope with the impossible and deliver from every conceivable difficulty.

c. To the command and the promise, the Lord added an important condition: the need to cleanse all personal relationships in order to clear divine relationships. It is sometimes proposed that v. 25 is misplaced (as in fact v. 26 is: see any recent translation). No textual evidence supports that conclusion, however. Prayer, to be effective, must have a proper foundation. The one who prays must be in harmony with God's will and in fellowship with his brother.

D. Edmond Hiebert has said it well: "Prayer cannot be used in the service of hate." When we pray, whether standing, kneeling, or prostrate, and recall a rupture in brotherhood, we are to forgive. The prayer of faith is limited only by the sovereignty of God, and our sovereign God requires holiness and peace among His children (Heb. 12:14).

The Contest over Authority

Mark 11:27-33

> 27 And they come again to Jerusalem: and as he was walking in the temple, there come to him the chief priests, and the scribes, and the elders,
>
> 28 And say unto him, By what authority doest thou these things? and who gave thee this authority to do these things?
>
> 29 And Jesus answered and said unto them, I will also ask of you one question, and answer me, and I will tell you by what authority I do these things.
>
> 30 The baptism of John, was it from heaven, or of men? answer me.
>
> 31 And they reasoned with themselves, saying, If we shall say, From heaven; he will say, Why then did ye not believe him?
>
> 32 But if we shall say, Of men; they feared the people: for all men counted John, that he was a prophet indeed.
>
> 33 And they answered and said unto Jesus, We cannot tell. And Jesus answering saith unto them, Neither do I tell you by what authority I do these things.

The conflict between Jesus and the leaders of Judaism was rapidly coming to a head. When He had cast out of the Temple area those who sold and bought and had overturned the tables of the money changers and of those who sold doves (15), Jesus had touched an exposed nerve: money.

The chief priests, the scribes, and the elders (the Sadducees, the Pharisees, and influential laymen), accosted Jesus as He was walking in the Temple (27), perhaps in the porches around the Court of the Gentiles. They were angered by His disruption of their activities, but were also afraid of Him because of His popularity (18). Their attempt to discredit His credentials, however, resulted in the impeachment of their own authority.

1. *The dilemma posed for Jesus.* The foes of Jesus asked the ultimate question: "What authority have you for what you are doing? And who gave you permission to do these things?" (28, Phillips).

a. Jesus had no "official" authority. He was not a member of the Sanhedrin, not even an "ordained" rabbi. But who delegates authority in any field? Surely it is God, the source of all truth and reality, who delegates authority. The truest music, art, writing, science, philosophy, or whatever, carry intrinsically their own credentials. "We cannot do anything against the truth, but only for the truth" (2 Cor. 13:8, NIV).

b. The authority of Jesus was intrinsic to His person and was self-authenticating. But how would He answer the question? (1) Would He claim divine authority, as the Son of God? A charge of blasphemy would then follow, as indeed it did later in the week. (2) Would He claim messianic authority, as the Son of David? A charge of treason, as a revolutionary, would then follow, as by implication it did later in the week. The enemies of Jesus believed they had impaled Him on the horns of a dilemma.

2. *The dilemma posed by Jesus.* It was common practice, especially in debate, to counter an insincere question with another question. Jesus had done this before (cf. 10:2-3).

a. The dilemma required confession. To their insincere question, "Jesus replied, 'I'll tell you if you answer one question! What about John the Baptist? Was he sent by God, or not? Answer me!'" (29-30, TLB). Suddenly, the tables were turned—the judge and the prosecutor had become the defendant! The leaders of Judaism were confronted by the Word of God:

> It cuts more keenly than any two-edged sword, piercing as far as the place where life and spirit, joints and marrow, divide. It sifts the purposes and thoughts of the heart. There is nothing in creation that can hide from him; everything lies naked and exposed to the eyes of the One with whom we have to reckon (Heb. 4:12-14, NEB).

The cause of Jesus and the cause of John were one. The rejection of John required the rejection of Jesus. But the people knew both were Prophets of God. The antagonists were not willing to confess. Their judgment was swift: said Jesus, *Neither do I tell you by what authority I do these things* (33).

b. What happens when one refuses to recognize the authority of truth? It would seem that a refusal to acknowledge the authority of truth would lead to total frustration. The leaders of Judaism had rejected John the Baptist and now were rejecting Jesus. If they were blind to the one, they would be blind to the other as well. Obedience is the organ of religious knowledge (F. W. Robertson). As Jesus said: "'If any of you really determines to do God's will, then you will certainly know whether my teaching is from God or is merely my own'" (John 7:17, TLB).

It is frightening to realize that it was the religious leaders of Israel who were guilty of rejecting the will of God. The parable of the rebellious tenants (12:1-12) compels that conclusion. How do we keep open to the authority of truth while we maintain loyalty and commitment to a cause? Only by obedience to *Jesus as Lord.*

MARK 12

Divine Judgment: A Serious Contemporary Blind Spot
Mark 12:1-12

> 1 And he began to speak unto them by parables. A certain man planted a vineyard, and set an hedge about it, and digged a place for the winefat, and built a tower, and let it out to husbandmen, and went into a far country.
> 2 And at the season he sent to the husbandmen a servant, that he might receive from the husbandmen of the fruit of the vineyard.
> 3 And they caught him, and beat him, and sent him away empty.
> 4 And again he sent unto them another servant; and at him they cast stones, and wounded him in the head, and sent him away shamefully handled.
> 5 And again he sent another; and him they killed, and many others; beating some, and killing some.
> 6 Having yet therefore one son, his wellbeloved, he sent him also last unto them, saying, They will reverence my son.
> 7 But those husbandmen said among themselves, This is the heir; come, let us kill him, and the inheritance shall be ours.
> 8 And they took him, and killed him, and cast him out of the vineyard.
> 9 What shall therefore the lord of the vineyard do? he will come and destroy the husbandmen, and will give the vineyard unto others.
> 10 And have ye not read this scripture; The stone which the builders rejected is become the head of the corner:
> 11 This was the Lord's doing, and it is marvelous in our eyes?
> 12 And they sought to lay hold on him, but feared the people: for they knew that he had spoken the parable against them: and they left him, and went their way.

The enemies of Jesus are closing in on Him. They have challenged His authority to cleanse the Temple (11:28). They will shortly involve Him in one debate after another, hoping to embarrass and discredit Him (13-37). They are ready to seize and destroy Him. Within a few hours, the leaders of Israel will wreak their malice upon the Lord of all!

In the midst of this swirling controversy, Jesus tells a story. We know it as the parable of the wicked husbandmen. Some call the story an allegory. The message is clear and powerful. It is needed today: rejection of the will of God brings disaster and judgment. That is a serious contemporary blind spot.

The parable tells us something about the relation of the Old Testament and the New Testament, about the relation of the history of Israel to the Christian era. It also teaches us a good deal about the nature of God, the mission of His Son, and the tragic spiritual blindness of men.

1. *The unity and continuity of the Old and New Testaments.* The people who gathered around Jesus in the Temple area would have understood many elements in the parable.

a. Many would have called to mind the Song of the Vineyard in Isa. 5:1-7: "Let me sing now for my well-beloved a song of my beloved concerning his vineyard.

My well-beloved had a vineyard on a fertile hill.
And he dug it all around, removed its stones,
And planted it with the choicest vine.
And he built a tower in the middle of it,
And hewed out a wine vat in it;
Then he expected it to produce good grapes,
But it produced only worthless ones" (Isa. 5:1-2, NASB).

The prophet plainly identified the vineyard as "the house of Israel, and the men of Judah" (7, ASV). The judgment promised was devastating: "I will lay it waste" (5, ASV).

b. The people were also familiar with the details of the parable of the rebellious tenants—the absentee landowner, the restless sharecroppers, the frequent conflict over the *fruit of the vineyard* (2), even the practice of murder to secure possession of the land. Large areas of the upper Jordan Valley and parts of Galilee had estates that were the property of someone in another country who maintained his land through agents. Labor-management struggles often ensued. The parable had the ring of truth about it.

c. The flow of the story moves from the prophets of the Old Testament, who were wounded and shamefully handled, to Jesus, who was the son and heir (4, 7): one owner, many servants, a Son.

Christians sometimes make the mistake of separating the New Testament from the Old. The unity of the parable before us makes it clear that the Bible is one book, and that the common theme of redemption ties the two Testaments together.

2. *The nature of God.* Behind and hovering over the action of the parable is the God and Father of our Lord Jesus Christ.

a. It was He who committed to Israel a trust. It was He who "'planted a vineyard, and put a wall around it, and dug a vat under the wine press, and built a tower'" (1, NASB). It was to Israel that God committed His Word. "Ye shall be unto me a kingdom of priests, and an holy nation" (Exod. 19:6). Israel was to be "as a light to the nations" (Isa. 42:6, NASB).

b. It was He who sent His servants the prophets (Jer. 7:25) "'to receive some of the produce of the vineyard from the vine-growers'" (2, NASB). As an absentee landowner would send an agent to his sharecroppers to receive some return on his investment, so the Lord sent His representatives to Israel. Jeremiah described the process with pathos: "Since the day that your fathers came forth out of the land of Egypt unto this day I have even sent unto you all my servants the prophets, daily rising up early and sending them" (Jer. 7:25).

c. It was He who at long last sent His Son, the Beloved. The character of the father in the parable shines through: he was patient, longsuffering, hopeful. Likewise also the Heavenly Father: "'He had one more to send, a beloved son; he sent him last of all to them saying, "They will respect my son"'" (6, NASB).

It is important to remember that the *mission* of the Son and the *motive* of the Father are not in conflict. The atonement for the sins of mankind first of all sprang out of the love as well as the holiness of the Father (John 3:16).

3. *The mission of His Son.* Several parallels between the son in the parable and Jesus are clear.

a. He represented the highest hopes of the father. As noted above, the patient persistence of the father is unparalleled, so also his hopefulness: *They will reverence my son* (6). Can we say less of the Heavenly Father? "When the fulness of the time was come, God sent forth his Son, made of a woman, made under the law" (Gal. 4:4). Moreover, this was while "we were yet without strength," while "we were enemies" (Rom. 5:6, 10). Evidently the Father has never given up hope on mankind.

b. He represented the fullest disclosure of the father's will. If any of the rebellious tenants had questioned what the intention of the owner was, the coming of the *one son, his wellbeloved* (6) would have erased that question. *The lord of the vineyard* (9) intended to require of the husbandmen an accounting of their stewardship. He intended to hold them responsible for his share of the fruit.

When the Heavenly Father sent His Son into the world, He disclosed His will, His nature and character on the highest possible level. As Jesus said to Philip: "He that hath seen me hath seen the Father; and how sayest thou then, Shew us the Father?" (John 14:9). This is why all supplemental "revelations" are both unnecessary and spurious. What is higher than highest? The apostle John has established this truth for all time to come: "No man hath seen God at any time; the only begotten Son, which is in the bosom of the Father, he hath declared him" (John 1:18); or as the NIV translates it, "has made him known."

4. *The stubborn blindness of men.* The language seems severe and the judgment which befell the tenants harsh, but so were the realities of the parable.

a. It was common knowledge that the prophets of Israel had not been popular with the ruling authorities. Amos came to Bethel with a word of judgment, but the high priest, Amaziah, rejected him: "the land is unable to endure all his words" (Amos 7:10, NASB). It was so also with other prophets, such as Jeremiah, who in the end was spirited away to Egypt.

b. The murder of the son and heir was a device to secure the property "legally." The wicked tenants may have presumed that the coming of the son alone meant his father was dead. When property was known to be "owner-less," it could be seized and claimed at will. The judgment which befell those wicked tenants was fierce: *The lord of the vineyard . . . will come and destroy the husbandmen, and will give the vineyard unto others* (9).

c. The chief priests, the scribes, and the elders (11:27) understood the point of the parable and were stung by it. *They sought to lay hold* on Jesus, *for they knew that he had spoken the parable against them* (12). Before the week was out, they had seized the Son, *killed him, and cast him out of the vineyard* (8).

d. When will we learn that the wrath of God is real (Rom. 1:18), that "sloppy agape" is unbiblical? When will sinful men learn that they are losers? "'"The stone which the builders rejected, this became the chief corner stone"'" (10, NASB; see Ps. 118:22).

Before the century was over, the Temple lay in ruins, the city of Jerusalem was destroyed, Israel ceased to exist as a nation, and the Kingdom had passed to the Gentiles. The vineyard had, in fact, been given unto others!

Hostile Groups with a Common Cause

Mark 12:13-17

> 13 And they send unto him certain of the Pharisees and of the Herodians, to catch him in his words.
> 14 And when they were come, they say unto him, Master, we know that thou art true, and carest for no man: for thou regardest not the person of men, but teachest the way of God in truth: Is it lawful to give tribute to Caesar, or not?
> 15 Shall we give, or shall we not give? But he, knowing their hypocrisy, said unto them, Why tempt ye me? bring me a penny, that I may see it.
> 16 And they brought it. And he saith unto them, Whose is this image and superscription? And they said unto him, Caesar's.
> 17 And Jesus answering said unto them, Render to Caesar the things that are Caesar's, and to God the things that are God's. And they marvelled at him.

The authorities, who were looking for a way to kill Jesus, now tried another approach. They sent representatives of two otherwise hostile groups to catch or trap (the word suggests fishing or hunting) Him in His words (13).

Earlier in his account, Mark recorded the collusion between the Pharisees and the Herodians (3:6). The Pharisees were defenders of the Jewish traditions and looked with disdain upon the Herodians for their support of the worldly-minded family of Herod. A common foe gave them a common cause—the destruction of Jesus.

1. *An amazing tribute from malicious enemies.* However insincere it may have been, their tribute was remarkably accurate.

a. Their tribute was true. They addressed Him as *Teacher* and as a "man of integrity" (14, NIV). Jesus was a teacher, the greatest who ever lived. He devoted much of His time to "teaching in their synagogues" (Matt. 4:23) and elsewhere. He thought of himself as a teacher (14:49). He did indeed teach *the way of God in truth* (14). From Him we learn the divine standards of faith and conduct, of doctrine and ethics.

Jesus was a man of integrity. The words of flattery were factually accurate: "You are truthful, and defer to no one; for You are not partial to any" (14, NASB). Jesus seemed never to be motivated by expediency, always by principle.

b. Their trap was vicious. The question of the Pharisees and the Herodians was loaded with trickery: "Is it right to pay taxes to Caesar or not?" (14, NIV).

Since the time of Herod's son, Archelaus, who was deposed in A.D. 6, the Roman governors had collected a poll tax from every adult male in Judea. The tax was hated as a symbol of Jewish submission to a foreign power. It was more than "taxation without representation." Judas of Galilee, the revolutionary alluded to in Acts 5:37, reportedly equated such taxation with slavery.

The enemies sought to discredit Jesus with the people (if He supported the tax) or to imperil Him with Rome (if He renounced it).

2. *An amazing reply from the Man of Nazareth.* Jesus responded to the hypocrisy of His enemies with several questions and an order: "'Why are you trying to trap me?'" (15, NIV). He then called for one of the coins used in payment of the tax. "'Whose portrait is this? And whose inscription?'" (16, NIV).

a. The coin offers a clue to the reply. The *denarius,* translated "penny" (15) in the KJV, was worth about 20 cents and represented a day's wage. Hendriksen offers this helpful description of the coin: "A denarius from the reign of the then ruling emperor Tiberius pictures on its *obverse side* the head of that ruler. On the *reverse side* he is shown seated on a throne. He is wearing a diadem and is clothed as a high priest."

The following is Hendriksen's translation of the abbreviated inscription:

Obverse side
TIBERIUS CAESAR AUGUSTUS
SON OF THE DIVINE AUGUSTUS

Reverse side
HIGHEST PRIEST

Caesar clearly did not recognize that his realm was subservient to the Kingdom of God.

b. The reply of Jesus evoked amazement. The reply was amazing because it released their trap, and because it was both clear and perplexing. In substance, Jesus said, "The coin you carry represents a government from which you receive benefits—some degree of order, protection, means of travel. Give that government its due." However, the deliberately ambiguous statement implied that the power of Caesar was a delegated one. As Jesus said to Pilate: "'You would have no power over me unless it had been given you from above'" (John 19:11, RSV).

The reply of Jesus still causes us to marvel: "'Give to Caesar what is Caesar's and to God what is God's'" (17, NIV). Who could find fault?

Light on Resurrection Life

Mark 12:18-27

> 18 Then come unto him the Sadducees, which say there is no resurrection; and they asked him, saying,
> 19 Master, Moses wrote unto us, If a man's brother die, and leave his wife behind him, and leave no children, that his brother should take his wife, and raise up seed unto his brother.
> 20 Now there were seven brethren: and the first took a wife, and dying left no seed.
> 21 And the second took her, and died, neither left he any seed: and the third likewise.
> 22 And the seven had her, and left no seed: last of all the woman died also.
> 23 In the resurrection therefore, when they shall rise, whose wife shall she be of them? for the seven had her to wife.
> 24 And Jesus answering said unto them, Do ye not therefore err, because ye know not the scriptures, neither the power of God?
> 25 For when they shall rise from the dead, they neither marry, nor are given in marriage; but are as the angels which are in heaven.
> 26 And as touching the dead, that they rise: have ye not read in the book of Moses, how in the bush God spake unto him, saying, I am the God of Abraham, and the God of Isaac, and the God of Jacob?
> 27 He is not the God of the dead, but the God of the living: ye therefore do greatly err.

The harrassment of Jesus by His critics increased. One Jewish party after another cornered Jesus in the Temple area, plied Him with catch questions, posed dilemmas and problems of biblical interpretation—all in order to embarrass and humiliate the Prophet of Nazareth.

The Sadducees now took their turn. Scribes were the official teachers and interpreters of the Law. Some were Pharisees, others were Sadducees. Among the powerful ideas to emerge from this passage is the truth that religious leaders can be in error. In this case, they were mistaken in their teaching about the resurrection. They understood neither *the scriptures* nor *the power of God* (24). Jesus linked the two in order to shed light on what the resurrection life will be like.

1. *The scepticism of the Sadducees.* Reliable information about this group is limited. Apparently the Sadducees were the priestly party with considerable control over the Temple and its revenue.

a. They were reactionary in their views. They were rationalistic conservatives. As the truth of God unfolded, they resisted the divine disclosure. For example, their doctrinal stance was in the Pentateuch alone, where, in their view, teaching on the resurrection did not occur. Israel as a whole had come to accept as authoritative not only the Law, but also the Prophets, and the Writings (Luke 24:44).

b. They rejected the Old Testament doctrine of the resurrection. In this position they were in conflict with the Pharisees. Paul, who was himself once a Pharisee, later turned this tension to his own advantage. "But when Paul perceived that one part were Sadducees and the other Pharisees, he cried out in the council, 'Brethren, I am a Pharisee, a son of Pharisees; with respect to the hope and the resurrection of the dead I am on trial'" (Acts 23:6, RSV). In the dissension which followed, Paul escaped further investigation by the council. It follows that if the Sadducees disputed the teaching of their Hebrew colleagues, they would have quarreled even more with Jesus.

2. *The key to understanding the Scriptures.* The story of the woman who had seven husbands, all of whom died childless, was typical of scribal debate and discussion. By

such means debaters expected to demolish an opponent and his argument. The Sadducees had never encountered an opponent like Jesus.

a. One must have a knowledge of the Scriptures. As noted above, the Sadducees accepted only the Pentateuch (the first five books of the Old Testament) as authoritative. It is significant that Jesus quoted from the second book of the Pentateuch and showed they did not know their own Scriptures: "'Now about the dead rising—have you not read in the book of Moses, in the account of the bush, how God said to him, "I am the God of Abraham, the God of Isaac, and the God of Jacob"? He is not the God of the dead, but of the living. You are badly mistaken!'" (24-27, NIV; cf. Exod. 3:6).

The God of the Patriarchs would keep His covenant as Helper, Redeemer, Savior, and would not terminate that covenant at the grave. It would be meaningless to say that He is *the God of the dead* (27).

b. One must also have a knowledge of the power of God. It is insufficient to have a knowledge of the facts of Scripture. Spiritual insight is essential. The work of scholarship is important. A grasp of the historical background and use of the original languages, for example, are valuable. However, without spiritual understanding, all of that evidence of learning will become fruitless, even hurtful, "for the letter kills, but the Spirit gives life" (2 Cor. 3:6, NASB). "The written Word rightly related to the living Word gives us our only sure hope for the preservation of pure religion" (BBC).

From the observation that Abraham, Isaac, and Jacob are *living* (27), Jesus drew the doctrine of the resurrection. It was as if God had said to Moses, "As I have been with your father, so also I will be with you in salvation, deliverance, and redemption." "It is in fidelity to His covenant that God will resurrect the dead" (William L. Lane).

H. Orton Wiley used to say that our faith is not only in the goodness of God but also in His power. God has power to create new orders of being. We have it on the infallible authority of His Son that the doctrine of the resurrection is true.

3. *"When the veil is lifted at last."* A divine parsimony limits what we can know about life beyond the resurrection. Some conclusions are certain, however.

 a. God will raise all men from the dead. This is a teaching of the Old Testament as well as of the New. "And many of them that sleep in the dust of the earth shall awake, some to everlasting life, and some to shame and everlasting contempt" (Dan. 12:2; cf. John 5:28-29). Anyone who denies these truths, in the words of Jesus, is badly mistaken!

 b. God will change the form and quality of our being. A continuity will remain. It is *we* who shall be changed, but we shall be *changed.* Paul wrote the Corinthians: "Behold, I shew you a mystery; we shall not all sleep, but we shall all be changed" (1 Cor. 15:51).

 The detail which Jesus did give, as to that change, was just enough to rebuke the Sadducees and to correct their error: "When people rise from the dead they neither marry nor are they given in marriage; they live like the angels in Heaven" (25, Phillips).

 What other changes will come? We cannot know now, "but we know that, when he shall appear, we shall be like him" (1 John 3:2).

The Heart of Biblical Religion

Mark 12:28-34

> 28 And one of the scribes came, and having heard them reasoning together, and perceiving that he had answered them well, asked him, Which is the first commandment of all?
> 29 And Jesus answered him, The first of all the commandments is, Hear, O Israel; The Lord our God is one Lord:
> 30 And thou shalt love the Lord thy God with all thy heart, and with all thy soul, and with all thy mind, and with all thy strength: this is the first commandment.
> 31 And the second is like, namely this, Thou shalt love thy neighbour as thyself. There is none other commandment greater than these.
> 32 And the scribe said unto him, Well, Master, thou hast said the truth: for there is one God; and there is none other but he:

33 And to love him with all the heart and with all the understanding, and with all the soul, and with all the strength, and to love his neighbour as himself, is more than all whole burnt offerings and sacrifices.
34 And when Jesus saw that he answered discreetly, he said unto him, Thou art not far from the kingdom of God. And no man after that durst ask him any question.

For a few fleeting moments, the atmosphere in the Temple area changed markedly. In the passing parade of hostile critics—priests, scribes, elders, Pharisees, Sadducees, and Herodians—one lone scribe broke through the barriers of blind prejudice and rage to see Jesus in a true light.

That nameless scribe articulated for all time the heart and essence of biblical religion. Jesus confirmed the truth of his statement and gave us the comforting, liberating word that His yoke is easy and His burden is light (Matt. 11:30).

1. *At last—a friendly question!* It is rewarding to ponder the question and comment of this sincere scribe. What qualities did he possess? He possessed an *open mind*. The scribe had come upon the crowd surrounding Jesus and had listened for a time to their questioning. He was favorably impressed, for he recognized that Jesus had answered them well. Unlike many, this man had not prejudged Jesus and His teaching.

He also possessed an *inquiring mind*. The question he had asked was a common one: "'What commandment is the foremost of all?'" (28, NASB). It was appropriate to ask such a question, for the Jews reputedly had some 613 laws and commandments to observe—365 negative and 248 positive. Eager and hungry minds sought some principle of classification in order to cope with such a maze of duties. Were some heavier than others? (cf. Matt. 23:23).

2. *The final, ultimate word.* Sensing the scribe's sincerity, Jesus gave him a straightforward answer—no need to grapple with duplicity and subterfuge.

a. The foremost commandment. In reply, Jesus quoted from the *Shema* (see Deut. 6:4-9), a precious creed, recited twice daily by all pious Jews. It describes the sovereignty of God and the plain, unadorned duty of man: "Hear, O Israel: the Lord your God is the only Lord; love the Lord your God with all your heart, with all your soul, with all your mind, and with all your strength" (29-30, NEB).

b. The second commandment in line. Jesus expanded on the reply and included more than the scribe requested: " 'The second is this: "Love your neighbour as yourself" ' " (31, NEB). So far as is known, Jesus was the first to link these two great commandments together (Deut. 6:4-5; Lev. 19:18). In so doing, He summarized the two tables of the Ten Commandments: duties to God (Exod. 20:1-11) and duties to man (Exod. 20:12-17).

c. The meaning of both. Now came an earthshaking, revolutionary word—*There is none other commandment greater than these* (31). Matthew's record of this comment enriches our understanding of it: "On these two commandments hang all the law and the prophets" (Matt. 22:40). Kenneth Taylor's paraphrase of that verse draws out the meaning: "All the other commandments and all the demands of the prophets stem from these two laws and are fulfilled if you obey them. Keep only these and you will find that you are obeying all the others" (Matt. 22:40, TLB).

3. *A warm response to a wise reply.* The response of the scribe to the reply of Jesus reveals even more his sincerity and integrity. The scribe recognized the truth of Jesus' words. Truth carries a self-authenticating quality about it. This scribe echoed the words of another: " 'Teacher, You have spoken well' " (Luke 20:39, NASB).

The scribe understood the implication of Jesus' words. He could see at once that Jesus had distilled from the detail of the Old Testament and other Hebrew law the essence of biblical religion: "To love Him with all the heart . . . and to love one's neighbor as himself, is much more than all burnt offerings and sacrifices" (33, NASB).

We are bound only by the holy "love of God flooding through our hearts by the Holy Spirit given to us" (Rom. 5:5, Phillips). But love is stronger than law, because the constraints move from the external to the internal, from *com*pulsion to *im*pulsion. What a liberating word is that! In one stroke Jesus cut away all the ecclesiastical rules and restraints which bound men in servitude. Observance of all lesser duties springs not from law but from love.

Jesus must have loved that scribe. "And when Jesus saw that he had answered intelligently, He said to him, 'You are not far from the kingdom of God'" (34, NASB). Did he one day enter in? (cf. Acts 6:7).

4. *Ominous silence.* For a short while the heavenly light of mutual understanding, love, and intelligent goodwill penetrated one part of the Temple area. The clouds and gloom soon returned. The enemies of Jesus had been silenced. "No one dared ask Him any more questions" (34, NIV). Their malice remained. In just a matter of hours it erupted in violence and death.

The Messiah: David's Son or David's Lord?

Mark 12:35-40

> 35 And Jesus answered and said, while he taught in the temple, How say the scribes that Christ is the son of David?
> 36 For David himself said by the Holy Ghost, The Lord said to my Lord, Sit thou on my right hand, till I make thine enemies thy footstool.
> 37 David therefore himself calleth him Lord; and whence is he then his son? And the common people heard him gladly.
> 38 And he said unto them in his doctrine, Beware of the scribes, which love to go in long clothing, and love salutations in the market-places,
> 39 And the chief seats in the synagogues, and the uppermost rooms at feasts:
> 40 Which devour widows' houses, and for a pretence make long prayers: these shall receive greater damnation.

Once more, Jesus took the initiative against His be-leaguered enemies (cf. 11:30). What was His motive? Was He teasing or tantalizing them? Was He seeking to correct misconceptions concerning the Messiah? Was He covertly leading the people to see His own Messiahship?

Whatever His purpose may have been, Jesus proposed a riddle and pronounced a judgment. The conundrum puzzled and delighted the *common people* (37). The promise of judgment seemed only to antagonize the scribes further.

1. *Jesus proposes a riddle.* It is fascinating to see how often, and with what variety, Jesus used questions in His teaching. Questions penetrate the mind and prod the thought processes.

   a. The standard teaching of the scribes. The Jews loved their Scriptures and apparently enjoyed considering certain popular messianic passages, including the psalm which Jesus quoted (36). The scribes regularly taught that the Messiah would be a Son of David. This teaching implied that the Messiah would be another political leader like David, that he would miraculously drive out the invader and bring in a new golden age.

   The question Jesus raised challenged that interpretation: "'How is it that the teachers of the law say that the Christ is the son of David?'" (35, NIV).

   b. The surprising prophecy of David. The riddle followed at once: If David, under the inspiration of the Holy Spirit, addressed the Messiah as Lord, how could he be David's son? (36-37; see Ps. 110:1). This overturned the teaching of the scribes, to their distress, but to the pleasure of the people. "The large crowd listened to him with delight" (37, NIV).

   One may inquire why Jesus was asking questions about the Christ, i.e., the Messiah. All along He had guarded the "messianic secret" with care. Had He now begun to release some hints for the disclosure of that secret? It seems so. He is now saying that the Messiah's "greatness is independent of David's prestige and actually prior to David" (IOC). The Messiahship of Jesus is of a different sort: "My kingdom is not of this world: if my kingdom were of this world, then would my servants fight" (John 18:36).

2. *Jesus pronounces a judgment.* A dominant note in the preaching and teaching of Jesus was the threat of divine judgment. That note is often missing in the contemporary proclamation of the gospel. Why is that so? It is important to "accentuate the positive." It is easy to become censorious, judgmental, self-righteous. It is also folly to ignore the plain warning that "God is not mocked: for whatsoever a man soweth, that shall he also reap" (Gal. 6:7), that the God of love is also "a consuming fire" (Heb. 12:29).

a. Beware: religious pretense. The scribes, who were the teachers of the law and, consequently, prominent leaders in Judaism, were excessively preoccupied with self-recognition. Jesus listed several aspects of this self-centeredness: "'They like to walk around in flowing robes and be greeted in the marketplaces, and have the most important seats in the synagogues and the places of honor at banquets'" (38-39, NIV). More devastating was Jesus' condemnation of their religious pretense, for they tried to cloak their avarice with pious forms—they seized widows' houses and made long prayers (40).

b. Beware: severe punishment. Judgment is certain to fall on religious leaders who are impostors. The scribes were vain, greedy, unscrupulous, vicious, and yet paraded under flowing robes of religiosity. "'Such men will be punished most severely'" (40, NIV). That was the last word of Jesus on the scribes!

How should we who are religious leaders relate to these warnings? We should not be defensive. The ignorant and the prejudiced will use them to club all religious leaders, the sincere with the insincere.

We should remember that all of us are under divine judgment, that death comes even for the bishop! We should emulate the example of Paul: "So whether you eat or drink or whatever you do, do it all for the glory of God. Do not cause anyone to stumble, whether Jews, Greeks or the church of God—even as I try to please everybody in every way" (1 Cor. 10:31-33, NIV).

Stewardship Under Scrutiny

Mark 12:41-44

> 41 And Jesus sat over against the treasury, and beheld how the people cast money into the treasury: and many that were rich cast in much.
> 42 And there came a certain poor widow, and she threw in two mites, which make a farthing.
> 43 And he called unto him his disciples, and saith unto them, Verily I say unto you, That this poor widow hath cast more in, than all they which have cast into the treasury:
> 44 For all they did cast in of their abundance; but she of her want did cast in all that she had, even all her living.

Jesus and the Twelve had left the Temple area known as the Court of the Gentiles and had gone into that section of the Temple proper known as the Court of Women. This outer court contained a room designated as the treasury (John 8:20). Thirteen trumpet-shaped receptacles were available for "freewill offerings," the words inscribed on some of the receptacles.

It was possible to sit nearby and watch the people as they gave their money. Quite possibly the donors announced the amount and purpose of their gifts.

1. *The Lord sees our gift.* What is striking is that *Jesus beheld how the people cast money into the treasury* (41). He saw the "much" of the rich and offered no criticism. The rich had plenty and gave much. This was commendable. But He also saw the "all" of the widow. Three words stress her poverty: *one widow, poor.* She came alone; she had lost her companion; she had the meagerest of resources.

The supernatural insight of Jesus is in evidence here. The woman probably never knew what happened, but the Lord of all saw her in her loneliness and her poverty. But she was *not* alone, and she was *not* poor.

2. *The Lord understands our motivation.* Every onlooker may have known the amount and purpose of each gift. Not even one onlooker, however, could have known the motivation of any donor. The rich may well have had laudable

motives. Nothing is said to the contrary. It is perhaps more than coincidental, however, that the previous section (35-40) carries a warning against the avarice of the scribes *which devour widows' houses* (40).

This one poor widow touched the heart of Jesus. It is clear from the action and comment of Jesus that He was deeply impressed. He made special mention of her gift. On other noteworthy occasions, Jesus "called his disciples to him" (43, RSV; cf. 6:7; 10:42), like a coach calling his team to the bench. The Twelve went into a "huddle" with their Master.

He extolled her sacrificial love. One can imagine that Jesus identified the woman as she went away unnoticed in the crowd. She could not have known that in the records of heaven her gift was larger than all the contributions of the "many rich people" with their "large sums" (41, RSV). Why? Because it was more costly.

Evidently the Lord has an interest in how much we have left after we have given. The widow had "put in everything she had, her whole living" (44, RSV). Jesus was about to give His all. He looked for disciples who would follow His example.

MARK 13

The End of the Age

Mark 13:1-37

> 1 And as he went out of the temple, one of his disciples saith unto him, Master, see what manner of stones and what buildings are here!
> 2 And Jesus answering said unto him, Seest thou these great buildings? there shall not be left one stone upon another, that shall not be thrown down.
> 3 And as he sat upon the mount of Olives over against the temple, Peter and James and John and Andrew asked him privately,
> 4 Tell us, when shall these things be? and what shall be the sign when all these things shall be fulfilled?
> 5 And Jesus answering them began to say, Take heed lest any man deceive you:
> 6 For many shall come in my name, saying, I am Christ; and shall deceive many.

7 And when ye shall hear of wars and rumours of wars, be ye not troubled: for such things must needs be; but the end shall not be yet.

8 For nation shall rise against nation, and kingdom against kingdom: and there shall be earthquakes in divers places, and there shall be famines and troubles: these are the beginnings of sorrows.

9 But take heed to yourselves: for they shall deliver you up to councils; and in the synagogues ye shall be beaten: and ye shall be brought before rulers and kings for my sake, for a testimony against them.

10 And the gospel must first be published among all nations.

11 But when they shall lead you, and deliver you up, take no thought beforehand what ye shall speak, neither do ye premeditate: but whatsoever shall be given you in that hour, that speak ye: for it is not ye that speak, but the Holy Ghost.

12 Now the brother shall betray the brother to death, and the father the son; and children shall rise up against their parents, and shall cause them to be put to death.

13 And ye shall be hated of all men for my name's sake: but he that shall endure unto the end, the same shall be saved.

14 But when ye shall see the abomination of desolation, spoken of by Daniel the prophet, standing where it ought not, (let him that readeth understand,) then let them that be in Judaea flee to the mountains:

15 And let him that is on the housetop not go down into the house, neither enter therein, to take any thing out of his house:

16 And let him that is in the field not turn back again for to take up his garment.

17 But woe to them that are with child, and to them that give suck in those days!

18 And pray ye that your flight be not in the winter.

19 For in those days shall be affliction, such as was not from the beginning of the creation which God created unto this time, neither shall be.

20 And except that the Lord had shortened those days, no flesh should be saved: but for the elect's sake, whom he hath chosen, he hath shortened the days.

21 And then if any man shall say to you, Lo, here is Christ; or lo, he is there; believe him not:

22 For false Christs and false prophets shall rise, and shall shew signs and wonders, to seduce, if it were possible, even the elect.

23 But take ye heed: behold, I have foretold you all things.

24 But in those days, after that tribulation, the sun shall be darkened, and the moon shall not give her light,

25 And the stars of heaven shall fall, and the powers that are in heaven shall be shaken.

26 And then shall they see the Son of man coming in the clouds with great power and glory.

27 And then shall he send his angels, and shall gather together his elect from the four winds, from the uttermost part of the earth to the uttermost part of heaven.

28 Now learn a parable of the fig tree; When her branch is yet tender, and putteth forth leaves, ye know that summer is near:

29 So ye in like manner, when ye shall see these things come to pass, know that it is nigh, even at the doors.

30 Verily I say unto you, that this generation shall not pass, till all these things be done.

31 Heaven and earth shall pass away: but my words shall not pass away.
32 But of that day and that hour knoweth no man, no, not the angels which are in heaven, neither the Son, but the Father.
33 Take ye heed, watch and pray: for ye know not when the time is.
34 For the Son of man is as a man taking a far journey, who left his house, and gave authority to his servants, and to every man his work, and commanded the porter to watch.
35 Watch ye therefore: for ye know not when the master of the house cometh, at even, or at midnight, or at the cockcrowing, or in the morning:
36 Lest coming suddenly he find you sleeping.
37 And what I say unto you I say unto all, Watch.

This discourse of Jesus, the longest in Mark, is a farewell address, in line with the parting words of other biblical leaders, such as Moses, Joshua, and Samuel (see Deuteronomy 31—32; Joshua 23—24; 1 Samuel 12, respectively). It marks the close of Jesus' public ministry and suffuses the impending events, however darksome, with light and glory. The final word with Jesus, the Christ, the Son of God (1:1), is one of triumph and victory, not of defeat and gloom.

Several factors should be kept in mind. (1) The chief purpose of this discourse is not to disclose mystery but to promote faithfulness and watchfulness in a time of upheaval and tumult. Vigilance, not calculation, is the aim of the Lord's message (William L. Lane). (2) Two themes appear alternately: the siege and fall of Jerusalem (A.D. 66-70); the Parousia (Second Coming) and final judgment. The first event was near; the second event lies in the future even yet. *No man, no, not the angels . . . neither the Son* (32) knows when *the Son of man* will return *in the clouds with great power and glory* (26).

It will, therefore, greatly help in the interpretation of this passage, to remember, (1) that Jesus predicted the fall of Jerusalem and the destruction of the Temple, (2) that He described conditions in the Church Age, which extends from the Resurrection to the Parousia, (3) that He made a solemn promise to return again, and (4) that the words of command and comfort, exhortation and consolation, interweave throughout the discourse.

1. *The fall of Jerusalem* (1-4). The immediate provocation for the discourse of Jesus on the end of the age was a comment and question by His disciples. As they left the Temple area, possibly on Tuesday evening, they looked back at the breathtaking sight of the Temple.

a. Herod's Temple, with its complex of ornate supporting structures, evoked admiration and awe even from the unfriendly. The rabbis, who had little respect for Herod, believed the city and the Temple were peerless. Later the Jewish historian, Josephus, and the Roman historian, Tacitus, alike described the Temple with its white marble and gold as an architectural wonder. Some of the stones were reported to be 40 feet long, 12 feet high, and 18 feet wide. The comment of the disciples was appropriate: "'Look, Teacher! What massive stones! What magnificent buildings!'" (1, NIV).

b. As the disciples looked with admiration on the beauty of the Temple, Jesus saw something else, a generation away. "'Do you see all these great buildings?' replied Jesus. 'Not one stone here will be left upon another; every one will be thrown down'" (2, NIV).

It is unlikely that we can imagine the reaction of the Twelve. It would be as if some responsible person were to predict the destruction of the U.S. Capitol building and Lincoln Memorial in Washington, D.C., or the Westminster Abbey and Houses of Parliament in London. However, 40 years later, when the Romans had broken the resistance of Jerusalem and were decimating the city, the legions of Titus set flame to the Temple and fulfilled to the last detail the awful prophecy of Jesus. Not one stone was left upon another, as archaeological evidence has shown.

Quite naturally, the startled disciples wanted to know when all these cataclysmic events would happen. "Tell us, when will this be, and what will be the sign when these things are all to be accomplished?" (4, RSV).

2. *The Church Age: "future shock"* (5-23). It is perhaps

surprising that Jesus did in fact answer the questions of the Twelve. He concludes this section with the words: "I have told you all these things beforehand" (23, RSV). In vv. 5-13, Jesus describes conditions in the Church Age generally. In vv. 14-23 He speaks more particularly of the generation just preceding the fall of Jerusalem (A.D. 70). Many details are imprecise, and interpretations vary. As a broad description this analysis seems valid and useful.

a. The role of the Church: redemptive suffering. It is helpful, even heartening, to note that Jesus described the period of the Church Age as one of fierce testing. Human existence is fraught with suffering and sorrow. Believers are not exempt. However, to be forewarned is to be fore-armed.

Jesus promised that His followers would be harassed by a variety of trials. Bogus messiahs will be successful in their work of deception (6). International turbulence and conflict will be alarming (7-8). Disturbances in nature (earthquakes) and in society (famine) will not be uncommon (8).

Moreover, disciples will experience suffering as a result of their discipleship. Persecution will be severe: trials, floggings, oppression. As the Jewish state fell away, these distresses moved from Hebrew hands to hostile Gentile authorities (9-11). Family treachery, betrayal of the worst sort, will sever the closest human ties (12).

The summary word of Jesus may be the harshest: "All men will hate you because of me" (13, NIV).

No period since Jesus spoke those words has been exempt from this category of woes. It is possible that our time has seen an intensification of every item. To cite a single fact: the free world has shrunk sharply in this century, and with that reduction in the number of free peoples has come a restriction on gospel work. Our period is indeed laden with *shock.* "Future shock" is present reality.

None of this should be surprising. In the words of James B. Chapman, "To bless is to bleed." Isaiah could foresee that the Messiah would be "a man of sorrows, and acquainted with grief" (Isa. 53:3). Repeatedly, Jesus told the Twelve that "the Son of Man must suffer many things . . . and that He must be killed." When the disciples gasped at the thought, and Peter rebuked Him, Jesus responded, "'Out of my sight, Satan!'" (8:31, 33, NIV). Moreover, He went right on to call His disciples to the same life of redemptive suffering: "'If anyone wants to follow in my footsteps, he must give up all right to himself, take up his cross and follow me'" (8:34, Phillips).

b. The hope of the Church: the divine promise. The last word for the Church, during the long period before the Lord's return, is not one of suffering and shock, but one of divine companionship, encouragement, strengthening, deliverance, and ultimate triumph.

The divine promise appears throughout the Olivet Discourse. The very first word is, "'Do not be alarmed'" (7, NIV). All the distress caused by false religions, by "'wars and rumors of wars . . . [by] earthquakes, famines, and troubles [is but] the beginning of birth pangs'" (7-8, NIV). These do not signal the end but the beginning of a new era.

In the midst of that maelstrom, the Great Commission continues to be the divine imperative: *And the gospel must first be published among all nations* (10). John Wesley was not the first to say, "The world is my parish." It was Jesus who said, "'The field is the world,'" and who commanded His disciples to broadcast "the good seed" (Matt. 13:38) among all nations.

When in the performance of that duty disciples are arrested and brought to trial, they are not to worry beforehand (11, NIV) about their witness. The Holy Spirit will testify through them.

However fierce the test, he who stands firm to the end will be saved (13). As Jesus said in another place, "Lo, I am with you alway, even unto the end of the world" (Matt. 28:20).

The account of the destruction and desecration of

Jerusalem and the Temple in A.D. 70 is another example of the divine promise. As the smoldering hatred of the Jews for Rome began to burst into flame, the Christian community somehow received the word of Jesus spoken a generation before: *Let them that be in Judaea flee to the mountains* (14). Jesus warned that nothing should delay their flight.

The early Christian historian, Eusebius, records that before the gates of Jerusalem were closed, permitting no one to leave, the Christians fled to Pella in Transjordan and escaped the massacre. Once more, as in 168 B.C., "the abomination that causes desolation" (14, NIV), defiled the Temple and its precincts. Both God and man fled.

In 168 B.C. the Syrians had desecrated the Great Altar by sacrificing on it a pig to Zeus and by other unholy acts. About A.D. 67-68 Jewish Zealots elevated a clown to the position of high priest and committed other acts of sacrilege in the Temple area. Luke cites the approach of the Roman armies as the source of desolation (Luke 21:20).

Whatever "the horrible thing" may have been "standing in the Temple" (14, TLB), desolation was the result. The Christian community was gone. The presence of God was gone (cf. Ezek. 7:14-23), but the divine promise had sheltered the Church (20).

3. *"That blessed hope"* (24-27). The Church Age, blending redemptive suffering and divine promise, moves on toward fulfillment—not toward *finis* (the end) but *telos* (completion).

a. He will come in power and glory. The Second Coming of Jesus Christ is a primary doctrine of the Bible. The Old Testament anticipates the Day of the Lord and the New Testament depicts it:

> *For the stars of heaven and their constellations*
> *Will not flash forth their light;*
> *The sun will be dark when it rises,*
> *And the moon will not shed its light.*

> *And the desert creatures shall meet with the wolves,*
> *The hairy goat also shall cry to its king;*
> *Yes, the night-monster shall settle there*
> *And shall find herself a resting place.*
> (Isa. 13:10; 34:14, NASB; see 24-25.)

The Parousia will resolve the contradictions and ambiguities of this present age. It is our loss if we are too sophisticated to appreciate the simple gospel song by C. A. Tindley:

> *By and by, when the morning comes,*
> *When the saints of God are gathered home,*
> *We'll tell the story how we've overcome;*
> *For we'll understand it better by and by.*

b. He will gather His elect in love and compassion. A divine reserve concerning the future events is everywhere present in the Scriptures. The Spirit refuses to satisfy idle curiosity about such matters. One detail is clear from this and other parallel passages: the Lord will gather *His elect from the four winds, from the uttermost part of the earth to the uttermost part of heaven* (27), i.e., from "everywhere."

During His ministry on earth, Jesus was largely unknown or misunderstood. That is true also of the people of God. Their significance as the salt of the earth and the light of the world (Matt. 5:13-14) is generally lost on the unbelieving world. We are "unknown, and yet well known" (2 Cor. 6:9).

The Second Coming will mean the complete vindication of the Son of Man and His elect. At that time, every knee shall bow and every tongue will confess that Jesus Christ is Lord (Phil. 2:10-11). Moreover, the people of God, who have been scattered to the four winds, sometimes in judgment (Jer. 18:17), will find great joy in their identification with the heavenly Son of Man (Dan. 7:13-14). One can only imagine what judgment that will mean for those not gathered.

4. *The time of His coming* (28-37). As noted earlier, the disciples were full of questions: "'When will these things be?'" (4, NASB). Jesus did not leave them without answers: "I have told you all things beforehand" (23, ASV). What did He disclose? What did He withhold?

a. No one knows the time. Although the future is veiled from us, we have biblical precedent for the search to understand it: "As to this salvation, the prophets who prophesied of the grace that would come to you made careful search and inquiry, seeking to know what person or time the Spirit of Christ within them was indicating as He predicted the sufferings of Christ and the glories to follow" (1 Pet. 1:10-11, NASB).

As we have seen, Jesus clearly predicted the fall of Jerusalem and the destruction of the Temple (4, 14-23). But we have also seen that no one can know when the Parousia will occur. What, then, can be the significance of the strong affirmation in v. 30: *Verily I say unto you, that this generation shall not pass, till all these things be done?*

The key may well be found in understanding the force of the phrases "these things" or "all these things" (see 4, 23, 29, 30). William L. Lane argues that these expressions refer to the woes to fall upon Jerusalem within a generation, and not to the Second Coming. The structure of the chapter seems to call for such a conclusion.

If one examines the disciples' question in v. 4 and the responses of Jesus in vv. 23 and 29, he is drawn to the conclusion that "all these things" in v. 30 cannot refer to the events associated with the Second Coming but to the demise of Jerusalem.

The *parable of the fig tree* (28) suggests *proximity* rather than *immediacy.* In a real sense, the rape of Jerusalem was impending. As Jesus said, *it is nigh, even at the doors* (29). In that light, "all these things," did come to pass within the generation of the disciples.

The Church has long puzzled over the unqualified statement that neither the angels in heaven, nor the Son knew the time of the Second Advent, but only the Father. The explanation is to be found in Phil. 2:5-8 and in the doctrine of the *kenosis*, the self-emptying of the Son when He came to earth: "Although He existed in the form of God, [He] did not regard equality with God a thing to be grasped, but emptied Himself, taking the form of a bond-servant . . . being made in the likeness of men" (Phil. 2:6-7, NASB). He accepted the limitations of human nature.

And then, as if to reinforce His word of caution, Jesus added the further insistence: *Ye know not when the time is* (33). Why do the "date-setters" attempt to ferret out information withheld from their Lord? A few days later, after the agony of the Cross and the glory of the Resurrection, just moments before the Ascension, Jesus said plainly to His disciples, "'It is not for you to know times or seasons which the Father has fixed by His own authority'" (Acts 1:7, RSV).

b. Everyone should be ready (33-37). The remainder of the Olivet Discourse is given over to a persistent appeal for the disciples to be alert, watchful, and prepared for that final hour. It grows on one, as he peruses these verses, how insistent Jesus was that His followers should be watchful and wary, almost like an animal of the wild who is sensitive to every sound, sight, and scent. At least six times in this discourse (5, 9, 23, 33, 35, 37) Jesus pressed the warning: *Take heed! Watch!*

The Twelve knew all too well about the presence of absentee landowners in Galilee and elsewhere, who would take journeys into far countries and delegate authority to their servants. These servants understood their stewardship. The master of the house would return suddenly and unexpectedly to ask for an accounting (34-36).

One need not look very far to discover a swarm of broken homes, broken vows, broken hearts. On the fringe of every fellowship are the alienated, the indifferent, the disgruntled. The "root of bitterness" has sprung up, defiling many persons (Heb. 12:15), often the youthful bystander.

However, we may also look for the positive implications in the warning of Jesus. It *is* possible to take heed, to be watchful, and to be ready. One may then look for the Parousia with expectation and joy. "Even so, come, Lord Jesus" (Rev. 22:20).

The Ministry in Passion and Power

Mark 14:1—16:20

MARK 14

Friends and Foes

Mark 14:1-11

1 After two days was the feast of the passover, and of unleavened bread: and the chief priests and the scribes sought how they might take him by craft, and put him to death.

2 But they said, Not on the feast day, lest there be an uproar of the people.

3 And being in Bethany in the house of Simon the leper, as he sat at meat, there came a woman having an alabaster box of ointment of spikenard very precious; and she brake the box, and poured it on his head.

4 And there were some that had indignation within themselves, and said, Why was this waste of the ointment made?

5 For it might have been sold for more than three hundred pence, and have been given to the poor. And they murmured against her.

6 And Jesus said, Let her alone; why trouble ye her? she hath wrought a good work on me.

7 For ye have the poor with you always, and whensoever ye will ye may do them good: but me ye have not always.

8 She hath done what she could: she is come aforehand to anoint my body to the burying.

9 Verily I say unto you, Wheresoever this gospel shall be preached throughout the whole world, this also that she hath done shall be spoken of for a memorial of her.

10 And Judas Iscariot, one of the twelve, went unto the chief priests, to betray him unto them.

11 And when they heard it, they were glad, and promised to give him money. And he sought how he might conveniently betray him.

The "countdown" had begun. It is now only two days until the Passover (1) when Jesus of Nazareth will literally become the Lamb of God (John 1:29), even as thousands of paschal lambs are also slain. The activity of friend and foe seems to quicken. In a sense, they both worked by stealth—the foes to avoid an uproar of the people (2), the friends for more kindly reasons. Jesus avoided unnecessary exposure.

1. *The sly work of foes* (1-2, 10-11). Jesus was always in close association with loving friends, but lurking nearby was a growing gang of malicious foes.

a. There were enemies on the outside. The die was cast. The leaders of Judaism long had mistrusted and hated Jesus. From the early days of His Galilean ministry, they had plotted how they might destroy Him.

Now Jesus had come to Jerusalem and was within their reach. Only the need for a convenient opportunity restrained them. How popular was the Prophet of Nazareth? If they seized Him in some public place, as in the Temple area, would they not risk a riot and the crushing power of Rome? They would have to wait and take Jesus quietly.

b. There was an enemy within. Evidently to their surprise, and certainly to their delight, the chief priests and the scribes discovered they could join forces with someone on the inside—"Judas Iscariot, he that was one of the twelve" (10, ASV).

The restraint of the biblical record is remarkable: no epithets or ugly adjectives, just the incredible words, "one of the twelve." Such betrayal breaks the heart, as when Julius Caesar gasped to see his friend among the assassins, "You also, Brutus my son."

What a sad, tragic figure is Judas, whose name (Judah) literally means, "praise"! He was disappointed and disillusioned. In his view, Jesus had taken the wrong course. How blind are those who forget or deny that "the heart is deceitful above all things, and desperately wicked: who can know it?" (Jer. 17:9).

2. *The beautiful work of friends* (3, 6, 9). Jesus was eating a meal with friends in the nearby village of Bethany. On this occasion, He was in the house of Simon the leper, about whom we are told nothing else. A woman, perhaps Mary (cf. John 12:3), having an alabaster cruse of oint-

ment of very costly nard, came near, broke the cruse, and poured it over His head. She had a treasure in her heart as well as in her hand.

a. It is startling to learn that the expensive perfume was indeed very precious. In the words of the grumblers, "'It could have been sold for more than a year's wages'" (5, NIV). Its purchasing power today would represent thousands of dollars.

Among those who were indignant and who scolded the woman was Judas, the treasurer of the Twelve, who was also a thief (John 12:6). Jesus came to the woman's defense with the sharp rebuke, *Let her alone* (6).

b. It would be instructive to ponder the significance of this lavish display of affection. How did Mary come to possess such an exquisite ointment, extracted from a plant native to India? Was it an heirloom? What special insight did she alone have that Jesus would soon lay down His life? She was an unusual person.

Not only did Jesus rebuke those who complained about this alleged waste, but He described the woman's "lavish display of affection" as a beautiful thing. The protestation that this ointment might have been sold in order to assist the poor has a twofold implication. It was customary to make special gifts to the poor at the Passover season. But more, it has been suggested that Jesus was himself poor, indeed, the poor righteous Man of Psalm 41, who was betrayed by a close friend but whom God vindicated. This unnamed woman had therefore fulfilled the command of Deut. 15:11—"Thou shalt open thine hand wide unto thy brother, to thy poor, and to thy needy in thy land."

c. The plotting of the chief priests and the scribes, along with the treachery of Judas, have been remembered in infamy all these centuries. It is a commentary on the grace of God that this beautiful deed of a nameless woman has also been remembered, but with blessing.

Moreover, Jesus gave His word that her kindness

would be remembered to the end of time: "'I tell you this in solemn truth, that wherever the Good News is preached throughout the world, this woman's deed will be remembered and praised" (9, TLB). (It may be noted from this promise that Jesus clearly expected an interval of time between His ministry and the Parousia, when the gospel would be preached worldwide.)

What a reward! The Lord will not be in anyone's debt. "Therefore, my beloved brethren, be ye stedfast, unmoveable, always abounding in the work of the Lord, forasmuch as ye know that your labour is not in vain in the Lord" (1 Cor. 15:58).

The Sacrament of the Lord's Supper

Mark 14:12-26

12 And the first day of unleavened bread, when they killed the passover, his disciples said unto him, Where wilt thou that we go and prepare that thou mayest eat the passover?

13 And he sendeth forth two of his disciples, and saith unto them, Go ye into the city, and there shall meet you a man bearing a pitcher of water: follow him.

14 And wheresoever he shall go in, say ye to the goodman of the house, The Master saith, Where is the guestchamber, where I shall eat the passover with my disciples?

15 And he will shew you a large upper room furnished and prepared: there make ready for us.

16 And his disciples went forth, and came into the city, and found as he had said unto them: and they made ready the passover.

17 And in the evening he cometh with the twelve.

18 And as they sat and did eat, Jesus said, Verily I say unto you, One of you which eateth with me shall betray me.

19 And they began to be sorrowful, and to say unto him one by one, Is it I? and another said, Is it I?

20 And he answered and said unto them, It is one of the twelve, that dippeth with me in the dish.

21 The Son of man indeed goeth, as it is written of him: but woe to that man by whom the Son of man is betrayed! good were it for that man if he had never been born.

22 And as they did eat, Jesus took bread, and blessed, and brake it, and gave to them, and said, Take, eat: this is my body.

23 And he took the cup, and when he had given thanks, he gave it to them: and they all drank of it.

24 And he said unto them, This is my blood of the new testament, which is shed for many.

25 Verily I say unto you, I will drink no more of the fruit of the vine, until that day that I drink it new in the kingdom of God.

26 And when they had sung an hymn, they went out into the mount of Olives.

Christians in general believe that Jesus instituted at least two sacraments: baptism and the Lord's Supper. Catholics, both Roman and Greek, hold to seven sacraments. Donald M. Baillie defines a sacrament as "a sacred sign which God uses for the strengthening of faith."

In the present passage, Mark describes the institution of the Lord's Supper, also known as Communion or the Eucharist. This significant event took place in the setting of the Jewish Passover and under the shadow of the Cross. Jesus observed that sacred feast alone with the Twelve, and by His touch transformed and made it His own.

1. *Plans for the Passover* (12-16). It was no simple matter to prepare for the eating of the Passover. Jesus and the Twelve were far from home and would have to depend upon friends for a spacious room with appropriate appointments. The meal itself was rather complex. D. Edmond Hiebert describes the details: "The work of preparation involved procuring and preparing the lamb, making the necessary room arrangements for the feast, and procuring unleavened cakes, wine, bitter herbs, and crushed fruit moistened with vinegar." The lamb came from the Temple where it was slain and prepared for roasting.

a. Preparations by stealth. It is clear that Jesus took precautions not to disclose where He would observe the Passover. He sent Peter and John (Luke 22:8) into the city, where they would find a man carrying a pot of water. This would be unusual. Normally women carried the water jars and men the water skins. They were to follow him through the labyrinthian streets to the designated house. Even Judas, who sought ways to deliver Jesus to His foes, would not know in advance the location.

b. Prior arrangements or prescience? One senses, as he retraces the steps of Jesus, that He always thought ahead and laid His plans carefully. He was efficient. It was so at the time of the "triumphal entry" (11:1-6). It was true in this instance as well. A place had to be chosen. A guide was ready to lead the "scouts" to the house. The

Upper Room was furnished and prepared (15). The owner of the house was not surprised when the callers arrived.

Was all of this by prior arrangement or because of foreknowledge? It does not reflect upon the supernatural qualities of Jesus to suppose that the details of preparation were by prearrangement. He did leave us an example that we should follow in His steps (1 Pet. 2:21). However, Mark seems to leave the impression that the foresight of Jesus was involved in the planning. Perhaps both elements were present.

It is pleasing to see with what loving cooperation the disciples followed Jesus' instructions. They went into the city, presumably from Bethany, and found everything just as Jesus had said. And so, *they made ready the passover* (16). The new Israel began to be. A new Exodus was in the making.

2. *Predictions of betrayal* (17-21). What were Jesus' thoughts as He came into the city of Jerusalem that fateful Thursday night? As a faithful member of the people of God, He anticipated with joy the Feast of the Passover. However, He looked not only backward to Moses and the mighty deliverance of Israel from the bondage of Egypt, but also into the future and the greater deliverance of all men from the bondage of sin. He knew that the cost to Him—betrayal, arrest, trial, crucifixion—would be very great. He never flinched. "Then said he, Lo, I come to do thy will, O God" (Heb. 10:9).

a. The effect on the disciples. During the course of the meal, Jesus shared with the Twelve the tragic word that one of them would betray Him: "As they were sitting around the table eating, Jesus said, 'I solemnly declare that one of you will betray me, one of you who is here eating with me.' A great sadness swept over them, and one by one they asked him, 'Am I the one?'" (18-19, TLB).

It is revealing that none of them said, "Is it he?" Their question could be worded, "It isn't I, is it?" Matthew (26:25) and John (13:26) record that Jesus pointed to

Judas as the betrayer. "Judas, too, asked him, 'Rabbi, am I the one?' And Jesus told him, 'Yes'" (Matt. 26:25, TLB). This fact was not generally understood by the group.

    b. Divine foreknowledge and human responsibility. These divinely established antinomies (apparent contradictions) are clearly affirmed in the experience of Jesus and Judas. All along Jesus understood that He was the fulfillment of Old Testament promises. *The Son of man indeed goeth, as it is written of him* (21). Jesus knew that He combined in His person the glorious Son of Man (Dan. 7:13) and the Suffering Servant (Isaiah 53). He had a sense of calling and destiny from which He never swerved. As He said on another occasion: "'Now my soul is deeply troubled. Shall I pray, "Father, save me from what lies ahead"? But that is the very reason why I came!'" (John 12:27, TLB).

    Nevertheless, the responsibility of Judas for his perfidy remained. Jesus felt deeply for that man: "'Oh, the misery ahead for the man by whom I am betrayed. Oh, that he had never been born!'" (21, TLB). Jesus never expressed anger for Judas, only grief, hurt, and sorrow. He loved him to the end, warned him, and sought to dissuade him. But Judas was free and responsible.

3. *Pronouncements for the future* (22-26). It is probable that Judas left the Upper Room before the institution of the Lord's Supper. The conversation and the events of the evening turned toward the future, both immediate and distant.

    a. Broken body, poured-out blood. In addition to Mark, Matthew (26:26-29), Luke (22:19-20), and Paul (1 Cor. 11:23-25) tell the story of how Jesus transformed the Feast of the Passover into the Eucharist (from a word meaning "to give thanks," v. 23), i.e., the sacrament of the Lord's Supper. Matthew and Luke are closely parallel; Luke and Paul, interestingly, have affinities.

    The unleavened cakes (the bread) were always broken in pieces, never cut. After asking God's blessing on it,

Jesus took the broken pieces *and gave to them, and said, Take, eat: this is my body* (22). So soon, and in such a brutal fashion, this would literally come to pass.

Later in the paschal meal, the pilgrims normally drank from a series of four cups to remind them of God's fourfold promise of deliverance from Egypt (Exod. 6:6-7). Jesus took one of these, gave thanks, and offered it to them. When they had all partaken, Jesus spoke the now timeless words, "'This is my blood, poured out for many, sealing the new agreement between God and man'" (24, TLB).

b. The new covenant. When ancient Israel came to Mount Sinai, following the miraculous events of the Exodus, the Lord entered into a covenant with His people. He would be their God if they would be His people (Exod. 19:5). That covenant was ratified by sacrifices, including the shedding of blood. But Israel broke that covenant. A new covenant, or agreement, became necessary, as the prophet Jeremiah said (Jer. 31:31-34). Jesus now instituted that new covenant and ratified it with His blood. "This is the covenant I will make with them after that time, says the Lord. I will put my laws in their hearts, and I will write them on their minds" (Heb. 10:16, NIV; cf. Jer. 31:34).

c. Future promise of fellowship. The last words of Jesus, before the group left for the Mount of Olives, are intriguing. We may draw at least two inferences. First, Jesus knew this would be the last Passover meal He would share with the disciples. His course was irrevocably set. He had already warned the Twelve: "Behold, we go up to Jerusalem; and the Son of man shall be delivered unto the chief priests, and unto the scribes; and they shall condemn him to death, and shall deliver him to the Gentiles: and they shall mock him, and shall scourge him, and shall spit upon him, and shall kill him: and the third day he shall rise again" (10:33-34).

Second, the Cross was not the end. Beyond the Cross was the Resurrection, the Ascension, and then something ineffable, unutterable: "'I shall never again taste wine until the day I drink a different kind in the Kingdom of God'" (25, TLB). What can that fellowship with the Lord be? "How beautiful heaven must be!"

The final scene fires the imagination. Those 12 men—Jesus and the Eleven—sang a hymn (probably from Psalms 113—118). Picture that! How often the musicians and poets have the last word!

> *O give thanks unto the Lord; for he is good:*
> *Because his mercy endureth forever.*
> *Let Israel now say,*
> *That his mercy endureth forever* (Ps. 118:1-2).

The Scattering and Gathering of the Sheep

Mark 14:27-31

27 And Jesus saith unto them, All ye shall be offended because of me this night: for it is written, I will smite the shepherd, and the sheep shall be scattered.
28 But after that I am risen, I will go before you into Galilee.
29 But Peter said unto him, Although all shall be offended, yet will not I.
30 And Jesus saith unto him, Verily I say unto thee, That this day, even in this night, before the cock crow twice, thou shalt deny me thrice.
31 But he spake the more vehemently, If I should die with thee, I will not deny thee in any wise. Likewise also said they all.

The last evening Jesus spent with His disciples combined light and darkness. The fellowship during the Passover meal must have been warm, friendly, healing. The announcement of betrayal and the departure of Judas cast a shadow. The singing of the Passover hymn and the walk to the Garden of Gethsemane must have been in sharp contrast with the insistence of Jesus that all of the disciples would defect and that their spokesman would both deny and forsake the Master. But even those darksome events were not the last word. We see both a scattering and a gathering of the sheep, both human failure and divine restoration.

1. *Human failure* (scattering). It is evidently important for us to see the "seamy" side of this situation in order to

appreciate the smoother, "finished" side later on. We need to see both.

a. The Lord's prediction. Jesus repeatedly saw His ministry as a fulfillment of scripture. The words, "I will strike the shepherd, and the sheep will be scattered" (27, RSV), are from Zech. 13:7. The message startles one. By God's command the shepherd is struck down and the sheep are scattered in panic. But this is part of a refining process: "I will . . . refine them as one refines silver, and test them as gold is tested." In the end, the Lord will say, "'They are my people'; and they will say, 'The Lord is my God'" (Zech. 13:9, RSV).

b. Peter's protestation. The language of Jesus is stern: "'You will all fall from your faith'" (27, NEB). And to Peter: "'You yourself will disown me three times'" (30, NEB). Protesting too loudly, Peter responded, "'Even if I must die with you, I will never disown you'" (31, NEB). The other disciples said the same. Earlier (8:32), Peter had rebuked Jesus for His prediction of suffering. Now he joins forces with Him!

2. *Divine restoration* (gathering). At the moment, Jesus and the disciples were going through a very dark and trying hour. The promise of a brighter day was probably not even noticed by the disciples. However, the promise was there, and it was powerful.

a. The coming Resurrection. Can we apprehend the unbelievable joy implied in the words of Jesus? "'Nevertheless, after I am raised again'" (28, NEB). How we need those words in the hour of trial! "Endure hardship as discipline; God is treating you as sons. For what son is not disciplined by his father? . . . No discipline seems pleasant at the time, but painful. Later on, however, it produces a harvest of righteousness and peace for those who have been trained by it" (Heb. 12:7, 10-11, NIV).

Nevertheless, afterwards! After the hurt, grief, and disappointment, if we are in Christ, will come healing, comfort, consolation. This, too, has "come to pass." The disciples were about to be plunged into an abyss of sorrow, despair, disillusionment. But after the Resurrection, there would be renewal; there would be hearts leaping for joy.

b. The coming recovery. Jesus had a further word for His disciples, and for us. "'I will go ahead of you into Galilee'" (28, NIV). After the betrayal and arrest, after the mockery of the trial and the scourging, after the Cross, the grave, and the Resurrection, Jesus would meet them in Galilee. He was making an appointment for a "family reunion, back home." Jesus had grown up in Nazareth. Peter and Andrew, James and John, at least, lived in Capernaum. Together they had all toured the province of Galilee preaching, teaching, healing.

Now Jesus asks them to look forward to a gathering with Him in familiar surroundings, "after the storms have passed." This they in fact did (16:7) and laid plans for the conquest of the world!

The Hour and Power of Darkness

Mark 14:32-42

> 32 And they came to a place which was named Gethsemane: and he saith to his disciples, Sit ye here, while I shall pray.
> 33 And he taketh with him Peter and James and John, and began to be sore amazed, and to be very heavy;
> 34 And saith unto them, My soul is exceeding sorrowful unto death: tarry ye here, and watch.
> 35 And he went forward a little, and fell on the ground, and prayed that, if it were possible, the hour might pass from him.
> 36 And he said, Abba, Father, all things are possible unto thee; take away this cup from me: nevertheless not what I will, but what thou wilt.
> 37 And he cometh, and findeth them sleeping, and saith unto Peter, Simon, sleepest thou? couldest not thou watch one hour?
> 38 Watch ye and pray, lest ye enter into temptation. The spirit truly is ready, but the flesh is weak.
> 39 And again he went away, and prayed, and spake the same words.
> 40 And when he returned, he found them asleep again, (for their eyes were heavy,) neither wist they what to answer him.
> 41 And he cometh the third time, and saith unto them, Sleep on now, and take your rest: it is enough, the hour is come; behold, the Son of man is betrayed into the hands of sinners.
> 42 Rise up, let us go; lo, he that betrayeth me is at hand.

The reality of Satan and the power of his dark kingdom are plainly evident in the Gospel record. Jesus did not go through the experiences of Gethsemane without a struggle. His encounter with Satan was fierce. Jesus found peace and power in submission to the Father's will, but the cup of suffering which He drank was bitter.

1. *Satan comes to collect.* When Jesus defeated Satan in the wilderness temptations (1:13), He chose the way of the Cross, rather than the way of the sensational, political Messiah. Satan has now come to collect on that choice. Jesus must engage the enemy in hand-to-hand combat.

a. Jesus endured loneliness. The place *named Gethsemane* (32) was a pleasant grove on the slopes of the Mount of Olives, ideal for "resting, sleeping, praying, and teaching" (Hendriksen). It now became something quite different. Jesus needed fellowship and stationed the disciples nearby as watchmen. But while He prayed, they slept. The lines by W. B. Tappan capture the meaning of that hour:

> 'Tis midnight; and on Olive's brow
>   The star is dimmed that lately shone;
> 'Tis midnight; in the garden now,
>   The suff'ring Saviour prays alone.
>
> 'Tis midnight, and from all removed,
>   Emmanuel wrestles lone with fears;
> E'en the disciple that He loved
>   Heeds not his Master's grief and tears.

b. Jesus endured treachery. Even as He prayed and the "watchmen" dozed, Judas and the ugly mob, representing *the chief priests and the scribes and the elders* (43), were on their way to Gethsemane. Judas had found a place of quiet and isolation where he could deliver Jesus to His enemies (see 14:1). Jesus "came unto his own, and his own received him not" (John 1:11).

c. Jesus endured the pain of vicarious atonement. The picture painted by the Synoptists is beyond our power to grasp: Mark's words are almost identical with Matthew's: "Horror and dismay came over him, and he said to them, 'My heart is ready to break with grief; stop here, and stay awake.' Then he went forward a little, threw himself on the ground, and prayed that, if it were possible, this hour might pass him by" (34-35, NEB).

Luke enriches our understanding with these words: "Now there appeared to him an angel from heaven bringing him strength, and in anguish of spirit he prayed the more urgently; and his sweat was like clots of blood falling to the ground" (Luke 22:43-44, NEB).

What was this great horror? Like the Psalmist, He could have said, "All thy waves and thy billows are gone over me" (Ps. 42:7). Other brave men have endured loneliness, treachery, and physical torture. No one else, however, has ever become a sin-offering for the world and in that capacity experienced abandonment by God. Only of Jesus was it said: "God made him who had no sin to be sin [a sin offering] for us, so that in him we might become the righteousness of God" (2 Cor. 5:21, NIV). The cry of desolation from the Cross, "'My God, my God, why have you forsaken me?'" (15:34, NIV), was surely the expression of Jesus as the sin offering for all men.

2. *The Son submits and conquers.* Three times Jesus went to the place of prayer, falling on His face (35), or kneeling (Luke 22:41), each time pleading with the Father, "Take away this cup from me" (TLB). Each prayer closed with an expression of submission: *Nevertheless not what I will, but what thou wilt* (36).

Jesus had a sense of destiny. He was dedicated without reservation to fulfill the Father's will. Jesus overcame temptation, as all of us may, by the constancy of His will. As a result, He came from the hour of intercession and submission with a sense of power and poise.

a. Jesus showed amazing patience with the bumbling disciples. Thrice He awakened them and urged them to be watchful. He especially chided Peter: "'Simon, are you asleep? Could you not watch one hour?'" (37, RSV). But when the struggle was over, His words were full of understanding. "'It is enough; the hour has come; the Son of man is betrayed into the hands of sinners. Rise, let us be going'" (41-42, RSV).

b. Jesus exhibited a quiet confidence and preparedness when the foe appeared (42). This was true throughout the long night to follow, and all the way, on the following morning, to the Cross. A knowledge of the will of God, coupled with a glad readiness to obey, brings peace, poise, and power.

> The hour of anguish or frightening responsibility is bearable when it is the God of holiness and love who beckons us to endure it. In the end one will be stronger if he accepts the cup than he will be if he refuses it. Submission to the will of God is the soul of a Spirit-filled life (BBC).

> *Shut in with Thee, O Lord, forever,*
> *My wayward feet no more to roam;*
> *What pow'r from Thee my soul can sever?*
> *The center of God's will my home*
>
> —Mrs. C. H. Morris

The Loneliest Hour

Mark 14:43-52

43 And immediately, while he yet spake, cometh Judas, one of the twelve, and with him a great multitude with swords and staves, from the chief priests and the scribes and the elders.
44 And he that betrayed him had given them a token, saying, Whomsoever I shall kiss, that same is he; take him, and lead him away safely.
45 And as soon as he was come, he goeth straightway to him, and saith, Master, master; and kissed him.
46 And they laid their hands on him, and took him.
47 And one of them that stood by drew a sword, and smote a servant of the high priest, and cut off his ear.
48 And Jesus answered and said unto them, Are ye come out, as against a thief, with swords and with staves to take me?
49 I was daily with you in the temple teaching, and ye took me not: but the scriptures must be fulfilled.
50 And they all forsook him, and fled.
51 And there followed him a certain young man, having a linen cloth cast about his naked body; and the young men laid hold on him:
52 And he left the linen cloth, and fled from them naked.

This may have been the loneliest hour of Jesus' Passion—that period in which His sufferings peaked to the point of agony. One of the Twelve betrayed Him with a sign of affection and discipleship. The henchmen of the Sanhedrin seized and arrested Him as if He were the leader of an insurrection. In a foolish act of misdirected loyalty, one of the disciples drew his sword and spilled blood. The posted "guards" forsook Him and ran for their lives. Against this somber background, the strengths of Jesus appear as light in darkness.

1. *The cowardice of the leaders.* The scene was bizarre—a reflection of twisted thought. Jesus had entered the city a few days before, enveloped in the symbols of a peaceful Messiah (11:7-10). Throughout the week following, He had taught openly in the spacious courts of the Temple. No wonder Jesus protested, "'Have you come out as against a robber, with swords and clubs to capture me?'" (48, RSV). The leaders of Judaism, safe in the city, had sent a small mob, protected by soldiers (John 18:12), to take Jesus.

2. *The perfidy of Judas.* The betrayer incarnates "the mystery of iniquity" (2 Thess. 2:7). How could he do it? The Evangelists describe their horror for his deed with the simple, brief, but devastating words: "one of the twelve" (Matt. 26:47; Mark 14:23; Luke 22:47). Judas had walked endless miles with Jesus, spent countless hours with Him, witnessed the miracles (perhaps was the instrument for some), heard the "wonderful words of life," listened to the parables; but in the end he lost faith and in disillusionment betrayed Jesus by guiding the mob to Him.

Few acts in human history have borne the brunt of such universal condemnation as the kiss of Judas and his deal for 30 pieces of silver (Matt. 26:15). Judas was efficient and effective. He led the Temple police through the crowded city, in the dark, to the One they could not have found nor identified. But his words, "take him, and lead him away safely" (44, ASV), are full of apprehension.

3. *The strengths of Jesus.* As one reads this account in the four Gospels, Jesus appears suffused in light, while the others move in the shadows. His strengths are awesome.

a. His total honesty. John tells us that as His adversaries approached, Jesus confronted them. "Who is it you want?" (NIV). When they said, "Jesus of Nazareth," Jesus identified himself: "I am he." At this they drew back and fell to the ground. Jesus identified himself again and interceded for the disciples. It was He who took the initiative, chided the mob for its cowardice, and made no attempt to escape.

b. His confidence in the divine plan. Perhaps because of his native bluster (31), or because of a natural desire to prove his loyalty, Peter drew a sword and cut off the ear of one Malchus, a servant of the high priest. (Only John names these persons.) One shudders to think what might have happened if Malchus had not ducked! Only "the beloved physician," Luke (Col. 4:14), records that Jesus touched Malchus' ear and healed him (Luke 22:51).

Jesus taught His disciples several lessons on the spot: (1) Force is counter-productive and is not an instrument for building the Kingdom. "'Put your sword back into its place; for all who take the sword will perish by the sword'" (Matt. 26:52, RSV). (2) Jesus had an alternative and could have escaped arrest: "'Do you think that I cannot appeal to my Father, and he will at once send me more than twelve legions of angels?'" (Matt. 26:53, RSV). (3) He would not, under any circumstances, deviate from the divine plan: "'How then should the scriptures be fulfilled, that it must be so? . . . But all this has taken place, that the scriptures of the prophets might be fulfilled'" (Matt. 26:54-56, RSV).

Predestinarians and those who believe that man is a free agent will perhaps always differ on the interpretation of these passages. God is sovereign and man is free. The scriptures stress both truths.

Kenneth Taylor has rendered Rom. 8:28 in a way that helps to resolve this apparent impasse: "We know that all that happens to us is working for our good if we love God and are fitting into His plans" (TLB).

4. *The testimony of an eyewitness* (51-52). Among those who forsook Jesus and fled was a certain young man whose identity is unknown. However, we are not without clues. The vignette appears only in Mark. Why did he include it? The youth had followed Jesus. The linen cloth which the young man had *cast about him, over his naked body* (ASV), implies that he was from a well-to-do family and that he had dressed hurriedly. As noted in the Introduction to this volume, these details suggest that it was John Mark who followed Jesus to Gethsemane.

The New Testament word translated "young man," according to William L. Lane, refers to one "exceptionally strong and valiant, or faithful and wise." A day had come when even the heart of the strongest had failed (see Amos 2:16).

Jesus Before the Sanhedrin

Mark 14:53-65

> 53 And they led Jesus away to the high priest: and with him were assembled all the chief priests and the elders and the scribes.
> 54 And Peter followed him afar off, even into the palace of the high priest: and he sat with the servants, and warmed himself at the fire.
> 55 And the chief priests and all the council sought for witness against Jesus to put him to death; and found none.
> 56 For many bare false witness against him, but their witness agreed not together.
> 57 And there arose certain, and bare false witness against him, saying,
> 58 We heard him say, I will destroy this temple that is made with hands, and within three days I will build another made without hands.
> 59 But neither so did their witness agree together.
> 60 And the high priest stood up in the midst, and asked Jesus, saying, Answerest thou nothing? what is it which these witness against thee?
> 61 But he held his peace, and answered nothing. Again the high priest asked him, and said unto him, Art thou the Christ, the Son of the Blessed?
> 62 And Jesus said, I am: and ye shall see the Son of man sitting on the right hand of power, and coming in the clouds of heaven.
> 63 Then the high priest rent his clothes, and saith, What need we any further witnesses?
> 64 Ye have heard the blasphemy: what think ye? And they all condemned him to be guilty of death.

65 And some began to spit on him, and to cover his face, and to buffet him, and to say unto him, Prophesy: and servants did strike him with the palms of their hands.

Those who took Jesus into custody led Him to the palace of the high priest where the Sanhedrin had already assembled, in expectation of His arrest and capture. It was irregular for the Sanhedrin to meet at night, especially at the Passover season, but not illegal in very serious cases. In such instances, a prompt trial was required. However, in areas of political unrest, such as Judah, Rome retained the power of the sword. The Sanhedrin could not carry out a sentence of death. Only the Roman governor could authorize an execution. We may draw several conclusions from Mark's account.

1. *The ecclesiastical trial was a farce.* According to John (18:12-14, 19-24), a preliminary hearing was held before Annas, the father-in-law of Caiaphas, and onetime high priest. The ecclesiastical trial was followed by two others: one before Pilate (15:1), another before Herod Antipas (Luke 23:6-12). Mark gives special attention to the trial before the Sanhedrin, which was farcical.

a. The "court" presumed the defendant to be guilty. The Sanhedrin, or *council* (55), was the supreme governing body of Judaism, and was composed of 70 members, presided over by the high priest. There were three groups in its membership: the chief priests, the elders, and the scribes (53). These were, respectively, former high priests, influential laymen, and lawyers. The first two groups were Sadducees, the third group Pharisees.

b. The prosecutors sought for evidence to support the presumption of guilt. *All the council sought for witness against Jesus to put him to death* (55). As with the Sanhedrin, witnesses had already assembled, expecting the arrest and arraignment of Jesus. The testimony of the witnesses did not agree and was inadmissable (see Deut. 17:6; Num. 35:30).

c. The Defendant was under pressure to testify against

himself. The council sat in a semicircle on elevated seats, with the accused and the witnesses positioned at the center. The arrangement was threatening to the defendant. When the witnesses failed to convict Jesus, the high priest, Caiaphas, proceeded with questions designed to incriminate Him.

d. The "court" condemned and mistreated the defendant. Once the verdict of "guilty" had been reached—*and they all condemned him to be guilty of death* (64)—it was appropriate for the members of the Sanhedrin to demonstrate their disapproval with cuffing, spitting, mocking.

One is appalled at the blindness, bigotry, depravity, and cruelty of man. It was the religious leaders of Judaism who were responsible for this display of injustice.

2. *The disciples were lurking, perhaps hopefully, in the shadows.* After the disciples as a body had forsaken Jesus and fled for safety (50), two of them recovered some of their poise and followed Jesus. These were Peter (54) and, presumably, John. (See John 18:15-16.)

We could wish for answers to a variety of questions. What association or relationship did John have with the high priest? The thought is startling. He was known to the servants of the high priest and had influence with them. Evidently there was an open court on the ground floor of the palace which was entered by permission through a gate or porch. The trial was in progress on a second or higher level, for "Peter was below in the courtyard" (66, RSV). And yet, later in the night, Jesus caught Peter's gaze: "The Lord turned and looked at Peter. And Peter remembered" (Luke 22:61, RSV).

Peter followed, but *afar off* (54). When he gained entrance to the courtyard, it must have been with a feeling of defeat. "He sat with the guards to see the end" (Matt. 26:58, RSV).

3. *The integrity of Jesus was like a shaft of light in the darkness.* A parade of false witnesses failed to agree (56).

According to pentateuchal law, witnesses were impeached whose testimony was not consistent, even in minor details.

a. The testimony of false witnesses. Another group of witnesses, however, brought a more serious charge. "We heard him say, 'I will destroy this man-made temple and in three days will build another, not made by man'" (58, NIV).

Throughout the Mediterranean world it was a serious offense to destroy or even desecrate a temple. Centuries before, when Jeremiah proclaimed the word of the Lord that judgment would fall upon Jerusalem, his countrymen accused him of blasphemy and treason. They would have taken his life if wiser heads had not intervened (Jer. 26:1-19).

The charge against Jesus was patently false and did not stand. Throughout the proceedings Jesus was silent. Despite the abuse, *he held his peace, and answered nothing* (61). The Evangelists clearly saw this as a fulfillment of messianic prophecy: "He was oppressed, and he was afflicted, yet he opened not his mouth" (Isa. 53:7).

b. The testimony of the Son of Man. What purloined testimony could not accomplish, the honesty and integrity of Jesus did accomplish, and to His hurt. Frustrated and angry, the high priest pursued the earlier messianic hints: "Are you the Christ, the Son of the Blessed One?" (61, NIV).

We have seen repeatedly that throughout His ministry Jesus guarded the messianic secret almost fiercely. He charged those whom He had healed to say nothing about their mighty deliverance (e.g., 1:44). When the disciples began to understand that He was the Christ, He "impressed it upon them that they must not mention this to anyone" (8:30, Phillips). He did not want to inflame nationalistic hopes nor encourage misconceptions of His messiahship.

However, "the hour [had] come, that the Son of man should be glorified." It was time for the grain of "wheat to fall into the ground and die" in order to bring "forth much fruit" (John 12:23-24).

Jesus could no longer remain silent. When Caiaphas probed imperiously, "Are you the Christ?" Jesus replied without hesitation, without equivocation, *I am* (62). The language is emphatic. He went on to describe the proof of His assertion: "'You will see the Son of man sitting at the right hand of Power, and coming with the clouds of heaven'" (62, RSV).

The Sanhedrin had now secured its purpose. They could charge Jesus with blasphemy. On what basis? The answer usually given is that Jesus identified himself with the Son of man in Daniel (7:13), who had divine authority. Another view is that only God could designate the Messiah, and that the claim of Jesus was "an infringement of God's majesty and a diminishing of his honor" (Lane).

The verdict was inevitable: "'What is your decision?' And they all condemned him as deserving death" (64, RSV).

An Experience of Failure

Mark 14:66-72

> 66 And as Peter was beneath in the palace, there cometh one of the maids of the high priest:
> 67 And when she saw Peter warming himself, she looked upon him, and said, And thou also wast with Jesus of Nazareth.
> 68 But he denied, saying, I know not, neither understand I what thou sayest. And he went out into the porch; and the cock crew.
> 69 And a maid saw him again, and began to say to them that stood by, This is one of them.
> 70 And he denied it again. And a little after, they that stood by said again to Peter, Surely thou art one of them: for thou art a Galilaean, and thy speech agreeth thereto.
> 71 But he began to curse and to swear, saying, I know not this man of whom ye speak.
> 72 And the second time the cock crew. And Peter called to mind the word that Jesus said unto him, Before the cock crow twice, thou shalt deny me thrice. And when he thought thereon, he wept.

Probably everyone has experienced failure in some form. Discouragement, depression, and frustration usually follow. "Nothing succeeds like success," and nothing fails like failure. All the species of positive and possibility thinking presume the negative side of defeat and offer brighter alternatives.

Failure is not uncommon among believers—failure in some aspect of Christian service, or failure in living the Christian life (see Gal. 6:1). Peter's experience of failure should convey both warning and hope to those who ponder his fall and restoration.

1. *The ambivalence of Peter.* It is painful to put this fact into words: at the moment, Peter was simultaneously attracted to and repelled by the Lord. But Peter had not yet built into his personality the controls necessary to integrity. He was strong enough to come near to the place where Jesus was under trial, but not strong enough to confess that he was a follower of the Nazarene. He would never find that strength, he would never build those controls into his personality, apart from the power of the Holy Spirit.

It was not characteristic of Peter to be lacking in courage. It was he who stepped out of the boat and, at the bidding of Jesus, walked on the water (Matt. 14:28). He was the first to see and declare the Messiahship of Jesus (Mark 8:29). It was he who drew blood in the Garden (John 18:10). And yet it was Peter who, in panic and fear of arrest (see John 18:26), denied his Lord.

2. *The identification of Peter.* The scene before us took place sometime during the long night between the Last Supper and the arraignment before Pilate (15:1). Peter had made his way to the palace of the high priest, where the trial of Jesus was in progress. The building must have been spacious. Entrance was through a gate under guard. Within was an open court large enough to accommodate a considerable number of people, some of whom were sitting about a fire. In the dim light, Peter moved through the crowd hoping to escape detection. Two factors led to the identification of Peter as one of the Twelve.

a. His association with Jesus. As Peter sat among the

guards, warming himself at the fire, one of the young women in the employ of the high priest noticed Peter. Her comment suggests that she had seen Peter in the company of Jesus: "You were with Jesus, the Nazarene" (67, TLB). How did she know that? Had she seen Peter during the week as Jesus taught in the temple?

Here was "guilt by association." That would be guilt every disciple should be glad to bear.

> *One of them, one of them.*
> *I'm so glad that I can say,*
> *I'm one of them!*

b. His speech. Despite Peter's protestations that he did not even know Jesus, indeed, because of his protestations, the challenge continued. Another maid saw Peter and said to those standing nearby, "This fellow was also with Jesus of Nazareth" (Matt. 26:71). Once again Peter denied it. A bit later these bystanders approached Peter and charged, "We know you are one of His disciples, for we can tell by your Galilean accent" (Matt. 26:73, TLB).

In a deeper sense Jesus said, "By thy words thou shalt be justified, and by thy words thou shalt be condemned" (Matt. 12:37).

Under such provocation, Peter "blew up" and began to curse and swear, saying that he did not know this man. This comment does not necessarily imply profanity, as more recent translations make clear. William Hendriksen has a helpful word:

He must have said something like, "May God do this or that to me if it be true that I am or ever was a disciple of Jesus." He stands there invoking on himself one curse after another. And the louder he talks, the more, without realizing it, he is saying to all those standing around, "I'm a liar."

3. *The repentance and restoration of Peter.* It is reassuring to realize that only Peter could have told the story of his denial. No one else would have known.

The goodness of God enveloped Peter before, after,

and during this experience of failure. Warnings came beforehand. "'Peter,' Jesus said, 'before the cock crows a second time tomorrow morning you will deny me three times'" (30, TLB). It was the cockcrowing, a proverbial indication of the night watches, that stabbed Peter's conscience. *He called to mind that word that Jesus said unto him* (73). Peter remembered and repented with bitter tears.

Luke recalls a startling event full of pathos and beauty. At the second crowing of the cock, "the Lord turned, and looked upon Peter" (Luke 22:61). It is not clear how that could have taken place. "It would seem that the Master, his trial ended, was being led across the court to his prison cell, from which within a few hours he would emerge once more to face the Sanhedrin" (Hendriksen).

What did that look convey? Jesus had already taken a good deal of abuse and must have shown the effects of the beatings and mistreatment. G. Campbell Morgan has a kind word for Peter at this juncture: "The look of Jesus would have been wasted on Peter, if it had not been that Peter was looking at Jesus."

Peter did repent and found restoration, as the later gathering of Jesus and His disciples in Galilee proves (John 21:1). What prevented Judas from finding a similar recovery? "Brothers, if a man is trapped in some sin, you who are spiritual should restore him gently. But watch yourself; you also may be tempted" (Gal. 6:1, NIV).

MARK 15

An Astonishing Confrontation

Mark 15:1-15

> 1 And straightway in the morning the chief priests held a consultation with the elders and scribes and the whole council, and bound Jesus, and carried him away, and delivered him to Pilate.
> 2 And Pilate asked him, Art thou the King of the Jews? And he answering said unto him, Thou sayest it.

3 And the chief priests accused him of many things: but he answered nothing.

4 And Pilate asked him again, saying, Answerest thou nothing? behold how many things they witness against thee.

5 But Jesus yet answered nothing; so that Pilate marvelled.

6 Now at that feast he released unto them one prisoner, whomsoever they desired.

7 And there was one named Barabbas, which lay bound with them that had made insurrection with him, who had committed murder in the insurrection.

8 And the multitude crying aloud began to desire him to do as he had ever done unto them.

9 But Pilate answered them, saying, Will ye that I release unto you the King of the Jews?

10 For he knew that the chief priests had delivered him for envy.

11 But the chief priests moved the people, that he should rather release Barabbas unto them.

12 And Pilate answered and said again unto them, What will ye then that I shall do unto him whom ye call the King of the Jews?

13 And they cried out again, Crucify him.

14 Then Pilate said unto them, Why, what evil hath he done? And they cried out the more exceedingly, Crucify him.

15 And so Pilate, willing to content the people, released Barabbas unto them, and delivered Jesus, when he had scourged him, to be crucified.

This was certainly one of the greatest confrontations in history: a Roman governor and the Son of God. One was talking, the other was silent, except to acknowledge true and damaging accusations (2).

But this confrontation is a reality for us as well: "Let your gentleness be evident to all. The Lord is near" (Phil. 4:5, NIV). Pilate and Jesus confronted each other in the presence of the religious leaders of Judaism. Their blindness provoked Pilate's moral compromises, while Heaven looked on in silence.

1. *When religious leaders are blind.* They were legally correct but morally wrong. Through the long night after the arrest, Jesus had been examined and harassed by the high priest, the chief priests, the elders, and the scribes, i.e., by *the whole council* (1), the supreme governing body of Judaism. It was unusual for them to meet at night, and illegal to pronounce sentence until after daybreak.

To conform to the letter of the law, they met *straightway in the morning* for *a consultation.* They bound Jesus, as if He were a dangerous criminal, and *delivered him to Pilate* for the execution they hoped he would carry out.

It is a testimony to the accuracy of the account that they sought audience with Pilate at dawn. Trials were regularly held at that hour. Pilate would not have interrupted his day later to see them.

They gave further evidence of their blindness in refusing to accompany Jesus into the judgment hall (palace) where Pilate sat, lest they become ceremonially defiled on a holy day (John 18:28). Once again they were legally correct and morally wrong.

2. *When government compromises.* Since 63 B.C. Israel had borne the yoke of Roman oppression. Since A.D. 6, Judea had been governed by Roman procurators or prefects, influential but minor Roman officials, whereas other segments of Israel were governed by puppet kings, members of Herod's family. The land was difficult to govern. The rulers were harsh, brutal.

a. The duty of Pontius Pilate. However roughhewn it may have been, justice was an ideal of the Romans (cf. Acts 16:37-38; 22:24-29). The procurator and his advisers sat as a bench of judges. It was required of the plaintiffs that they prepare specific charges and that these should be of a serious nature. The tribunal then heard witnesses and examined the defendant. Acquittal or execution of sentence followed at once.

It is clear even from Mark's stark account that Pilate followed this procedure. The other Gospels give more detail. Pilate was apparently prepared to carry out his duty.

b. The dilemma of Pilate. During the ecclesiastical trial, the Sanhedrin had charged Jesus with blasphemy. "'Are you the Christ, the Son of the Blessed One?' And Jesus said, 'I am'" (14:61-62, NASB). The affirmation of Jesus that He was the Messiah, the Son of God, aroused the wrath of the council.

However, the members of the Sanhedrin knew that

such a charge would carry no weight with Pilate. The charge would have to be political rather than religious. Instead, the adversaries of Jesus accused Him of treason. Pilate's question, *Art thou the King of the Jews?* (2), presumes such an accusation.

Pilate soon discovered that Jesus was no revolutionary and that "the chief priests had delivered Him up because of envy" (10, NASB). However, the clamor of the crowds, stimulated by the priests, suggested the likelihood of a riot. Pilate could not risk his reputation further. His name was already synonymous with cruelty (see Luke 13:1-2). The emperor would not hesitate to remove and banish him. Pilate therefore temporized and looked for a way out of his dilemma.

Matthew and Luke record two dramatic interruptions in the legal proceedings. Matthew tells us that Pilate's wife sent word to her husband not to have anything to do with "that just man." She had "suffered many things" in a dream because of Him (Matt. 27:19). Luke tells us that when Pilate discovered Jesus was from Galilee, he sent Him to Herod Antipas, the ruler of that province, who was then in the city (Luke 23:6-16).

Pilate gained nothing from either interruption. He ignored the warning of his wife and learned nothing from Herod's fruitless and contemptuous examination of Jesus. Ironically, "Herod and Pilate became friends with each other that very day," ending a personal feud (Luke 23:12, RSV).

Pilate saw one last alternative: his practice of releasing a political prisoner at the Passover season. Amnesty for political prisoners was often associated with festivals in many cultures. Apparently the multitude reminded him of this custom (8). One wonders why they brought up the subject.

The procurator called for Barabbas, a notorious prisoner, guilty of insurrection and murder. Pilate "nominated" the two—Jesus Bar-Joseph and Jesus Barabbas (as some manuscripts have it). The "vote" of the multitude astonished Pilate. Three times the governor attempted to free Jesus (Luke 23:22).

The Sanhedrin had charged Jesus with the crime of which Barabbas was guilty. Barabbas was released. Jesus was slain.

When the people shouted him down with the demand that he crucify Jesus, Pilate replied with an unanswerable question, *Why, what evil hath he done?* (14). The answer lay in Pilate's own twisted soul: "I must save my own skin."

3. *When Heaven is silent.* When religious leaders are blind, and government compromises moral principle, Heaven looks on in grieved silence—for a time. Judgment falls at last. On all three occasions—before the Sanhedrin, before Pilate and later Herod—Jesus spoke only to acknowledge true and damaging accusations.

When the Sanhedrin asked whether or not He was the Messiah, Jesus said simply, "I am." When Pilate pressed the question, "Are you the King of the Jews?", Jesus replied in veiled language, deliberately ambiguous: "You have said so," or possibly, "It is as you say." In other words, Jesus would claim to be the King of the Jews only in a sense Pilate would not understand.

In the presence of Herod, who had long wanted to see Jesus do something sensational, He said nothing at all. Silence! The Sanhedrin never really knew the truth. Nor did Pilate, who had asked, "What is truth?" and then turned on his heel without waiting for an answer. And so with Herod, who treated Jesus with contempt and sent Him back to Pilate.

Is it possible that silence is the last and final word for the unbeliever? The thought makes one shudder. God reveals His will only to those who are willing to do His will (John 7:17).

However, Paul instructs us on that question: "Therefore God exalted him to the highest place and gave him the name that is above every name, that at the name of Jesus every knee should bow, in heaven and on earth and under the earth, and every tongue confess that Jesus Christ is Lord, to the glory of God the Father (Phil. 2:10, NIV; cf. Isa. 45:23; Rom. 14:11).

The Weapons of Ridicule and Mockery

Mark 15:16-20

16 And the soldiers led him away into the hall, called Praetorium; and they call together the whole band.
17 And they clothed him with purple, and platted a crown of thorns, and put it about his head.
18 And began to salute him, Hail, King of the Jews!
19 And they smote him on the head with a reed, and did spit upon him, and bowing their knees worshipped him.
20 And when they had mocked him, they took off the purple from him, and put his own clothes on him, and led him out to crucify him.

Pilate had sentenced Jesus to death by stages. The intermediate step was scourging. In the hands of the insensitive Roman soldiers a beaded whip left the flesh in shreds. Men often died under the lash. Perhaps this hastened the death of Jesus. After that ordeal, if the victim survived, came the cross. No instrument of capital punishment has ever been more inhumane. The Roman statesman Cicero described crucifixion as a "most cruel and hideous punishment."

The darkness of the human heart has never been plumbed. Self-centeredness is there. Cruelty is there. The sufferings of Jesus revealed that darkness. Another factor intensified all other pain—the atmosphere of ridicule and mockery. "He is despised and rejected of men; a man of sorrows, and acquainted with grief" (Isa. 53:3).

1. *"Beyond the line of duty."* It is not uncommon for brave and loyal soldiers, who have gone beyond the line of duty, to be cited for meritorious service. The scene before us is a dreadful perversion of that custom. After the scourging, which evidently took place in an open courtyard, the soldiers led Jesus back into the palace for some merriment.

The troops were assigned to the governor and would

have accompanied him from Caesarea, Pilate's chief place of residence. A battalion, or cohort, numbered about 500 men. They saw in Jesus a typical Jewish revolutionary and a pretender to the emperor's throne. Their masquerade of mockery was their tribute of malice to a puppet king. Each item of ridicule—the robe, the crown of thorns, the reed, the homage—was a debasement of regal insignia.

In the words of William L. Lane:

> In imitation of the purple robe and the gilded wreath of leaves which were the insignia of the Hellenistic vassal kings . . . , they threw around Jesus' naked body a faded scarlet cloak (cf. Mt. 27:28) or some shabby purple rug, and pressed down on his head a wreath plaited from the branches of some available shrub such as acanthus or of palm-spines. The pretendant to the throne would be both a vassal prince and a figure of fun.

2. *The "Emperor" incognito.* What the Roman soldiers could not have known was that the Man whom they mocked, ridiculed, demeaned, and crushed was in fact royalty far above their emperor. Multiplied millions of all times and climes have acclaimed Him as "King of kings, and Lord of lords." They ascribe to Him honor and eternal dominion (1 Tim. 6:15-16, RSV).

The stature of Jesus has grown through the centuries as mankind has marveled that He returned good for evil, blessing for cursing, that "when he was reviled, reviled not again" (1 Pet. 2:23). He overcame evil with good.

Jesus must have been praying, even through this ordeal, "Father, forgive them" (Luke 23:34). But how can one redeem man except by entering into his need to illuminate, cleanse, and heal? "To bless is to bleed" (J. B. Chapman).

The persecuted and suffering Christians of Rome, reading these words about the suffering of Jesus, must have found heart and strength to encounter and endure their own ordeal. After all, Jesus had warned them—and us—that "the servant is not greater than his lord. If they have persecuted me, they will also persecute you" (John 15:20).

The Crucifixion and Death of Jesus

Mark 15:21-41

21 And they compel one Simon a Cyrenian, who passed by, coming out of the country, the father of Alexander and Rufus, to bear his cross.
22 And they bring him unto the place Golgotha, which is, being interpreted, The place of a skull.
23 And they gave him to drink wine mingled with myrrh: but he received it not.
24 And when they had crucified him, they parted his garments, casting lots upon them, what every man should take.
25 And it was the third hour, and they crucified him.
26 And the superscription of his accusation was written over, THE KING OF THE JEWS.
27 And with him they crucify two thieves; the one on his right hand, and the other on his left.
28 And the scripture was fulfilled, which saith, And he was numbered with the transgressors.
29 And they that passed by railed on him, wagging their heads, and saying, Ah, thou that destroyest the temple, and buildest it in three days,
30 Save thyself, and come down from the cross.
31 Likewise also the chief priests mocking said among themselves with the scribes, He saved others; himself he cannot save.
32 Let Christ the King of Israel descend now from the cross, that we may see and believe. And they that were crucified with him reviled him.
33 And when the sixth hour was come, there was darkness over the whole land until the ninth hour.
34 And at the ninth hour Jesus cried with a loud voice, saying, Eloi, Eloi, lama sabachthani? which is, being interpreted, My God, my God, why hast thou forsaken me?
35 And some of them that stood by, when they heard it, said, Behold, he calleth Elias.
36 And one ran and filled a spunge full of vinegar, and put it on a reed, and gave him to drink, saying, Let alone; let us see whether Elias will come to take him down.
37 And Jesus cried with a loud voice, and gave up the ghost.
38 And the veil of the temple was rent in twain from the top to the bottom.
39 And when the centurion, which stood over against him, saw that he so cried out, and gave up the ghost, he said, Truly this man was the Son of God.
40 There were also women looking on afar off: among whom was Mary Magdalene, and Mary the mother of James the less and of Joses, and Salome;
41 (Who also, when he was in Galilee, followed him, and ministered unto him;) and many other women which came up with him unto Jerusalem.

Man's inhumanity to man was never more obvious than in the scene before us. Insensitivity, savagery, and moral blindness were among the expressions of that inhumanity. Small wonder that men give up on man!

Unfortunately, such cruelty has been common in history. What is *uncommon* is the contrast among the persons and in the events around the Cross. The sordid side of human darkness is "not worthy to be compared with" the brighter side of divine promise.

1. *The sordid side of human darkness.* The Cross has become the focal point and the principal symbol of the Christian faith. On Golgotha, however, it was the insignia of shame.

a. *The ugly act of crucifixion* (24). As noted earlier, crucifixion was regarded as the ugliest form of execution and death. The Jewish historian and soldier, Josephus, described it as "wretched." The pagans shuddered at the mention of the word "cross." Roman citizens were exempt from crucifixion, and Jewish law allowed for no such provision. To be hanged on a tree was the fate of one already dead and for the purpose of public disgrace (Deut. 21:23).

All of this notwithstanding, Jesus was condemned by the Sanhedrin, sentenced by Pilate, and led to the Cross by a quartet of Roman soldiers and their commanding officer, the centurion.

The restraint of the Evangelists in their account of the Crucifixion is notable. They said simply, "And they crucified him" (24, RSV). Recent discoveries in the vicinity of Jerusalem confirm the usual description: an iron nail pierced the overlapping feet through the heel. The arms were fastened to the crossbeam in a similar fashion. The body was supported by a block of wood midway on the upright beam. Death came, often slowly, by exhaustion, loss of blood, exposure, and maltreatment, including fracture of the legs.

b. *The identification with robbers* (27). Jesus did not go to Golgotha alone. In addition to the soldiers and the large crowd, two thieves accompanied Him and suffered the same fate. Robbery, even with violence, was not a capital offense. Their crimes were therefore probably associated with political rebellion. Like Jesus, they were sentenced to death for a political offense. Unlike Jesus, they were guilty. The Zealots, a party seeking the forcible overthrow of Roman rule in Israel, were regularly put to death by crucifixion.

The writers of the New Testament saw the Old Testament fulfilled repeatedly in the works and words of Jesus. "And so the Scripture was fulfilled that said, 'He was counted among evil men'" (28, TLB).

c. The callous greed of the soldiers (24). Persons condemned to the cross for crimes against the state normally suffered the further humiliation of nakedness. The Jews allowed victims a loincloth.

The clothing of Jesus was meager, probably under and outer garments, plus other items such as a belt, sandals, and head covering (W. L. Lane). John tells us that the soldiers "took his garments and made four parts, one for each soldier. The tunic," or outer garment, "was without seam, woven from top to bottom." For this they "cast lots to see whose" it would be (John 19:23, RSV).

Psalm 22 figured largely in the story of the Crucifixion, as John notes. "This was to fulfill the scripture,

'They parted my garments among them
and for my clothing they cast lots'" (John 19:24, RSV).

The helplessness of Jesus could scarcely have been more eloquently expressed than in the lament of the Psalmist (see Ps. 22:18).

According to legal texts recovered from that period, the property of a condemned person became the property of the state. It was accepted practice for the executioners to claim the minor possessions of the one executed.

d. The cruelty of the taunts (29, 31-32). Matthew and Luke record that when the soldiers had crucified Jesus they and the people sat down or "stood by, watching" (Luke 23:35, RSV).

To this crass indifference, the religious leaders, the

soldiers, and the people generally added derision and ridicule. It is difficult to undergo suffering, even when compassionate friends and family are nearby. What was it like to suffer and to die with cruel taunts ringing in one's ears? "Let the Christ, the King of Israel, come down now from the cross, that we may see and believe" (32, RSV).

Among those who came by, wagging or shaking their heads in self-righteous condemnation, was someone who unwittingly declared a profound truth, however cruel: *He saved others; himself he cannot save* (31). Jesus himself knew that to be true. He was indeed the grain of wheat which would "fall into the ground and die" in order to bring "forth much fruit" (John 12:24).

2. *The brighter side of divine promise.* The darkness of human cruelty must have shadowed Golgotha many times before and after the death of Jesus. But never before or again was *the place of the skull* (22) illumined with such heavenly light.

a. *The experience of Simon of Cyrene* (21). Condemned criminals were required to carry the horizontal beam of their cross through the busy streets to the place of execution. This was to intimidate the public and discourage any would-be revolutionaries. Suspended from the victim's neck was a placard bearing the accusation. As Jesus approached the city gate, He must have fallen. The crossbeam was heavy and the ordeal of the trials and the scourging debilitating.

A marvel took place at that point. "Simon of Cyrene, who was coming in from the country," was compelled "to carry his cross" (21, RSV). Years later his sons, Alexander and Rufus, were well known in the Christian community to which Mark wrote (cf. Rom. 16:13).

> *Must Jesus bear the cross alone,*
> *And all the world go free?*
> *No, there's a cross for ev'ry one,*
> *And there's a cross for me.*
>
> —Thomas Shepherd

b. The refusal of an opiate (23). It had become a humane tradition to offer a narcotic to those suffering crucifixion in order to ease their pain. This practice grew out of the injunction in Prov. 31:6-7: "Give strong drink unto him that is ready to perish. . . . Let him drink . . . and remember his misery no more." Myrrh was a drug containing such properties.

But Jesus would not receive the *wine mingled with myrrh* (23). He had already determined that He would drink the cup of suffering the Father proffered Him. He had asked James and John, "Can ye drink of the cup that I drink of?" (10:38). And only the night before He had prayed, "Father . . . take away this cup from me: nevertheless not what I will, but what thou wilt" (14:36). He would bear the burden of the Cross fully aware.

c. The hours of darkness and the cry of dereliction (33-34). However dark these events may have seemed to be, they were in fact lined with heavenly sunshine and bright with divine promise.

At about noon, midway between the crucifixion and death of Jesus, the light of the sun failed, enveloping the whole land in darkness for three hours. No natural explanation is sufficient. "The darkening of the sun marks a critical moment in history and emphasizes the eschatalogical and cosmic dimensions of Jesus' sufferings upon the cross" (Lane).

Amos saw such a day: "It shall come to pass in that day, saith the Lord God, that I will cause the sun to go down at noon, and I will darken the earth in the clear day: . . . and I will make it as the mourning of an only son (8:9-10).

At the close of that long period of darkness, Jesus cried out from the bitter experience of His own darkness: "My God, my God, why have you deserted me?" (34, TLB; cf. Ps. 22:1).

How are we to explain these strange, perplexing words? Do they represent only the typical cry of a believer in time of deep trouble? Surely the New Testament doctrine of the atonement calls for something deeper. William L. Lane believes that the cry

> must be understood in the perspective of the holy wrath of God and the character of sin, which cuts the sinner off from God (cf. Isa. 59:2). . . . His cry expresses the profound horror of separation from God. . . . The sinless Son of God died the sinner's death and experienced the bitterness of desolation.

> *There is a green hill far away,*
> *Without a city wall,*
> *Where the dear Lord was crucified,*
> *Who died to save us all.*

> *We may not know, we cannot tell,*
> *What pains He had to bear,*
> *But we believe it was for us*
> *He hung and suffered there.*

> —CECIL ALEXANDER

d. The tearing of the temple curtain (38). At the moment that Jesus expired, another supernatural portent took place: "The curtain of the temple was torn in two from top to bottom" (38, NIV).

Two colorful curtains marked boundaries in Herod's temple. One separated the outer court from the sanctuary, another the holy place from the holy of holies. In either case the symbolism was powerful. If it was the outer curtain which was rent asunder, the symbolism points to the destruction of the Temple. The death of Jesus did in fact seal the fall of the Temple (cf. 14:58; 15:29).

If it was the inner curtain which was torn, the symbolism suggests that all men now have access into the very presence of God, no longer through a high priest once a year, but through Jesus who opened up "a new and living way." The veil which was torn was His flesh. "Having therefore, brethren, boldness to enter into the holiest by the blood of Jesus . . . let us draw near with a true heart in full assurance of faith" (Heb. 10:19-22).

e. The confession of the centurion (39). The hardened commander of the Roman execution squad must have watched Jesus throughout that first "Good Friday." Seven times Jesus spoke from the Cross, but never once with anger, cursing, or screams of pain so typical of such victims.

When Jesus finally did die, suddenly and with a cry full of trust (Luke 23:46), the centurion could not restrain a resounding affirmation of faith: *Truly this man was the Son of God* (39). Some eyewitness, perhaps one of the women (John 19:25), heard that testimony and preserved it for all time.

In one sense Mark at this point reached a climax in his account. He began by proclaiming Jesus to be the "Christ, the Son of God" (1:1). By midpoint in his Gospel, Peter and the Twelve had responded, "Thou art the Christ" (8:29). And now, near the close, a Roman soldier declares that Jesus is the Son of God. Thus Jew and Gentile with one voice confirm what Mark had confessed, that Jesus is indeed the Messiah, the Christ, the Son of God, and Lord of all.

f. The compassionate care of the women (40-41). The presence of a large group of women among the disciples and supporters of Jesus is a fact deserving special notice. The compassion, tenderness, and understanding of Jesus drew these gentle persons to Him. The rights of women in that period were meager. They had followed Him in Galilee and provided for Him and the Twelve "out of their means" (Luke 8:3, RSV). Now the disciples were out of sight, but these were near (John 19:25) and would be the first at the tomb.

For all time to come, "Mary Magdalene and Mary the mother of James the younger and Joses, and Salome" (40, RSV), would be remembered not only for their undying love but also as unimpeachable witnesses.

The sordid side of human darkness is always conquered by the brighter side of divine promise.

Joseph of Arimathea: Friend and Disciple

Mark 15:42-47

> 42 And now when the even was come, because it was the preparation, that is, the day before the sabbath,
> 43 Joseph of Arimathaea, an honourable counsellor, which also waited for the kingdom of God, came, and went in boldly unto Pilate, and craved the body of Jesus.
> 44 And Pilate marvelled if he were already dead: and calling unto him the centurion, he asked him whether he had been any while dead.
> 45 And when he knew it of the centurion, he gave the body to Joseph.
> 46 And he bought fine linen, and took him down, and wrapped him in the linen, and laid him in a sepulchre which was hewn out of a rock, and rolled a stone unto the door of the sepulchre.
> 47 And Mary Magdalene and Mary the mother of Joses beheld where he was laid.

The body of Jesus hung lifeless from the Cross. Who would arrange for a respectable burial? His mother had gone home with John (John 19:27) and must have been distraught. The disciples had fled, and no other member of the family was near. Time was of the essence. Jewish law required burial the same day (Deut. 21:22-23).

Jesus had a friend—one Joseph of Arimathea, i.e., from Ramah, 20 miles northwest of Jerusalem, the birthplace and hometown of the prophet Samuel. Heretofore a secret disciple, Joseph now came forward boldly and requested the body of Jesus for burial. The witness of the centurion and the permission of Pilate made his request possible.

1. *Joseph: a secret disciple.* Joseph was a remarkable person with many commendable qualities and powers. He was a man of noble character. Luke describes him as "a good and righteous man, who had not consented" to the "purpose and deed" of the council (23:50-51, RSV).

He was an influential man. The record is that he was not only a member of the Sanhedrin but a respected member. In addition, he was wealthy (Matt. 27:57). He was spiritually-minded, one who *waited for the kingdom of God* (43). He expected the Kingdom to come and to flourish. Clearly he knew of Jesus and had received His message.

He was a disciple of Jesus, "but secretly because he feared the Jews" (John 19:38, NIV). Does that secrecy negate all the other good qualities? The pressure was severe (see John 9:22; 12:42). We might also ask what influence he exerted in the Sanhedrin on behalf of Jesus. What matters is that ultimately his "faith concealed" became "faith revealed" (Hendriksen).

2. *Joseph: a bold disciple.* Authorities agree that it was an act of courage for Joseph to request the body of Jesus and take responsibility for His burial. More recent translations highlight that fact: "He summoned up courage" (Hendriksen). "He gathered up courage" (NASB). Why?

Quite literally, he *came forward.* At the least, Joseph must have had knowledge of the Jewish and Roman trials. He must have mingled with the large and hostile crowd on Golgotha. Nevertheless, at a crucial point, Joseph stepped out from that crowd and identified himself as a friend of Jesus. He may well have approached the centurion on the spot.

Further, he went to Pilate with his request. It is a testimony to his social and political influence that Joseph gained such an audience without delay. It was also a testimony to everyone, including his peers on the Sanhedrin, that he had made common cause with Jesus of Nazareth. Let us not slight the New Testament record: Joseph was a disciple of Jesus.

Lovingly, and sparing no expense, Joseph prepared the body of Jesus for burial "and laid it in his own new tomb" (Matt. 27:60, RSV). Nicodemus, another "secret disciple," assisted Joseph (John 19:39-40). The Evangelists add a significant footnote: Mary Magdalene and the other Mary, as well as other women who had followed Jesus from Galilee, looked on and observed thoughtfully, carefully. The details of the death, burial, and resurrection of Jesus could be substantiated by their witness.

The Cornerstone of Our Faith

Mark 16:1-8

> 1 And when the sabbath was past, Mary Magdalene, and Mary the mother of James, and Salome, had bought sweet spices, that they might come and anoint him.
> 2 And very early in the morning the first day of the week, they came unto the sepulchre at the rising of the sun.
> 3 And they said among themselves, Who shall roll us away the stone from the door of the sepulchre?
> 4 And when they looked, they saw that the stone was rolled away: for it was very great.
> 5 And entering into the sepulchre, they saw a young man sitting on the right side, clothed in a long white garment; and they were affrighted.
> 6 And he saith unto them, Be not affrighted: Ye seek Jesus of Nazareth, which was crucified: he is risen; he is not here: behold the place where they laid him.
> 7 But go your way, tell his disciples and Peter that he goeth before you into Gailiee: there shall ye see him, as he said unto you.
> 8 And they went out quickly, and fled from the sepulchre; for they trembled and were amazed: neither said they any thing to any man; for they were afraid.

No one has said it better than St. Paul: "And if Christ has not been raised, your faith is futile; you are still in your sins" (1 Cor. 15:17, NIV). The resurrection of Jesus from the dead is indeed the cornerstone of our faith and the validation of His person, for "he was declared Son of God by a mighty act in that he rose from the dead" (Rom. 1:4, NEB).

But what we now accept so readily, the first disciples could not understand nor anticipate. They were not prepared for the death of Jesus. How could they have expected His rising from the dead?

1. *The loving but downcast followers.* The first incident in all the Gospel accounts of the Resurrection is the coming of the women to the tomb. Mary Magdalene, who owed so much to Jesus for a mighty deliverance (Luke 8:2), heads the list in every case.

The suggestion is that the sabbath had been a period of impatient waiting. Joseph had buried Jesus sometime between 3 p.m. and 6 p.m. on Friday. The women would not have been able to buy the spices until after sundown on Saturday. In the meantime, they had rested on "the sabbath day according to the commandment" (Luke 23:56).

And now, as early as feasible on the following morning, the first day of the week, the women had come from their abode in Jerusalem, or perhaps Bethany, to express their love and grief.

2. *The divine disclosure.* How can we possibly relive the experience of the first witnesses to the Resurrection? The news was stupendous and left them trembling and awe-stricken.

The first discovery of the two Marys and Salome was that the very large stone, sealing the entrance to the tomb, had been wrenched aside. It is worth repeating that this heavenly action was not to release Jesus but to let the disciples in!

Upon entering the spacious tomb, the women received the divine word: *Jesus of Nazareth, crucified, dead, and buried, has risen—that's why He is not here. You can see the place where He once lay.*

As throughout the Gospel, this amazing event is told with restraint, without embellishment. The facts alone were enough. Nevertheless, the effect was overwhelming.

3. *Marching orders!* One could say that the Great Commission was anticipated by the angel: "But go, tell his disciples and Peter" (7, RSV). Paul Minear makes a worthy point: "God does not disclose the Resurrection fact except to enlist people in a task."

The women from Galilee were the last ones to leave the Cross, the first at the tomb, and the first to receive the revelation that Jesus had arisen from the dead. But their reward carried a special responsibility—to bear that word to the defeated disciples and to the despondent Peter. That the heavenly messenger singled out Peter was an expression of the Lord's mercy. It was Peter who vehemently protested his loyalties and who just as vehemently repudiated them.

The women were also instructed to carry a reminder of a forgotten appointment with Jesus. "'He is going before you into Galilee; there you will see Him, just as He said to you'" (7, NASB). Jesus had promised this reunion much earlier, but the disciples could not receive the word of His death, much less of His resurrection (see 14:28; Matt. 26:32).

This passage ends abruptly: ". . . they went out and fled . . . trembling and astonishment had come upon them . . . they said nothing . . . they were afraid" (8, RSV). As we shall see in the next section, this in all likelihood closes the Gospel of Mark. It is appropriate to recall that the natural reaction to a divine disclosure is fear and speechlessness, as on the Mount of Transfiguration: Peter and his comrades "did not know what to say, they were so frightened" (9:6, NIV).

Mary and her friends did carry out their assignment; "with fear and great joy," they "ran to tell his disciples" (Matt. 28:8, RSV). Messengers of that glad news have never ceased to run and to tell that same message.

An Early Epilogue

Mark 16:9-20

> 9 Now when Jesus was risen early the first day of the week, he appeared first to Mary Magdalene, out of whom he had cast seven devils.
> 10 And she went and told them that had been with him, as they mourned and wept.
> 11 And they, when they had heard that he was alive, and had been seen of her, believed not.
> 12 After that he appeared in another form unto two of them, as they walked, and went into the country.
> 13 And they went and told it unto the residue: neither believed they them.
> 14 Afterward he appeared unto the eleven as they sat at meat, and upbraided them with their unbelief and hardness of heart, because they believed not them which had seen him after he was risen.
> 15 And he said unto them, Go ye into all the world, and preach the gospel to every creature.
> 16 He that believeth and is baptized shall be saved; but he that believeth not shall be damned.

17 And these signs shall follow them that believe; In my name shall they cast out devils; they shall speak with new tongues;

18 They shall take up serpents; and if they drink any deadly thing, it shall not hurt them: they shall lay hands on the sick, and they shall recover.

19 So then after the Lord had spoken unto them, he was received up into heaven, and sat on the right hand of God.

20 And they went forth, and preached every where, the Lord working with them, and confirming the word with signs following. Amen.

Evangelicals and non-evangelicals agree that these verses present a problem. They have been described as a *cause célèbre* ("celebrated case") of New Testament textual criticism.

1. *A review of the facts.* Succinctly stated, these verses are not found in the earliest and most respected manuscripts of the New Testament, nor in the earliest and leading commentaries and versions. They are, however, found in numerous other later manuscripts and were apparently known to church fathers in the latter half of the second century. A fact seldom reported is that two or more different endings to the Gospel have been discovered in the various manuscripts (see such recent versions as the NIV, NEB, and NASB).

Scholarly discussion and debate continue concerning the authorship, date, and purpose of these verses. Interested readers should consult the selected bibliography of this volume for technical details. The reviews by Ralph P. Martin and William L. Lane are recent, comprehensive, accurate, and fair. In view of the avalanche of data, Lane's conclusion may be noted here: "The evidence allows no other assumption than that from the beginning Mark circulated with the abrupt ending of Ch. 16:8."

2. *How these facts are presently interpreted.* Questions for which we have no clear answer include: Did Mark intend to close his Gospel at v. 8, or was he hindered in his purpose? Why do so many later manuscripts and versions include these verses?

In reply, the prevailing consensus is apparently: (1) Mark was hindered in his work, evidently by something very serious, such as persecution or death; (2) the Early Church felt a sense of incompleteness about the Gospel and made a conscientious attempt to complete the account. This came about very early and soon became "standard" in the later manuscripts.

3. The following material from *Beacon Bible Commentary,* described as a "handy summary," may be useful in understanding the content of the closing verses of Mark as they appear in the KJV (a translation based upon medieval, i.e., late manuscripts).

9-11 are an abridged version of John 20:11-18 (the Rabboni story).

12-13 summarize Luke 24:13-35 (the walk to Emmaus).

14-15 recall Luke 24:36-49 and Matt. 28:16-20.

17-18 most of the signs here described can be paralleled in the Acts.

19-20 cf. Acts 1:9-11

It may be helpful to consult the exposition of these parallel passages in the corresponding volumes of *Beacon Bible Expositions.*

In commenting on the closing verses of this "early epilogue" (19-20), William Hendriksen concludes his exposition with these inspiring words:

Speaking in general, there is nothing in the entire *ending* (verses 9-20) that is more serene, uplifting, true, and beautiful than these final two verses. They point to the Lord Jesus as the One who, from his position at the right hand of God, tenderly watches over, guides, and energizes, and governs his church.

A Selected Bibliography*

Barker, Glenn W., et al. *The New Testament Speaks.* New York: Harper and Row, Publishers, 1969.

Hendriksen, William. *New Testament Commentary: Exposition of the Gospel According to Mark.* Grand Rapids: Baker Book House, 1975.

Hiebert, D. Edmond. *Mark: A Portrait of the Servant.* Chicago: Moody Press, 1974.

Lane, William L. "The Gospel According to Mark." *The New International Commentary on the New Testament.* Grand Rapids: Wm. B. Eerdmans Publishing Company, 1974.

Martin, Ralph P. *New Testament Foundations: A Guide for Christian Students. Vol. I: The Four Gospels.* Grand Rapids: Wm. B. Eerdmans Publishing Company, 1975.

———. *Mark: Evangelist and Theologian.* Grand Rapids: Zondervan Publishing House, 1973.

Ogilvie, Lloyd J. *Life Without Limits: The Message of Mark's Gospel.* Waco, Tex.: Word Books, Publisher, 1975.

Pherigo, Lindsey P. "The Gospel According to Mark." *The Interpreter's One-Volume Commentary on the Bible.* Edited by Charles M. Laymon. New York: Abingdon Press, 1971. (Referred to herein as IOC.)

Sanner, A. Elwood. "Mark," *Beacon Bible Commentary,* Vol. 6. Kansas City: Beacon Hill Press of Kansas City, 1964. (Referred to herein as BBC.)

Schürer, Emil. *A History of the Jewish People.* Abridged edition. Edited by Nahum N. Glatzer. New York: Schocken Books, 1961.

Smith, Thomas J. *The Mighty Message of Mark.* Winona, Minn.: St. Mary's College Press, 1974.

*The reader may refer to the *Beacon Bible Commentary,* Vol. 6, pp. 415-16, for a more detailed bibliography on the Gospel of Mark compiled by the present author.